THOMAS ANSHUTZ

Artist and Teacher

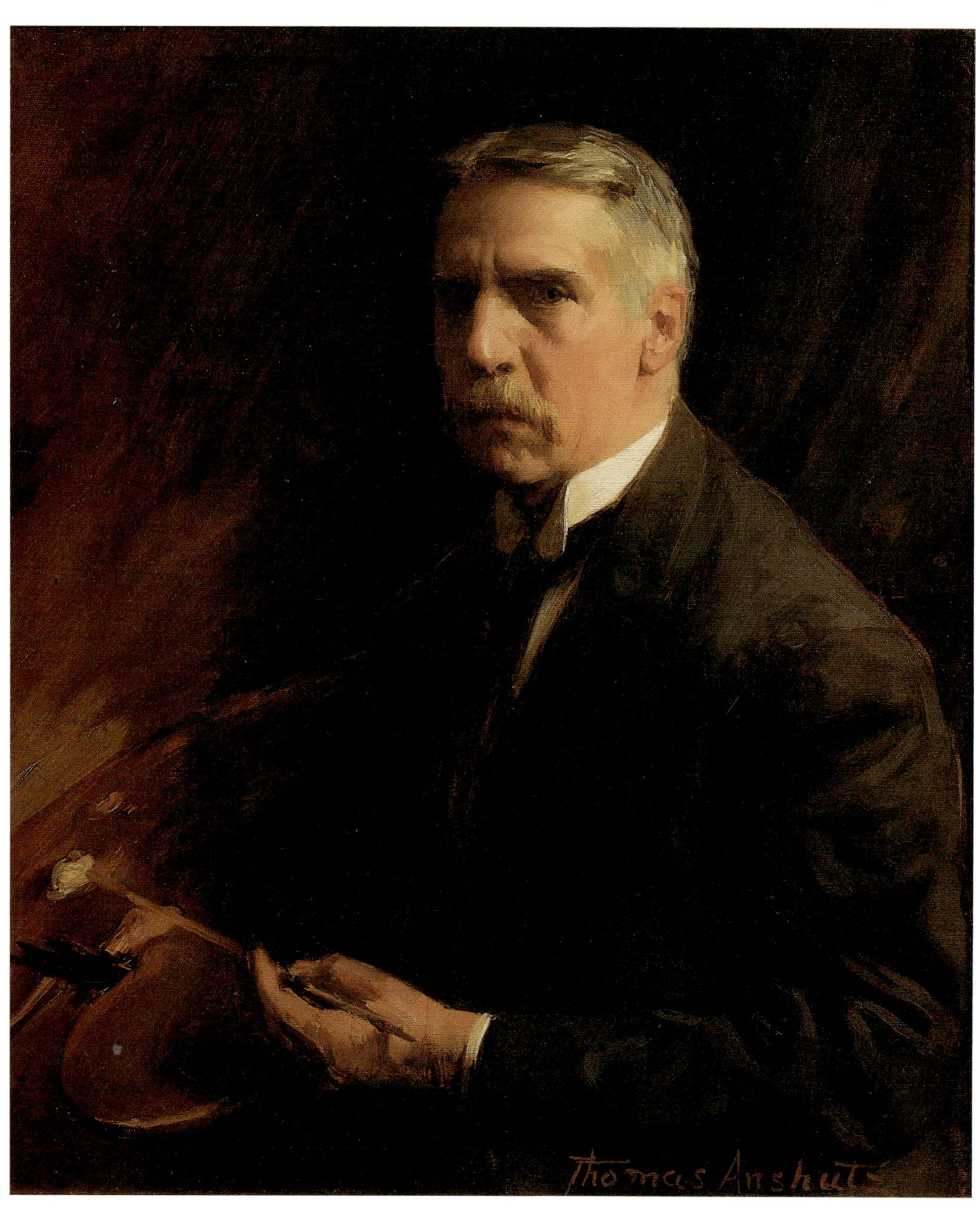
Thomas Anshutz

THOMAS ANSHUTZ
Artist and Teacher

RANDALL C. GRIFFIN

WITH A PREFACE BY WILLIAM INNES HOMER

PUBLISHED BY THE HECKSCHER MUSEUM IN ASSOCIATION WITH
THE UNIVERSITY OF WASHINGTON PRESS, SEATTLE

First Edition

Library of Congress Catalogue Card Number: 94-077597

ISBN: 0-295-97413-3

This book has been published in conjunction with the exhibition *The Art of Thomas Anshutz,* organized by Randall C. Griffin, Guest Curator, Heckscher Museum, Huntington, New York. The exhibition was on view from September 3 through November 20, 1994.

The exhibition and book are made possible by generous grants from the Henry Luce Foundation, Inc., the John Sloan Memorial Foundation, the National Endowment for the Arts, the New York State Council on the Arts and by general operating support provided by the Town of Huntington.

Book Design: ABGraphics, Port Washington, NY
Color separations: Electronic Separations Plus, Plainview, NY
Printed by: Design Art Ltd., New York, NY

Cover:
Thomas Anshutz, *The Farmer and His Son at Harvesting,* 1879, oil on canvas, 24¼ × 17¼," Courtesy Berry-Hill Galleries, Inc., New York

Frontispiece:
Thomas Anshutz, *Self-Portrait,* ca. 1909, oil on canvas, 30 × 25," National Academy of Design, New York

Contents

List of Lenders

Allentown Art Museum
Archives of American Art, Smithsonian Institution
Baker/Pisano Collection
Berry-Hill Galleries, Inc., New York
Brandywine River Museum
Byron Collection
The Hon. Joseph P. Carroll and Mrs. Carroll
The Corcoran Gallery of Art
The Fine Arts Museums of San Francisco
James Graham & Sons Gallery, New York
Hirshhorn Museum and Sculpture Garden, Smithsonian Institution
Mr. and Mrs. Raymond J. Horowitz
The Metropolitan Museum of Art
Mr. and Mrs. Samuel F. Mirabito
National Academy of Design
The Pennsylvania Academy of the Fine Arts
Private Collection
Private Collection, Riverhead, New York
Reading Public Museum
Mr. and Mrs. Richard Waitzer
Westmoreland Museum of Art
Yale University Art Gallery

In Honor of
Helen Farr Sloan,
Friend and Supporter
of American Art

Foreword

In its almost 75 years as a cultural institution, the Heckscher Museum has demonstrated a longstanding commitment to the history of American art. Its programs and publications have included pioneering work on Thomas Moran and family, Louis Comfort Tiffany, the students of William Merritt Chase, Eduard Steichen, Arthur Dove and Helen Torr, and many others. So it was with great excitement and anticipation that the Heckscher Museum embarked in 1989 on a project focusing on the nineteenth-century American painter Thomas Anshutz. A critical reevaluation of the artist had long been overdue, as Anshutz is one of the last major figures in nineteenth-century American art to lack a thoroughly researched exhibition and scholarly monograph. No museum retrospective of Anshutz's work had been held since the 1973 Pennsylvania Academy of the Fine Arts exhibition, which was accompanied only by a very small catalogue. Since then, new archival material has surfaced and previously unknown paintings have also come to light.

We are extremely proud of the resulting exhibition *The Art of Thomas Anshutz* and this monograph *Thomas Anshutz, Artist and Teacher,* curated and written by Randall C. Griffin, Assistant Professor in the Department of Art History at Southern Methodist University. As guest curator of the exhibition and author of this fine monograph, Professor Griffin has manifested his superb scholarship, fluid writing, and discriminating connoisseurship, all the while juggling a full-time academic schedule of teaching, publishing and lecturing. Without his in-depth knowledge, unflagging commitment and tireless efforts, this project would not have come to fruition. We owe him a tremendous debt of gratitude.

Further thanks must be extended to Helen Farr Sloan, whose exemplary support of the field of American art history is well known. It was early conversations with her that helped to shape the focus of our project and through her that Professor Griffin's expertise on Thomas Anshutz became known to the Museum. Helen Farr Sloan's generosity also extends to financial support as well, with exhibition and catalogue grants from the John Sloan Memorial Foundation. It is to her that we dedicate this publication.

For his insightful essay and ongoing interest in the Anshutz project, we would like to thank William Innes Homer, H. Rodney Sharp Professor, Department of Art History at the University of Delaware. His guidance has informed this endeavor on many levels.

Additional evidence of the importance of Thomas Anshutz and recognition of the need for a reevaluation of his role in American art history came in the form of grants from the National Endowment for the Arts, the New York State Council on the Arts, and the Henry Luce Foundation, Inc. In this time of financial strain, it was the monumental generosity of the Luce grant, the largest ever received by the Heckscher Museum for a special exhibition, that enabled us to produce the exhibition and publication of our dreams.

Of course, no exhibition is possible without lenders and we wish to thank the many institutions and individuals who have so generously parted with their precious works to make *The Art of Thomas Anshutz* possible. Enthusiasm for Anshutz's work and encouragement of our efforts were forthcoming from all we contacted, museum colleagues, private collectors and galleries alike. All of our generous lenders are listed on a separate page, but a few individuals deserve special mention here: the Hon. Joseph P. Carroll and Mrs. Carroll, who were early and avid supporters of the project and who have lent extensively from their considerable collection of Anshutz works; Virginia Dunning and the staff of James Graham & Sons Gallery, New York, who mined archives, storage, and sales records in an effort to locate sought-after works for the exhibition; and Marc Simpson, The Edna Root Curator of American Paintings at the M.H. de Young Memorial Museum, The Fine Arts Museums of San Francisco, who, as guardian of Anshutz's masterpiece, *The Ironworker's Noontime,* was able to build institutional support for our exhibition. To part with the pivotal work in his care, in fact to remove it early from an exhibition at his own institution, attests to his extreme generosity as a colleague, his superb skills as a negotiator, and his commitment as a scholar to the history of American art.

We are appreciative of the support of the Board of Trustees and staff of the Heckscher Museum, particularly William H. Titus, Registrar, who coordinated the many intricate details of borrowing and transporting the art works. Amy Berger and the staff at ABGraphics are to be commended for the beautiful design of this publication and for overseeing its production. Sincere thanks go to Pat Soden, Associate Director and General Manager of the University of Washington Press, whose distribution of this publication assures that Thomas Anshutz's reputation will receive the widespread recognition that it has so long deserved.

John E. Coraor, Ph.D.
Director

Anna C. Noll
Curator/Anshutz Project Director

Acknowledgments

A project of the scope of this landmark exhibition and monograph on Thomas Anshutz requires the participation and help of many individuals and institutions. I am especially indebted to the staff of the Heckscher Museum for their assistance in producing this publication, *Thomas Anshutz, Artist and Teacher* and for organizing the accompanying exhibition *The Art of Thomas Anshutz*. Their hard work has assured the success of this project. I owe special thanks to project director Anna C. Noll, Curator of the Heckscher Museum, for her guidance, knowledge and friendship. Her assistance in developing the exhibition, raising funds, editing the catalogue, and hanging the pictures has been crucial. I would like to gratefully acknowledge the Henry Luce Foundation, Inc., the John Sloan Memorial Foundation, the National Endowment for the Arts, and the New York State Council on the Arts for their generous grants that have made this exhibition and catalogue possible.

Many people and organizations have contributed to my research on Anshutz. For funding my earlier dissertation work, from which this publication and exhibition grew, I would like to thank the Henry Luce Foundation, Inc., the John Sloan Memorial Foundation, and the National Gallery of Art's Center for Advanced Study in the Visual Arts. Others who have contributed to this project include: David Brownlee, the Hon. Joseph P. Carroll and Mrs. Carroll, Sarah Cash, Wayne Craven, Lois Marie Fink, Jean Fitzgerald, Mary Anne Goley, Mr. and Mrs. Raymond J. Horowitz, Liza Kirwin, Sandra Leff, Cheryl Leibl, Henry A. Millon, Phyllis D. Rosensweig, Wilford W. Scott, Peggy Seegrist, David Sellin, Victor Spark, Damie Stillman, John Tagg, Barbara A. Wolanin, Saul Zalesch, Judith K. Zilczer, the staff of the Center for Advanced Study in the Visual Arts, and the staff of the National Gallery of Art's Library. I was also graciously assisted by a number of institutions: Archives of American Art, Corcoran Gallery of Art, Delaware Art Museum, James Graham & Sons Gallery, Hirshhorn Museum and Sculpture Garden, National Academy of Design, the National Gallery of Art's Photographic Archives, the National Museum of American Art's Index of American Painting, Pennsylvania Academy of the Fine Arts, Philadelphia Museum of Art, and the Philadelphia Sketch Club.

This catalogue is especially indebted to the pioneering scholarly work of Sandra Lee Denney and Ruth Bowman. Their theses on Thomas Anshutz and Ruth Bowman's articles have provided an invaluable foundation for my work. Ruth Bowman also kindly provided me complete access to her Anshutz materials.

I also benefited greatly from the comments, observations, and kindness of Helen Farr Sloan. Without her assistance, this project would never have been possible. She provided me with a wealth of information and insight concerning John Sloan and the Ashcan School, assisted me in contacting scholars and collectors in the field, and helped fund both my dissertation research and this exhibition and catalogue.

I offer very warm thanks to Dr. William Innes Homer. He encouraged me to begin this project. As my dissertation advisor his guidance, support, and patience have benefited me in so many respects. He allowed complete access to his large collection of Anshutz research materials. His many color and black and white reproductions of Anshutz's paintings, and letters from the artist, his family, and former students, have proved exceptionally helpful. Moreover, Dr. Homer's numerous inciteful comments have profoundly and indelibly shaped my work. Yet he always granted me the autonomy I needed to work through questions and issues on my own.

Finally, I want to thank my wife, Carol Griffin. Her ideas, critical feedback, invaluable editorial assistance, unflagging support, and love have made this project possible. In so many respects, she has strengthened this writing.

Randall C. Griffin
Guest Curator

Chronology

1851	Born in Newport, Kentucky.
ca. 1863	Moved with family to Wheeling, West Virginia.
1871	Summer, traveled down the Ohio and Mississippi Rivers; September, arrived in Brooklyn, New York.
1872	Entered the National Academy of Design.
1875	Moved to Philadelphia and studied with Thomas Eakins at the Philadelphia Sketch Club.
1876	Entered the Pennsylvania Academy of the Fine Arts.
1878	Made an assistant demonstrator in the dissecting room under Thomas Eakins.
1880	Was made Chief Demonstrator of Anatomy under Dr. William W. Keen.
1881	Joined the faculty of the Pennsylvania Academy of the Fine Arts.
1892	1 September, married Effie Shriver Russell; December, traveled to Paris, where he enrolled in the Académie Julian.
1893	Spring, saw Post-Impressionist art in Paris; traveled in Italy, Switzerland, and England; returned to Philadelphia in September and to his teaching position at the Pennsylvania Academy of the Fine Arts in the fall.
1894	The painter's only child, Edward Russell Anshutz, was born; Anshutz rented a summer home in Holly Beach, New Jersey.
1897	Traveled down the Delaware River in the summer.
1898	With Hugh Breckenridge, founded the Darby School of Painting, a summer school located in Darby, Pennsylvania.
1899	The Darby School moved to Fort Washington, Pennsylvania.
1904	Awarded silver medal at the St. Louis World's Fair for his portrait of John E.D. Trask.

1909 Became Head Instructor of the Pennsylvania Academy of the Fine Arts; was awarded the Academy's Gold Medal of Honor and the Walter Lippincott Prize for *The Tanagra*.

1910 Awarded gold medal at the Buenos Aires International Exposition; made an associate member of the National Academy of Design; named President of the Philadelphia Sketch Club; became increasingly ill with heart disease; traveled to Bermuda in the summer.

1911 Summer, traveled to Bad Neuheim, Germany for the "cure;" visited Lyman Saÿen in Paris and toured many art galleries; stopped in London before returning to Philadelphia in August; forced by illness to stop teaching by November; hospitalized in Philadelphia for a month.

1912 16 June, died at home of heart disease and bronchial illness.

Color Plates

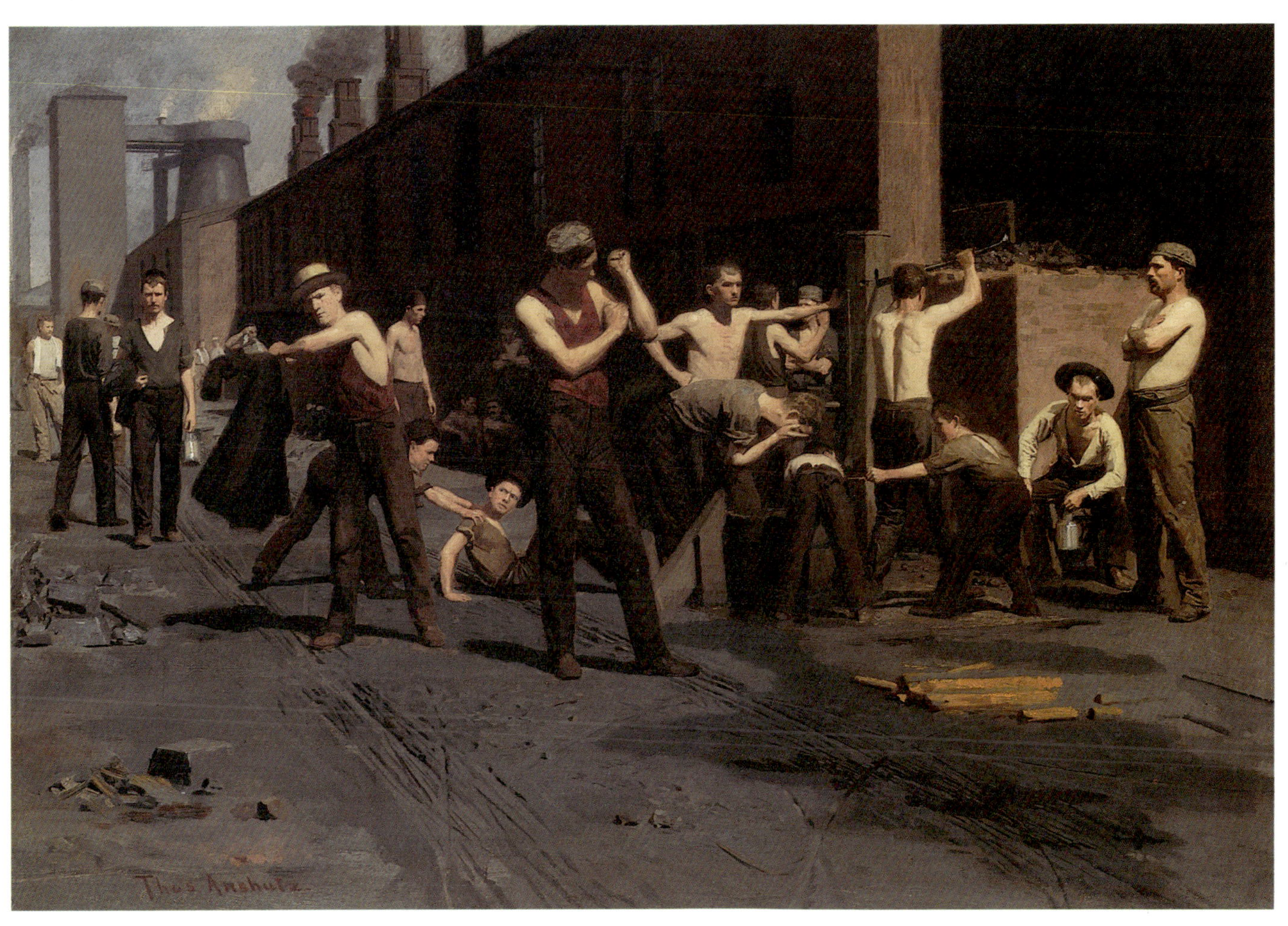

PLATE 1. *The Ironworkers' Noontime,* 1880
oil on canvas, 17⅛ × 24"
The Fine Arts Museums of San Francisco,
Gift of Mr. and Mrs. John D. Rockefeller 3rd, 1979.7.4

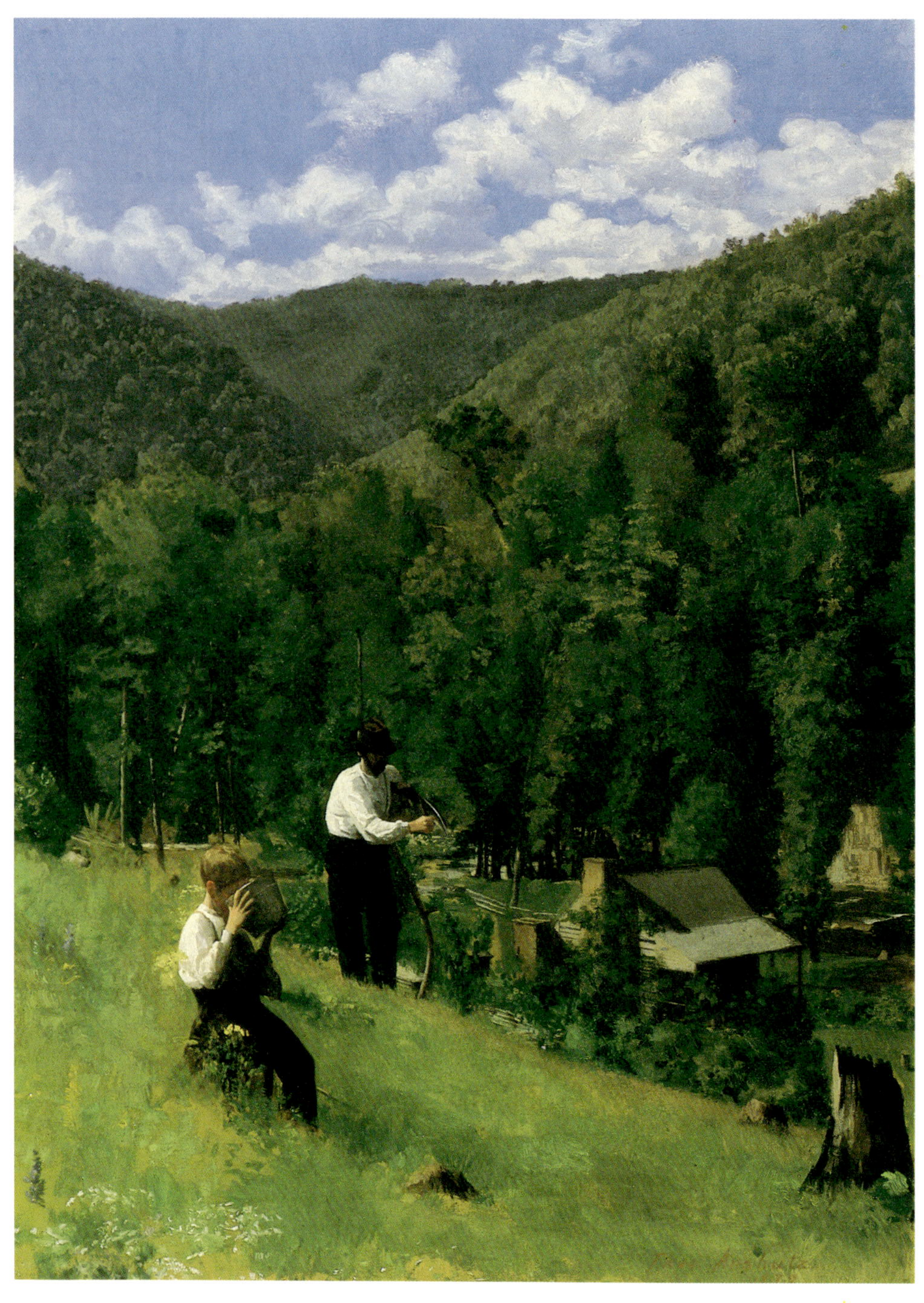

PLATE 2. *The Farmer and His Son at Harvesting,* 1879
oil on canvas, 24¼ × 17¼"
Courtesy Berry-Hill Galleries, Inc., New York

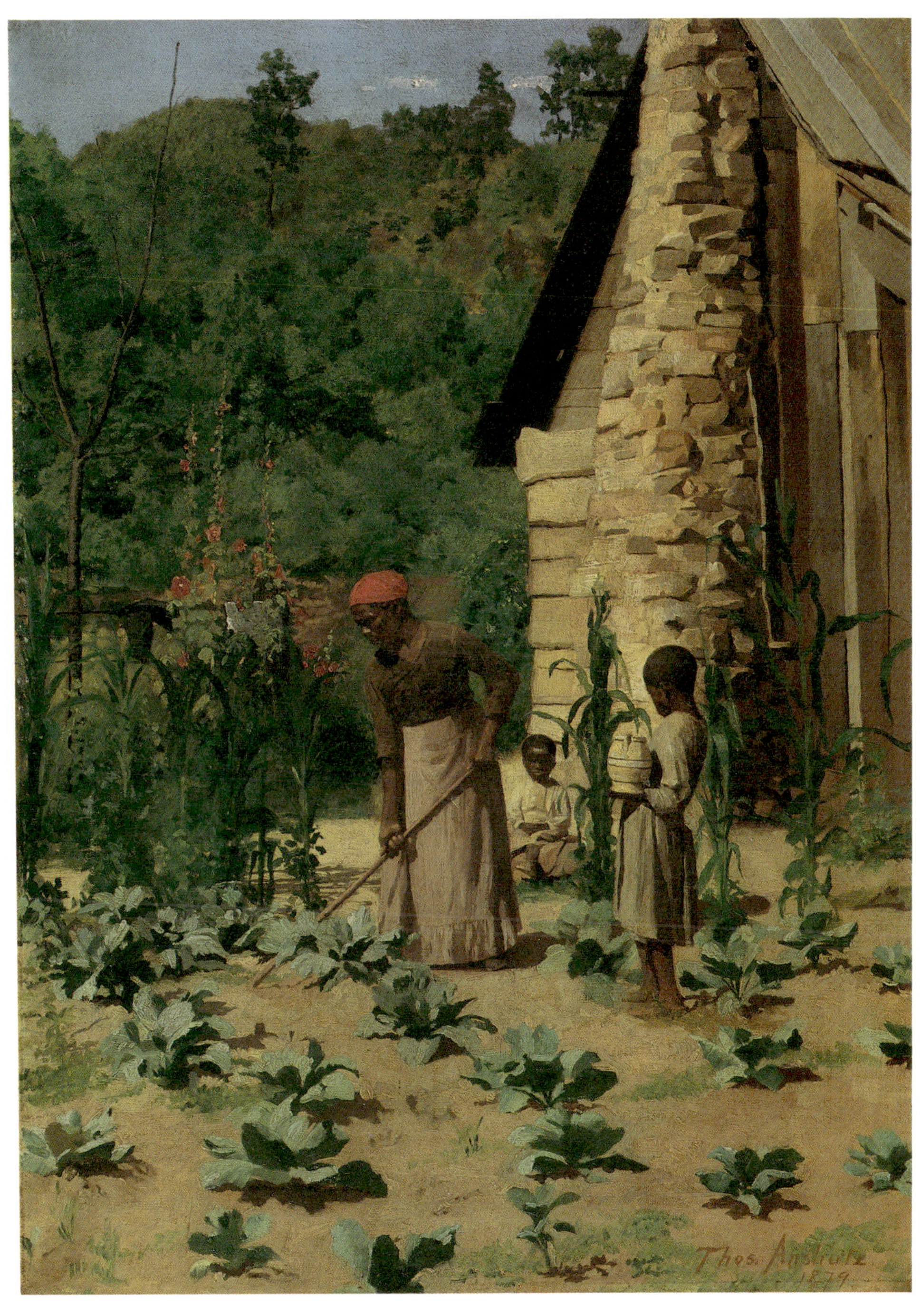

PLATE 3. *The Way They Live,* 1879
oil on canvas, 24 × 17"
The Metropolitan Museum of Art, Morris K. Jesup Fund, 1940

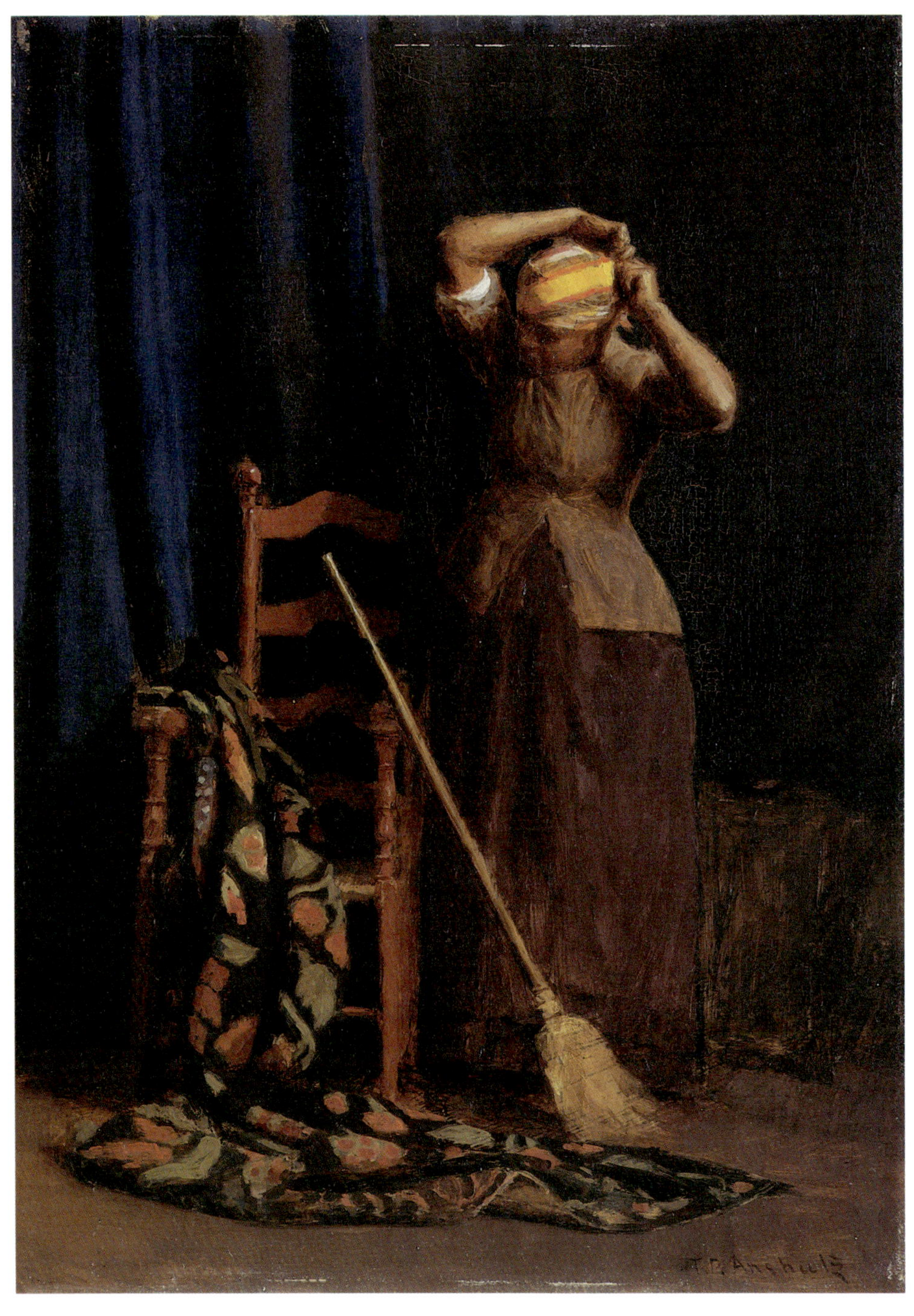

PLATE 4. *The Chore,* 1888
oil on canvas, $14\frac{1}{16} \times 9\frac{7}{8}$"
Allentown Art Museum: Gift of J. I. and Anna Rodale, 1961 (61.26)

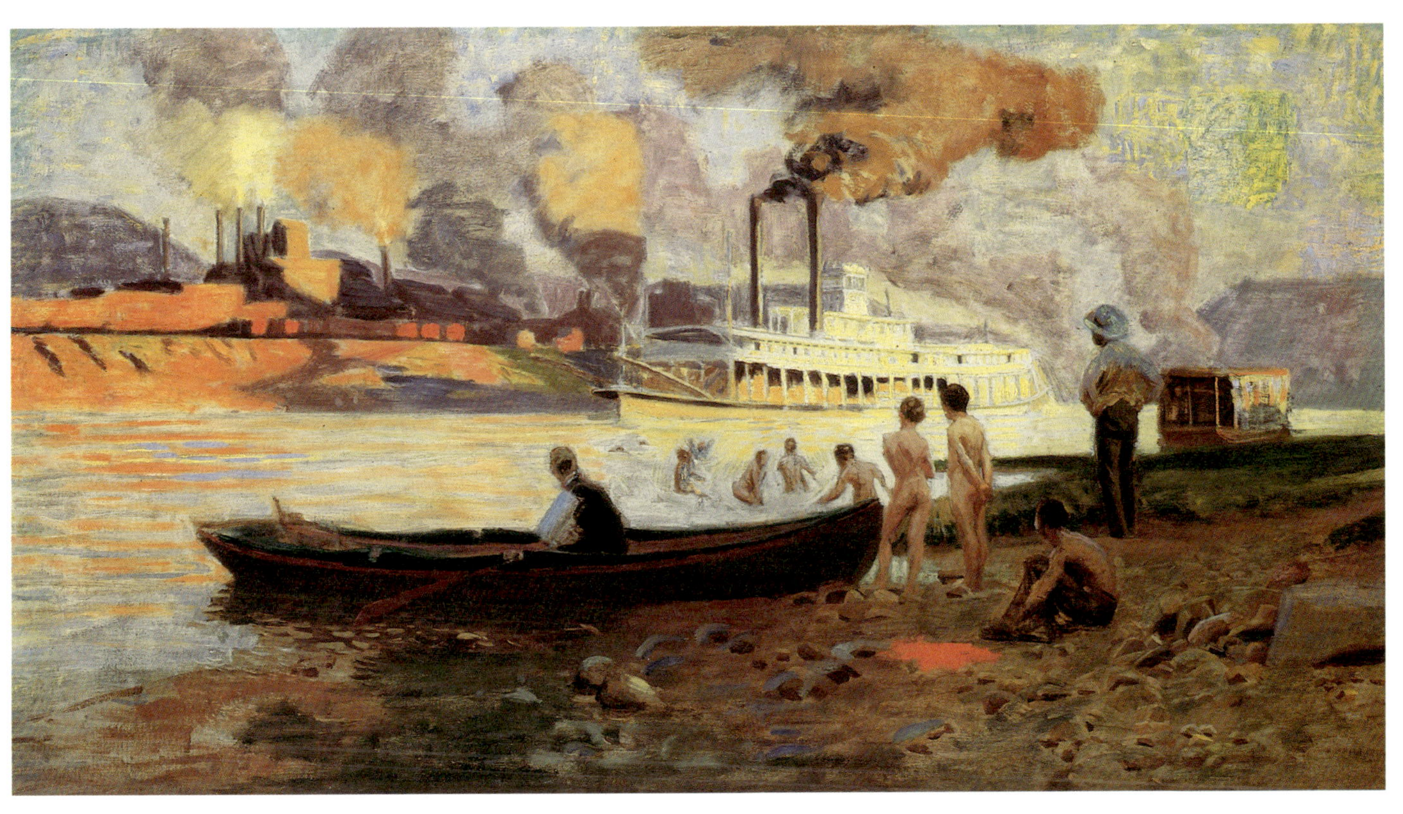

PLATE 5. *Steamboat on the Ohio,* ca. 1900-08
oil on canvas, 27¼ × 48¼"
The Carnegie Museum of Art; Patrons Art Fund, 57.36

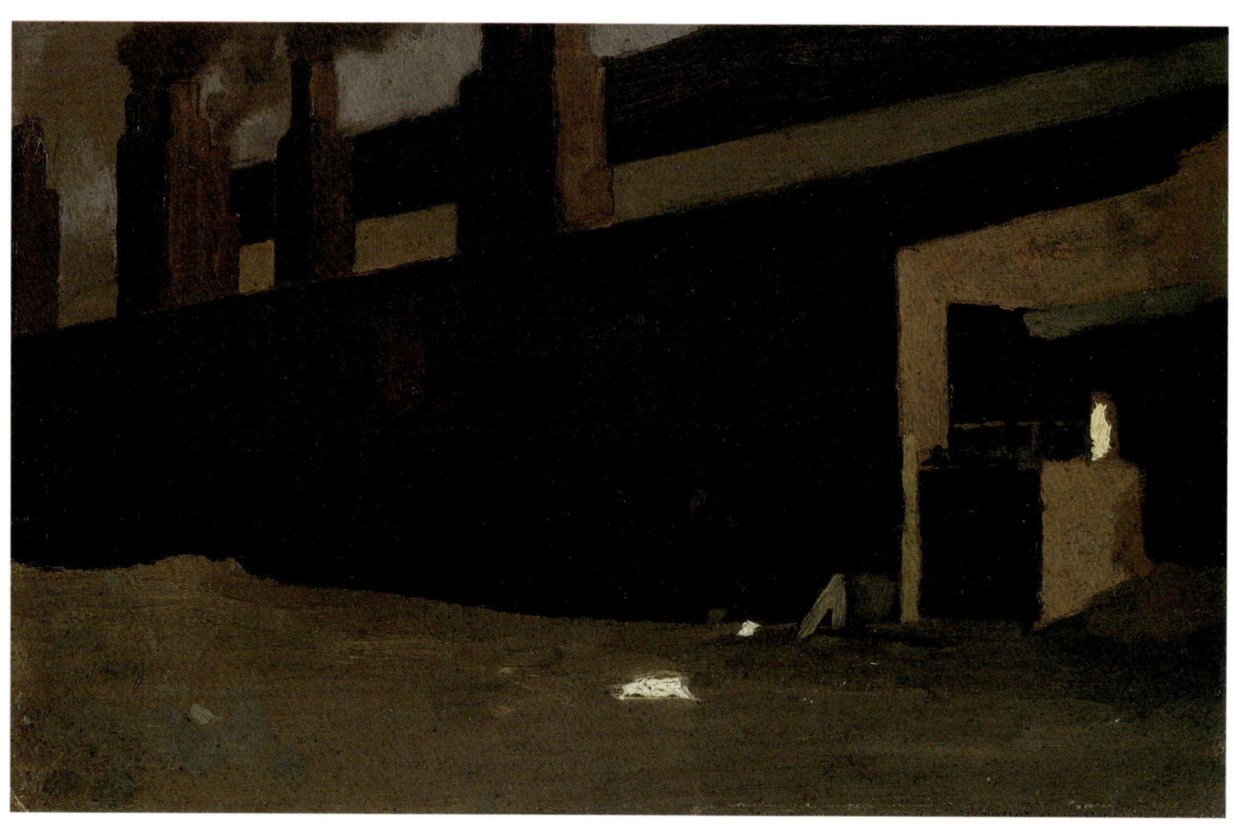

PLATE 6. *Factory-Study for The Ironworkers' Noontime,* 1880
oil on paperboard, 8½ × 12⅞"
Hirshhorn Museum and Sculpture Garden, Smithsonian Institution.
Gift of Joseph H. Hirshhorn, 1966.

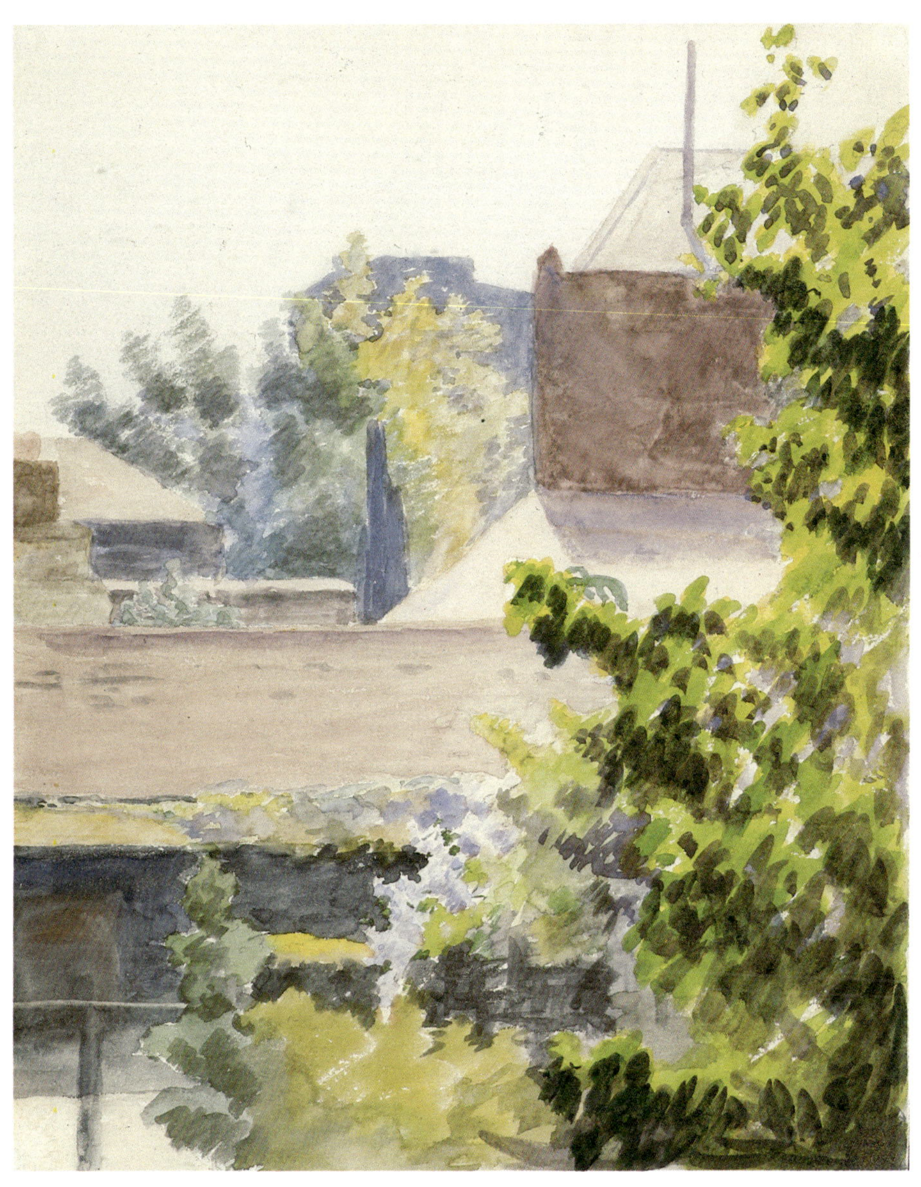

PLATE 7. *St. Cloud near Paris,* ca. 1893
watercolor on paper, 10½ × 8¼"
The Hon. Joseph P. Carroll and Mrs. Carroll, New York

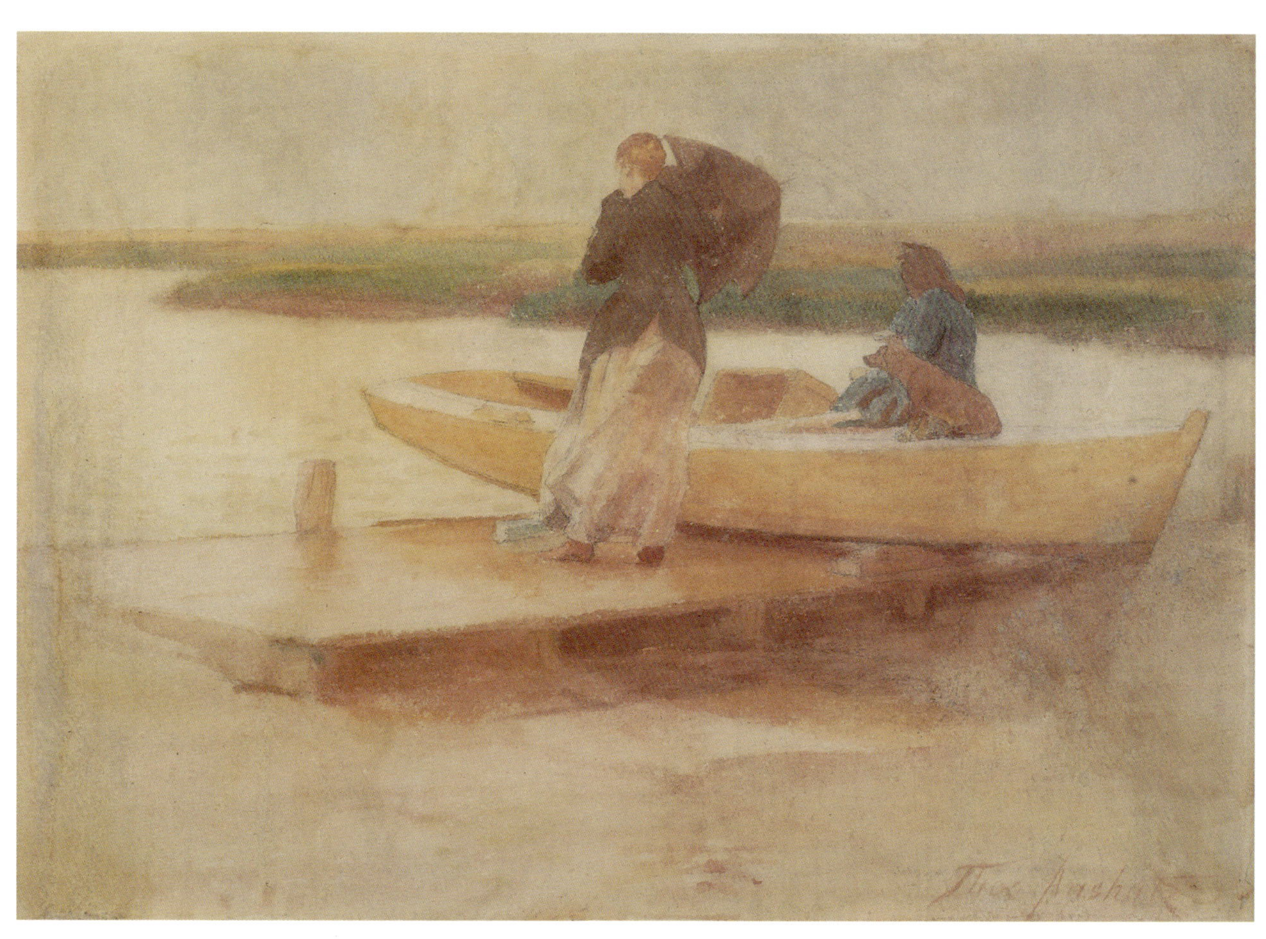

PLATE 8. *North East Weather,* ca. 1893
watercolor on paper, 10¾ × 14½"
Baker/Pisano Collection

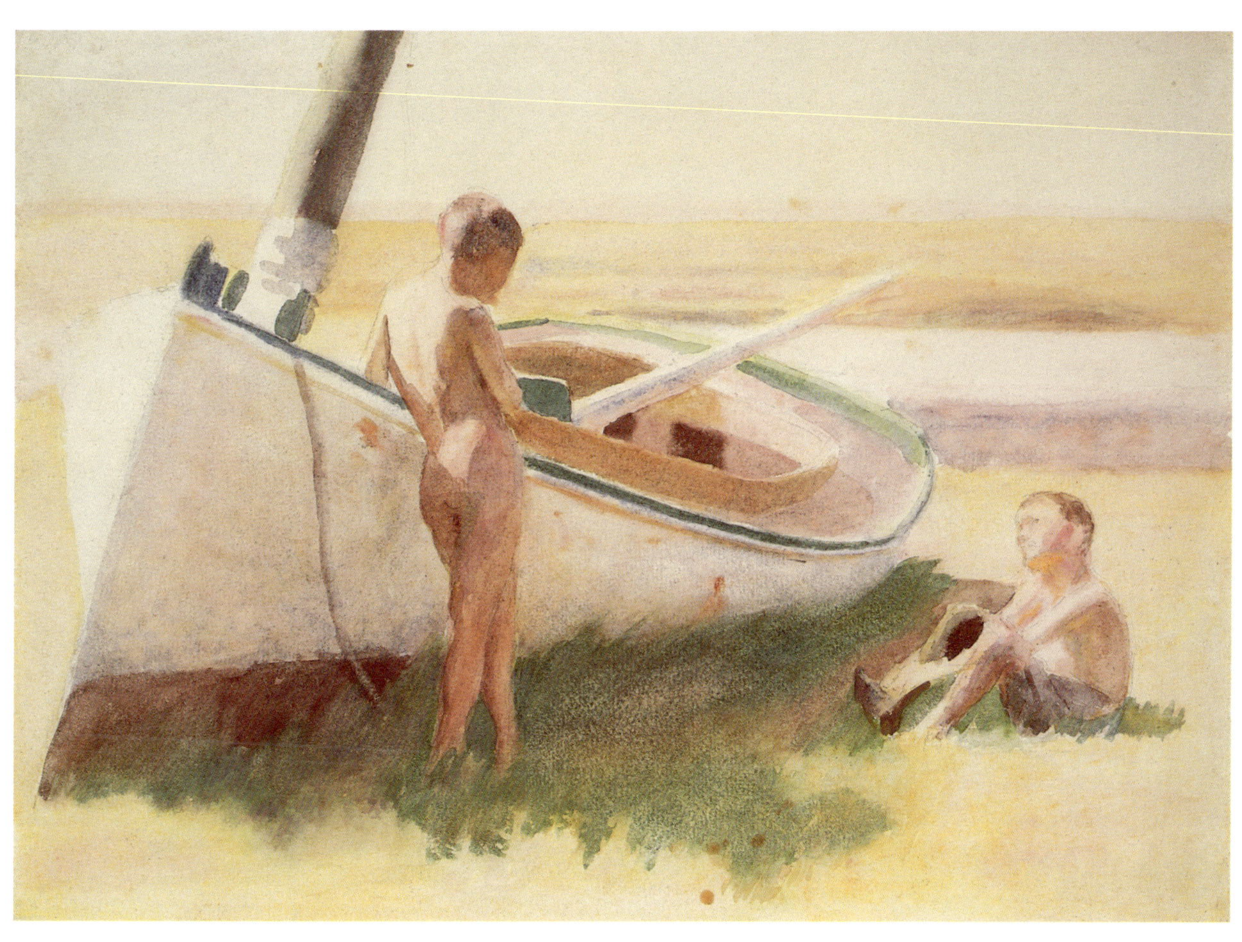

PLATE 9. *Two Boys by a Boat,* ca. 1894
watercolor on paper, 10 × 13⅜"
The Carnegie Museum of Art;
Gift of Mrs. Carl Selden, 82.100

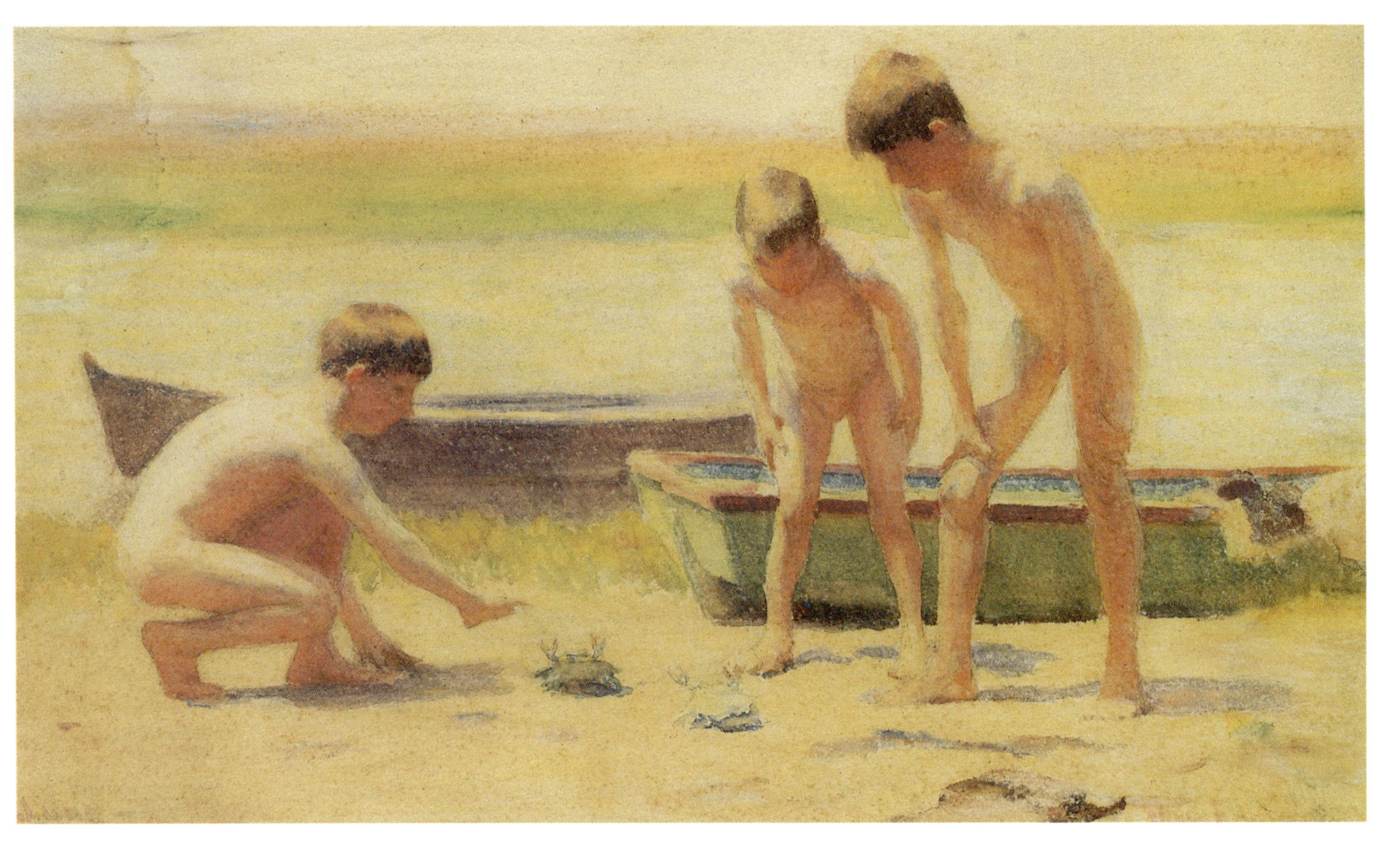

PLATE 10. *Boys Playing with Crabs,* ca. 1894
watercolor on paper, 14 × 20"
Private Collection

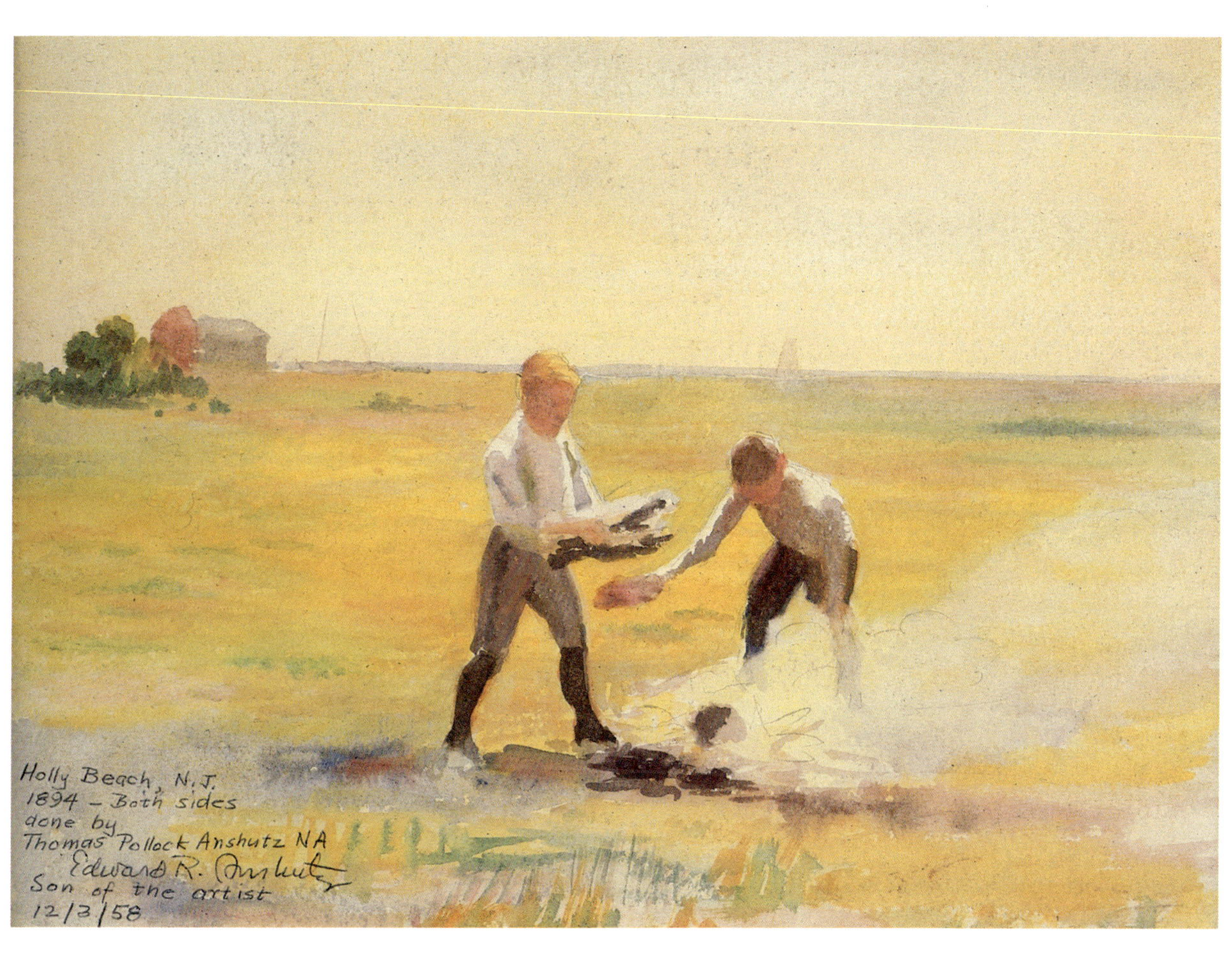

PLATE 11. *Boys by a Fire,* ca. 1894
watercolor on paper, 9¾ × 13¼"
Location unknown

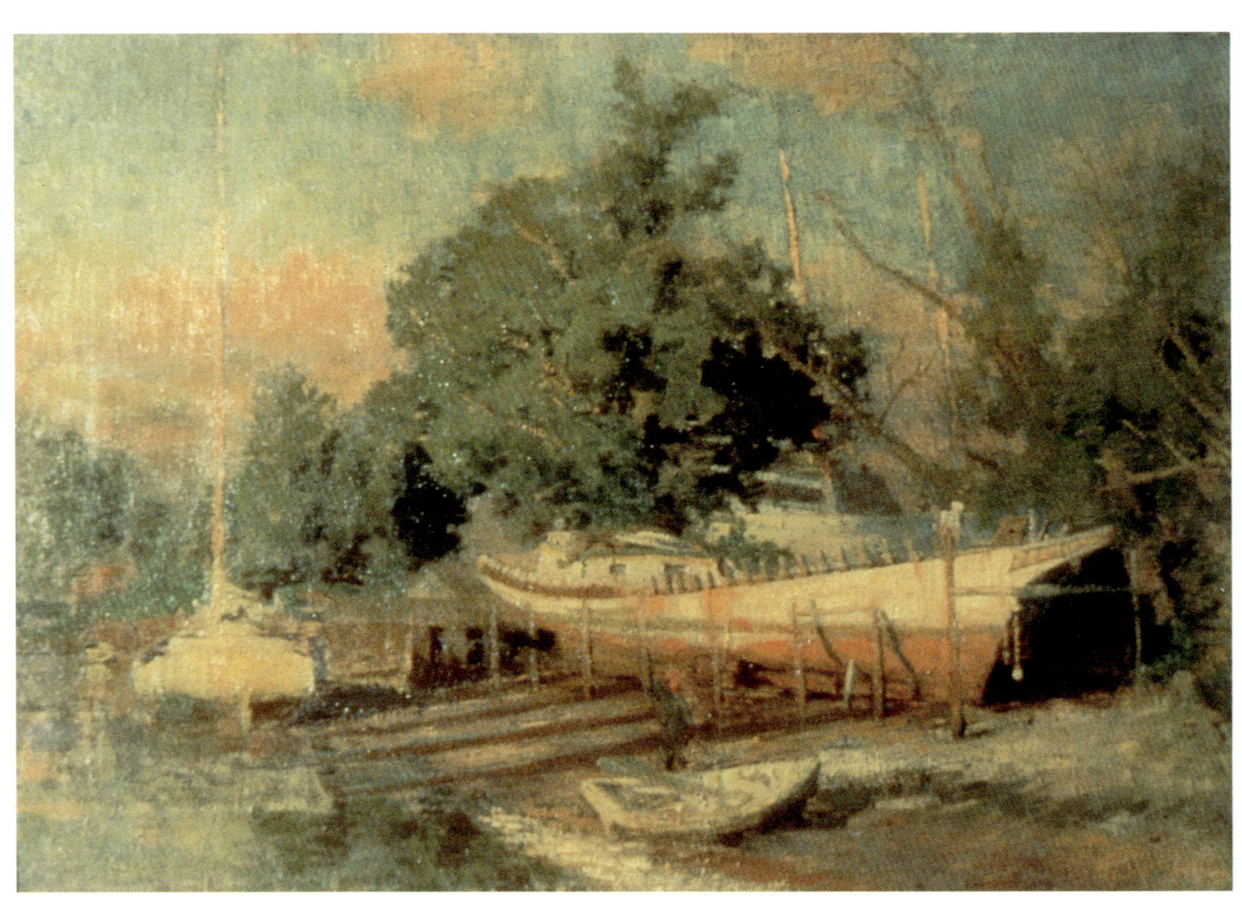

PLATE 12. *Down the Delaware Bay*, ca. 1897
oil on canvas, 26 × 36"
Location unknown

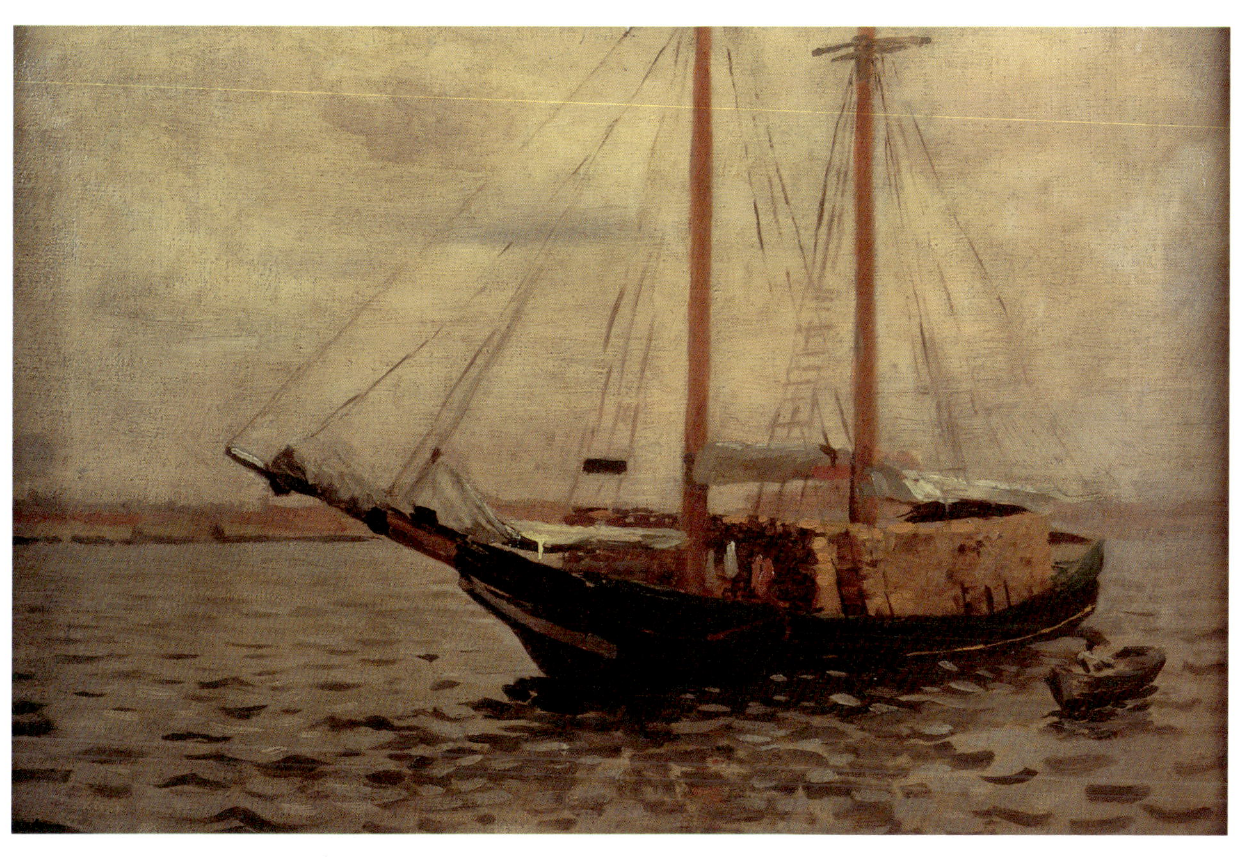

PLATE 13. *The Lumber Boat*, ca. 1897
oil on canvas, 16¼ × 24⅛"
Private Collection, Riverhead, New York

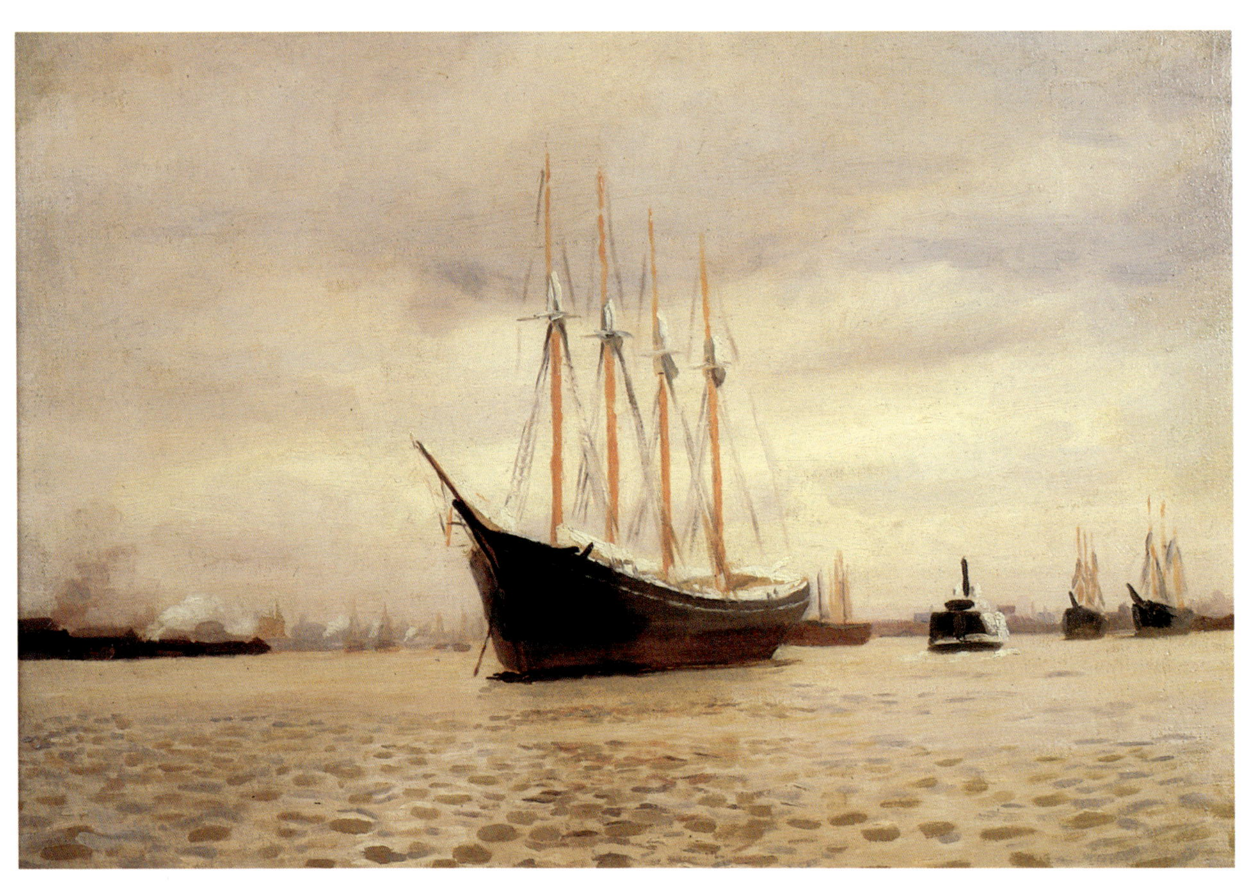

PLATE 14. *On the Delaware at Tacony,* ca. 1897
oil on canvas, 16⅛ × 23⅛"
The Hon. Joseph P. Carroll and Mrs. Carroll, New York

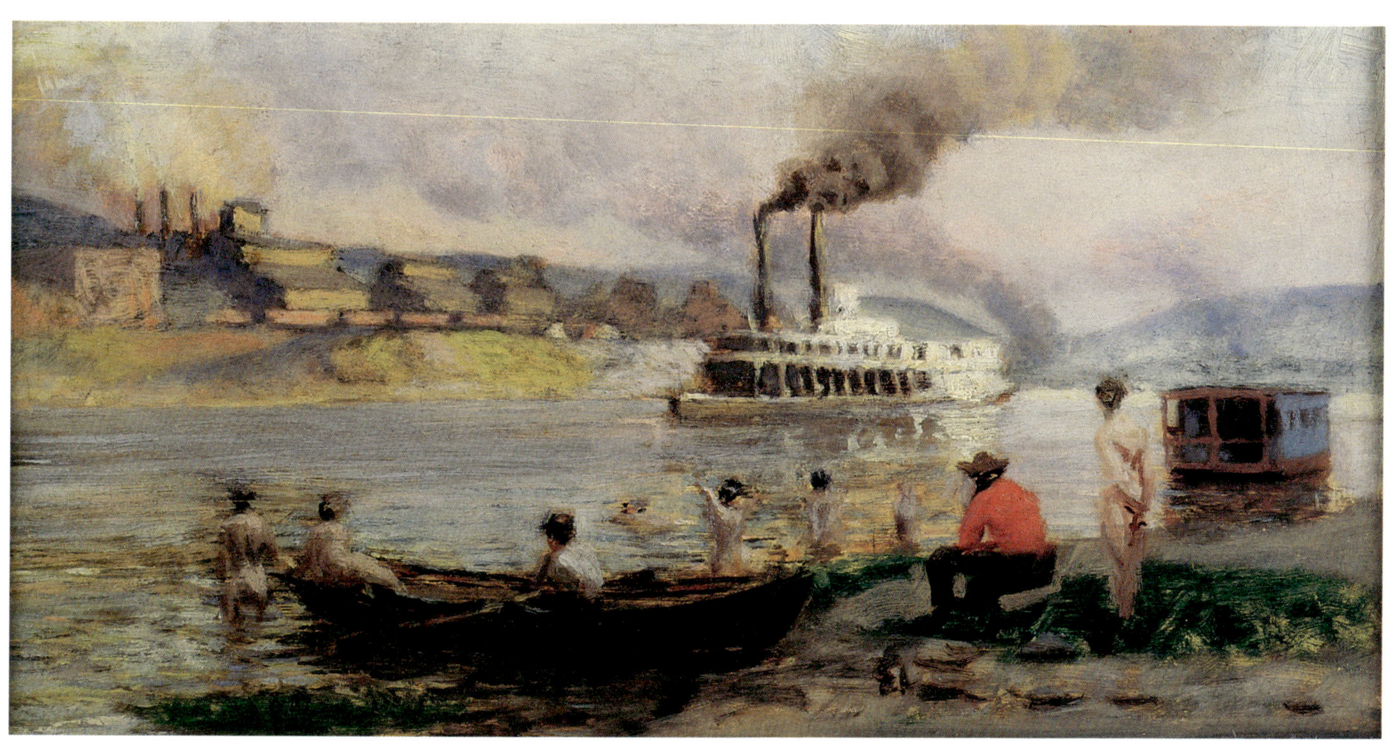

PLATE 15. *Steamboat on the Ohio,* ca. 1900
oil on canvas, 10 × 15"
Mr. and Mrs. Richard Waitzer

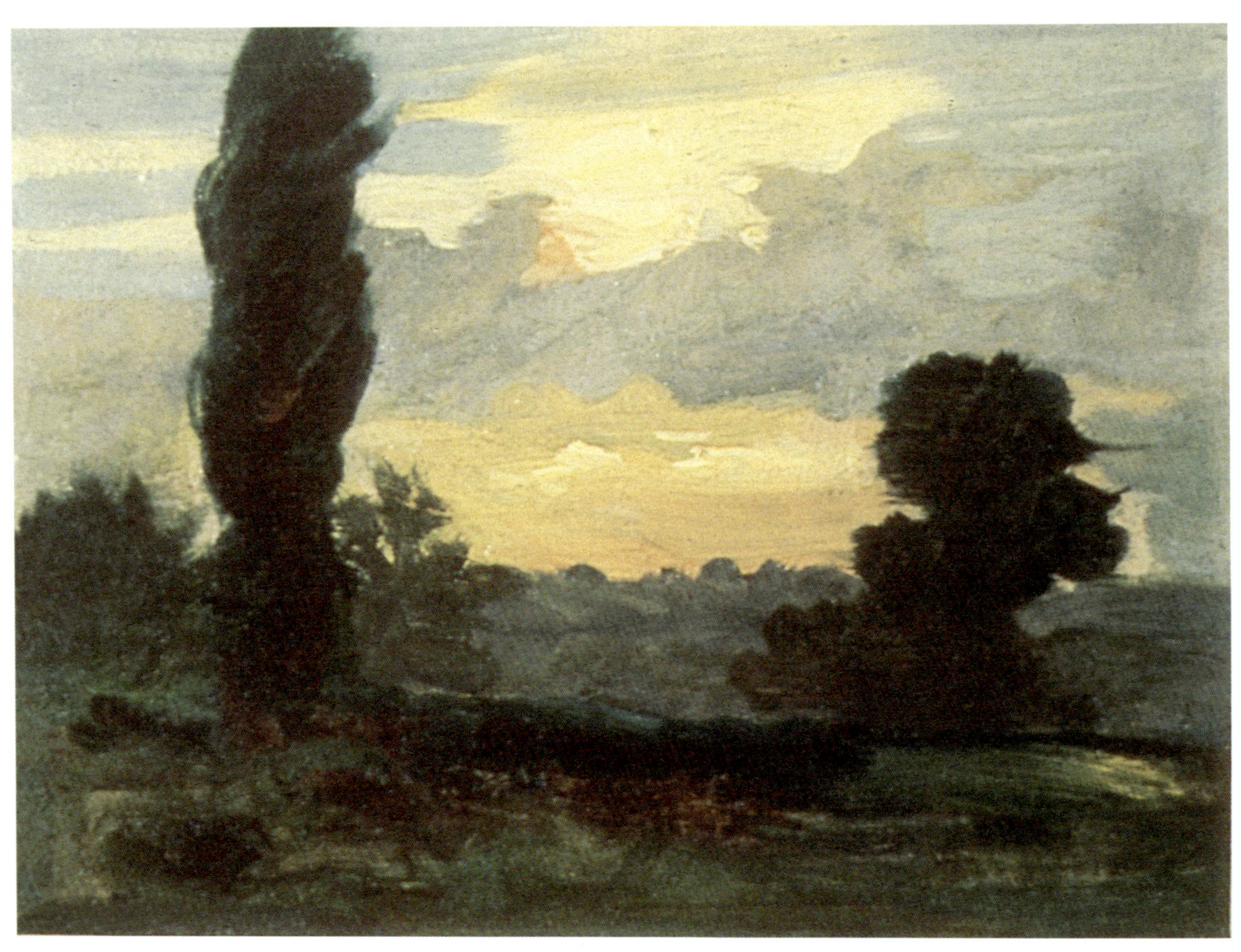

PLATE 16. *Landscape,* ca. 1898
oil on board, dimens. unknown
Location unknown

Preface

BY WILLIAM INNES HOMER

From time to time, worthy but little-known painters are rediscovered. Thomas Anshutz is one of these. An unusually talented artist whose achievements in painting have been overshadowed by his distinguished reputation as a teacher, Anshutz produced works that often are of very high quality, distinctly expressive, and technically proficient. It is amazing to realize that such an artist could have remained in relative obscurity, but such is the case.

There is a small but loyal Anshutz following among art historians and collectors. He has been celebrated in private, one might say, and those who have admired him have often communicated with each other and shared their enthusiasm. My own interest in Anshutz, for example, dates back to my years as a graduate student in the mid 1950s. Subsequently, I was able to discover a few others between that time and the present who also cared for the artist's work. One of these was Ruth Bowman, who wrote her master's thesis on Anshutz in 1971; and another was Sandra Denney, the author of a master's thesis written under my direction in 1969. More recently Randall Griffin, also formerly a student of mine, became an Anshutz devotée and wrote his doctoral dissertation on the artist's life and work; it became the basis for the text of the present catalogue.

Anshutz's admirers have included the dealer Robert C. Graham and the collectors Victor Spark and the Hon. Joseph P. Carroll and Mrs. Carroll. These individuals have provided building blocks of various kinds that have helped make this exhibition a reality. Then there is the commendable enthusiasm of Anna C. Noll, curator of the Heckscher Museum, who has demonstrated unwavering faith in the project.

Why is Anshutz worth recovering? There are a number of answers to this question, but the principal one is that his best work is at such a high level and so original that it is truly deserving of attention. One of his earliest efforts, for example, *The Ironworkers' Noontime,* has become an icon in American art history, a startlingly fresh painting and a revealing social document as well. His early works also include amazingly original pictures, acutely perceived transcriptions of city scenes that anticipate such twentieth-century masters as Charles Demuth and Charles Sheeler.

In many of the genre pieces—mostly figures in interiors—that he did under the influence of his teacher Thomas Eakins, Anshutz created his own personal variations, not slavish copies or echoes of the work of Eakins. In the 1890s and early 1900s, Anshutz also made large-scale portraits of women that are handled in a traditional style that is still indebted to Eakins; yet Anshutz's interpretation of his female subjects is uniquely his own. He enjoyed painting tall, elegant young women in long dresses, standing or seated in quiet Victorian interiors, with almost no background to compete with their dignity and presence. There is a kind of magical stillness to some of these pieces, an echo no doubt of the sedate Philadelphia world in which Anshutz lived and worked.

Gradually moving away from Eakins' dominant influence, Anshutz decided to find his own path and shaped a new idiom influenced by the French Impressionists and the Nabis. Some of his watercolor exercises, reflecting these influences of the 1890s, are stunningly beautiful—radiant, liquid efforts that sing with sensual color. In his last years, just prior to his death in 1912, Anshutz experimented with Neo-impressionist and Fauve color, producing pathfinding pictures that seem almost unbelievable for an artist who came out of the tradition of Philadelphia realism.

Thomas Anshutz possessed an independent cast of mind. As an art student at the National Academy of Design in New York, he was not satisfied with the status quo but sought, instead, a fresher, more realistic style than what he was being taught to imitate. When he arrived in Philadelphia, he became a student of Eakins, then in the most revolutionary phase of his development, practicing a kind of realism that Anshutz had already dreamed of while in New York. Attaching himself to Eakins in the mid 1870s, when that artist was teaching at the Pennsylvania Academy of the Fine Arts, Anshutz became something of a protégé. Eakins saw to it that Anshutz would become demonstrator of anatomy at the school, then a member of the teaching staff. The younger man's skill as an instructor must have pleased Eakins, who was no doubt impressed, too, by Anshutz's ability as an artist (though we have no exact records of what Eakins thought in this matter). In any case, the two men were close, and it is a tribute to Anshutz that he should have won the confidence and support of one of America's greatest painters and teachers.

For a time, Anshutz worked under Eakins' shadow. The younger man gradually became dissatisfied with his master's philosophy of art and teaching, however, and by the early 1880s he was beginning to move in his own direction. Anshutz had been responsive to ideas generated among his fellow art students and artist friends at the Philadelphia Sketch Club, and these newer notions of aesthetics seem to have gone against Eakins' grain. While Eakins had been revolutionary in his view of art and instruction in the 1870s, by the mid 1880s his methods had hardly changed at all, and younger artists, including Anshutz, were beginning to turn to more advanced aesthetic principles, including art-for-art's-sake,

Symbolism, and Impressionism. Therefore, it is not surprising to find Anshutz among the young rebels who turned against Eakins and were partially responsible for his expulsion from the Academy in 1886. This is not the place to recount the story of Eakins' resignation in detail, but it should be said that it was based not only on his libertarian handling of the nude in his teaching but also on his reluctance to embrace newer aesthetic standards that were being upheld by Anshutz and his young contemporaries. Anshutz was one of those who were asked to take over at the Academy, no doubt in response to his own offer to help. What at first might have seemed a stopgap measure expanded and developed into Anshutz's long term association with the Academy: he taught there for the rest of his life.

Although it is impossible to portray fully the importance of any teacher through an exhibition, Anshutz's instructional skills deserve to be taken into account as part of the whole picture. In the eyes of many of his protégés, he was a superb teacher, not in a flashy way but as someone who could draw out the best in his students as unique individuals. Again and again his pupils praised him for his openness to new ideas and his receptiveness to their individuality. Although he had been brought up in the academic tradition and never abandoned this foundation, Anshutz increasingly allowed his students to work in their own way and express themselves in the manner they thought best, hoping to encourage some spark of talent or genius. He did not impose his own style or anyone else's upon them. This openness toward his students' innate abilities came at the right time in the history of American art, because he had in his classes a group of young men who were destined to make their names as artists just after the turn of the century—they were the Philadelphia core of the New York Realists, or Ashcan School, and a sizeable number of those who became noted modernists. These artists needed freedom to work within the growing experimental climate in the creative arts, and Anshutz both allowed them that freedom and nurtured their unique talents.

Thomas Anshutz was unusual in that he associated with his own students as an equal and learned from them. For example, he maintained cordial relationships with Robert Henri and John Sloan when these two became established leaders of the New York Realists. They would often visit Anshutz at his home in Fort Washington, Pennsylvania, in a spirit of homage and friendship. In turn, Henri hired Anshutz to lecture on anatomy from time to time at the New York School of Art, an assignment commemorated in Sloan's etching of the subject. In a similar fashion, Anshutz kept up with his students who were following more advanced currents than the Ashcan School—for example, H. Lyman Saÿen, whom he visited in Paris and with whom he discussed various forms of contemporary art.

In 1892, Anshutz decided that he would need to gain a better understanding of recent developments in French painting. Thus he made his way to Paris to become a student once again, enrolling at the Académie Julian. Although he found this schooling unrewarding, he nonetheless benefitted from his Parisian sojourn. It was here that his eyes were opened to works in a Symbolist mode by the Nabis, and he learned a great deal from them. Indeed, these French painters' achievements corresponded to ideas that were already stirring within Anshutz, as we know from his letters of the mid 1880s, in which he wrote of subjectivity and the importance of intuition. Paris, then, not only helped Anshutz develop a more modern style of painting, it also gave him the basis for a broader aesthetic theory.

Part of the reason for the freshness of Anshutz's imagery (given that he was also capable of traditional painting) was his independence of mind and his willingness to forge ahead without concern for public taste or artistic precedent. He was a true American independent, sufficiently confident of his artistic vision that he could produce works of unusual freshness and originality. Perhaps he was able to proceed on this route so vigorously because he cared little about commercial success and wide popularity. Whatever the reason, it is now time to celebrate Anshutz's accomplishments and to view them not only for what they are, but also in a historical context, to measure them against the work of his contemporaries and his successors.

Introduction

Thomas Anshutz has remained a painter in art-historical limbo, his life, ideas, and imagery rarely examined in any depth. No monograph has previously focused on his work.[1] He has wrongly been viewed, on the basis of his well-known *The Ironworkers' Noontime,* as a one-picture artist (plate 1). Although he did not possess the prodigious talent of Thomas Eakins, William Merritt Chase, or Winslow Homer, he was a gifted draftsman and fine colorist who produced a number of exceptional pictures. Scholars have previously concentrated on the limited range of Anshutz's works that closely resemble those of his teacher, Eakins. Such a selective examination offers a distorted, monolithic record of Anshutz's art. Encompassing a wide range of styles and themes, Anshutz's work is in fact as diverse as that of any American artist of his era.

The eclectic range of his artistic production sets him apart from many of his contemporaries. Driven both by curiosity and insecurity, he assimilated—throughout his career—one style after another (never really finding his own), exploring everything from the naturalism of Eakins and Homer to the modernism of the Nabis and the Fauves. Especially in his late work, he is an unusual example of an early twentieth-century American artist who blurred categories of realist and modernist, conservative and avant-garde, thus complicating traditional art historical dualisms.

Even some of Anshutz's early pictures exhibit an unorthodox conflation of artistic concerns. *The Ironworkers' Noontime,* his best-known and most compelling image, is founded on a thorough academic knowledge of classical art, perspective, and anatomy, yet offers a starkly unidealized and innovative portrayal of factory life. Even today, the workers, in their blasted factory landscape, seem so viscerally present that the painting is somewhat unsettling. My discussion of *The Ironworkers' Noontime,* in chapter one, differs significantly from the rest of the text in its length and methodology, this more comprehensive treatment justified by the painting's uniqueness among Anshutz's work, and, indeed, among American paintings of its time. In addition, the artist's highly unusual treatment of industrial subject matter makes this image ideally suited for a social-contextual analysis. Unlike the other chapters, which seek to construct an overall historical narrative of Anshutz's art and teaching, emphasizing biography and artistic style—this section examines one image in greater detail in an effort to illuminate both its implications on and the nature of late nineteenth-century American culture.

Although *The Ironworkers' Noontime* was a hymn to Anshutz's mentor, Thomas Eakins, Anshutz spent much of the remainder of his artistic career attempting to distance his art from Eakins' naturalistic style, which Anshutz came to view as too "scientific" and analytical. Even in the early 1880s, when his art was closest to Eakins,' Anshutz never mimicked his mentor's severe "scientific" form of realism. Nevertheless, Anshutz's art almost always constituted a dialogue with Eakins' painting. Consistent in all of Anshutz's imagery is an interest, inspired by Eakins' teaching, in depicting underlying structures, especially the anatomical structure of the human figure.

In a similarly ambiguous manner, Eakins also strongly influenced Anshutz's teaching at the Pennsylvania Academy of the Fine Arts. Anshutz will probably always be considered as important a teacher as a painter. Instructing such students as John Marin, Charles Demuth, Robert Henri, William Glackens, and John Sloan, Anshutz acted as an important link between his own instructor, Thomas Eakins, and "The Eight" of 1908 and as a catalyst for the beginnings of early American modernism in Philadelphia. According to both students and critics, he attempted to encourage the development of students' idiosyncratic artistic visions, unfettered by emphasis on tradition. Anshutz's most telling contribution to the history of American art was to provide artists with training that joined the ideas of Eakins to much more "progressive" late nineteenth-century notions of art. He was especially gifted at recognizing student talent and at encouraging artistic individuality. In class assignments and in numerous out-of-class discussions, he emphasized the necessity for artistic change, experimentation, and the questioning of accepted conventions, thus paralleling his own developments as a painter. As his imagery became increasingly adventurous, so did his teaching. A man whose ideas of art spanned two generations of American artists, Anshutz was a painter and instructor who, especially after his first trip to Paris in 1892, attempted to reconcile tradition with innovation, and a belief in artistic rules with acceptance of aesthetic relativity. Throughout his late career, he grappled with this problem of balancing two seemingly antithetical views of art.

In writing this catalogue, I have attempted to avoid producing a history of Anshutz and his art that would either spuriously romanticize his life or glorify his art. The single-artist study is especially prone to consisting of fiction masquerading as truth, in its seamless narrative, selective inclusion, and uncritical acceptance of the autonomy of the individual. This study is no different. Although the examination of one historical thread is always—in some sense—inherently distortive, this genre of scholarship, nonetheless, provides a necessary and important foundation for future research. As Virginia Woolf wrote of a related form of scholarship—though she was speaking as the omniscient narrator of a fictive, not to say blatantly fantastic, character!—the biographer's task is "to plod, without looking to right or left, in the indelible footprints of truth; unenticed by flowers; regardless of shade; on and on methodically till we fall plump into the grave and write *finis* on the tombstone above our heads."[2]

CHAPTER 1

ANSHUTZ'S ART AND LIFE THROUGH 1891

Thomas Pollock Anshutz was born on October 5, 1851, in Newport, Kentucky, to Jacob Anshutz and Abigail Jane Anshutz, née Pollock. By Thomas Anshutz's early teens, his family had moved to the industrial town of Wheeling, at that time in Virginia, where his mother had lived before her marriage. Thomas Anshutz had two brothers, Edward and Sidney, and a sister, Edith. All the family were members of the Swedenborgian New Church.[1]

Very few primary documents survive from Thomas Anshutz's childhood, and his own later accounts of his early life lack detail. As an adult he wrote that during youth, he "...showed no decided artistic bent," but "had seen paintings in Cincinnati...which made a tremendous impression upon [him]," though what or where these paintings were is not known.[2] His parents, however, had encouraged his sketching, and one of his public school teachers had been favorably impressed by his artistic talents. Anshutz's uncle, a Mr. Peters from Brooklyn who worked for the *Brooklyn Times,* suggested that he be trained as an artist after seeing his nephew's drawings and paintings of boats on the Ohio River.[3] Thomas Anshutz began his formal career as an artist in his early twenties. He moved from his parents' home in Wheeling to Brooklyn in 1871, where he lived with his aunt and uncle, Mrs. and Mr. Peters, in order to study art.[4] There seems to be no record of his activities during his first two years' residence in Brooklyn, but at some point he became a member of the Brooklyn Art Club, and in 1873 he enrolled as a student at the National Academy of Design in New York, where instructors included Daniel Huntington, William Rimmer, Eastman Johnson, and Lemuel Everett Wilmarth.[5]

The teaching philosophy at the National Academy of Design, under the influence of Wilmarth, was modeled after art academies in Munich and Paris, where Wilmarth had trained. He was Anshutz's principal instructor at the National Academy. That institution's records show that Anshutz enrolled in an "antique" class—in which students sketched casts of ancient Greek and Roman sculptures—taught by Wilmarth that began on October 6, 1873.[6] At least initially, and perhaps in a characteristically new-student response, Anshutz lacked any enthusiasm whatsoever for his courses:

> The National Academy of Design is a rotten old institution supported and controlled by lovers of art and by artists whose principal skill consists in uncorking champagne bottles and sliding home on window shutters.... Well when the promising young genius enters the acad. with the idea of at once making his mark and fortune, he goes into this branch [the antique classes] where he is given some head with strongly marked features which he works at from two to three weeks immensely to his own satisfaction. Then there comes in an art critic (he comes 3 times per week) who probably says, "Well your drawing has some good points but you had better not waste any more time on it as it is hopelessly spoiled." So you work away at other heads which he suggests giving you more difficult and delicate faces until you are thoroughly convinced that you are an ass. When you are driven entirely mad and are suicidal he deals out some encouragement and points out your defects in a mild manner.... Drawing alone is taught or rather studied.[7]

Because so little of Anshutz's correspondence from this period survives, it is impossible to say whether his attitude toward the National Academy became more sanguine. He did, however, continue to take classes there for approximately two more years. He registered in Wilmarth's advanced life class on March 8, 1875. This spring term was the last he spent at the National Academy of Design.

None of Anshutz's drawings or paintings seem to have survived from his New York student years. Undoubtedly, given the National Academy's emphasis on draftsmanship and Anshutz's later, attested, proficiency, he acquired at least basic skills at this time.

During the years Anshutz resided in New York (1871-1875), he occasionally traveled to Wheeling and spent summers with his parents and siblings in Holly Beach, New Jersey. There, he sketched and practiced *plein-air* painting, which he described in late 1873 as follows:

> [I would] get up an outfit for outdoor work, go out into some woebegotten, turkey chawed, bottle-nosed, hen pecked country and set myself down. Get out my materials and make as accurate a painting of what I see in front of me as I can.[8]

Anshutz's preoccupation with naturalistically depicting the outdoors continued throughout much of his later life, changing only around 1905, when he began to experiment with landscapes inspired by James Abbott McNeill Whistler and the Nabis.

In the fall of 1875, after the National Academy of Design closed for the year, Anshutz moved to Philadelphia. There he enrolled in the life class of the Philadelphia Sketch Club, taught by Thomas Eakins, who was to become the dominant influence on Anshutz's early art and teaching.

Anshutz did not record why he chose to study in Philadelphia. The best-known art school in the city, the Pennsylvania Academy of the Fine Arts, had been closed for five years and did not reopen until a year after Anshutz's arrival, when its new building, at Broad and Cherry Streets, was completed.

After the Pennsylvania Academy reopened in October 1876, Anshutz enrolled in classes taught by Christian Schussele. The Philadelphia institution's curriculum at this time was somewhat similar to that of the National Academy of Design. Yet there were significant differences between the two schools: the Pennsylvania Academy offered a larger selection of courses, and, due to Eakins' influence, it emphasized to a greater extent study from life and anatomy classes.

In the same year (1876) in which Anshutz began his studies at the Pennsylvania Academy, Dr. William W. Keen, a noted Philadelphia surgeon who was the institution's Professor of Artistic Anatomy, appointed Eakins Chief Demonstrator of Anatomy. In 1878 and 1879 Anshutz was made an assistant demonstrator to Eakins. Then, in 1880, Anshutz himself became chief demonstrator, replacing Eakins, who, in the fall of 1879, had been named Professor of Drawing and Painting, after Schussele's death that August.[9] Beginning in the fall of 1881, Anshutz was promoted to the position of full-time faculty member at the Academy.

Eakins' focus on dissection and anatomy instruction made the Pennsylvania Academy unique among American art schools. He believed that good painting and sculpture were based on a thorough understanding of anatomy and that only by attaining a detailed anatomical knowledge of skeletal and muscular structure could a student properly conceptualize how the body moved and shifted weight. Eakins viewed dissection as a necessary pedagogical experience, which enabled students to come closer to an "objective" understanding of nature. He thought that, by comparison, it taught them to see more critically what was "false" and convention-ridden in art. Eakins justified the study of anatomy as an exercise in careful perception that enabled the student "to observe more closely, and the closer his observation is the better his drawing will be...."[10] Eakins had no difficulty reconciling an analytical "scientific" study of the body with an aesthetic and artistic one.

During the years 1878 to 1881, in accordance with Eakins' teachings, Anshutz studied human and animal anatomy assiduously. He spent hours each week assisting with anatomy classes, and also produced images representing those experiences. His no longer extant *Plaster Cast from Original Model of a Horse,* which he exhibited in 1879 at the Pennsylvania Academy, must have exemplified this interest.[11] One of Anshutz's sketchbooks, now in the collection of the Pennsylvania Academy of the Fine Arts, contains anatomical drawings of a horse, which, presumably, were produced while dissecting a horse at the Academy, a practice Eakins commonly required of advanced students. An article published in September 1879 in *Scribner's Monthly* contained

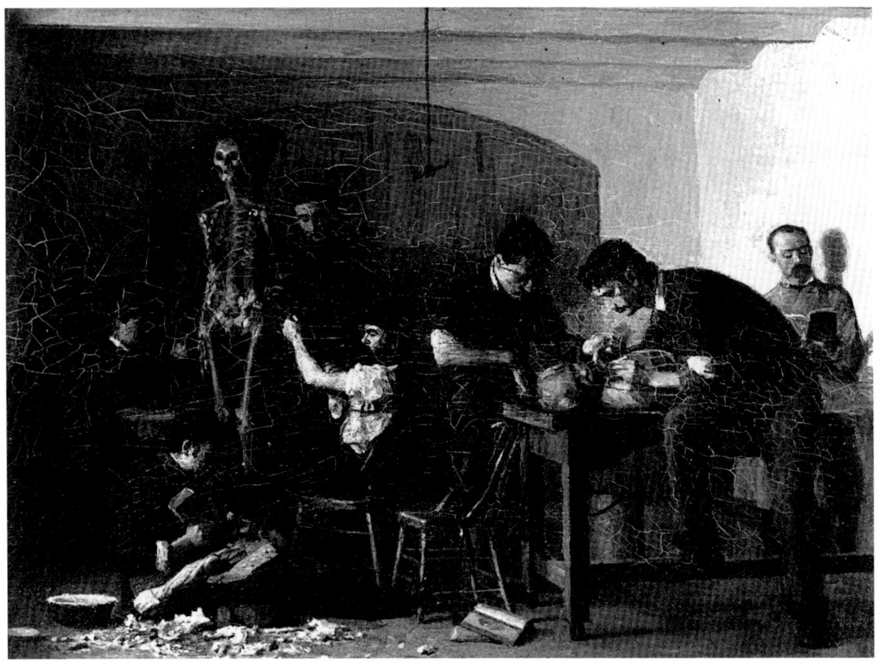

Figure 1.
The Dissecting Room, 1879
oil on canvas on wood, 10 × 12½"
The Pennsylvania Academy of the Fine Arts, Philadelphia. Gift of the Artist

a scene painted and contributed by Anshutz to illustrate teaching methods of the Pennsylvania Academy.[12] His *The Dissecting Room* shows two pyramidal groups of figures: one studying a skeleton on the left and the other dissecting a human cadaver on the right (fig. 1). On the far right a man appears to be reading instructions aloud from an anatomy book. Another student in the lower left is pictured making a cast of an arm or leg. As is typical of Anshutz's paintings from this period, the figures themselves are simplified, static, and sculptural. Anshutz continued to value knowledge of anatomy in artistic training, as is evident from John Sloan's etching *Anshutz on Anatomy,* which depicts the older artist giving a lecture at the New York School of Art much later, in 1906 (fig. 2).

As a teacher, Eakins rejected any lengthy study of antique casts, stressing instead study of the live model, as well as classes in dissection. Eakins' insistence on the study of the nude, as with dissection, exemplified his belief in various types of empirical study, and their value to painters. In order to be able to render the human figure accurately, he felt that the artist should dissect it, model it in clay or wax, and repeatedly depict its unclothed form.[13] Anshutz never focused as intensively on the nude, either in his art or teaching, as Eakins. However, the human figure is consistently central in Anshutz's art from the late 1870s through the end of his life.

At this time Anshutz embraced, as well, Eakins' rejection of what they both saw as affectation and falseness in art. Technical tricks and painterly flourishes such as *trompe l' oeil* polish or bravura displays of loose brushwork were considered insincere and superficial. According to both men, honesty and truth to one's *own* perceptions of nature constituted the only legitimate approach to art. That "sincerity" and "truth to one's observations" were thought preeminent by a range of contemporary artists, from Eakins and Anshutz to William Morris Hunt and Claude Monet, illustrates how a ubiquitously accepted philosophical concern could be inflected in varying ways.

Eakins' and Anshutz's notion of truth-and-art at this time could be summarized in this statement by the nineteenth-century French realist Gustave Courbet:

> Painting is an essentially concrete art and can only consist of the presentation of real and existing things. It is a completely physical language, the words of which consist of all visible objects; an object which is abstract, not visible, non-existent, is not within the realm of painting.[14]

Eakins' dislike of idealization prompted him to write:

> Get the character of things.... If a man's fat, make him fat. If a man's thin, make him thin. If a man's short, make him short. If a man's long, make him long.[15]

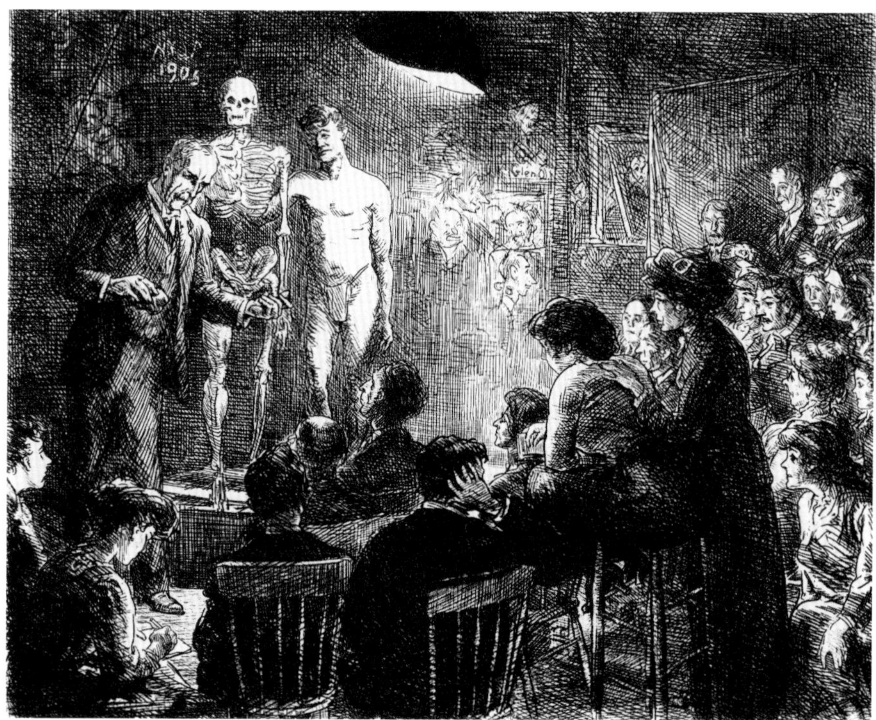

Figure 2.
John Sloan (1871-1951)
Anshutz on Anatomy, 1912
etching, 8th state, 12¾ × 14½" (sheet)
The Pennsylvania Academy of the Fine Arts, Philadelphia. Gift of Helen Farr Sloan

Anshutz, much later, similarly wrote, "The true artist aims for a simple, direct expression of this interest in things."[16]

Eakins' observation that "there are no lines in nature" also profoundly affected Anshutz's work.[17] Anshutz always employed broad, general areas of light and dark when drawing or painting, instead of rendering what he saw in detailed, linear fashion. Both he and Eakins considered such meticulousness of style superficial, a show of artistic virtuosity for its own sake, emphasizing merely surfaces. They wanted instead to capture underlying mass and structure. In their art and teaching, both men emphatically stressed the plastic structure of the figure. In order to achieve this "grand construction of a figure," a student was told by Eakins "to block up his figure rapidly, and then give to any part of it the highest finish without injuring its unity."[18] Anshutz similarly blocked in figures quickly. His occasional preparatory oil sketches, throughout his life, resemble Eakins' in their emphasis on basic masses of form.

This attempt to reconstitute the weight and mass of nature in paint is a principal element in both Eakins' and Anshutz's work. According to

Figure 3.
On the Ohio, ca. 1880
oil on fabric on composition board, 9 × 13½"
In the Collection of The Corcoran Gallery of Art, Washington, DC, Museum Purchase through the Gift of Joseph Sanders

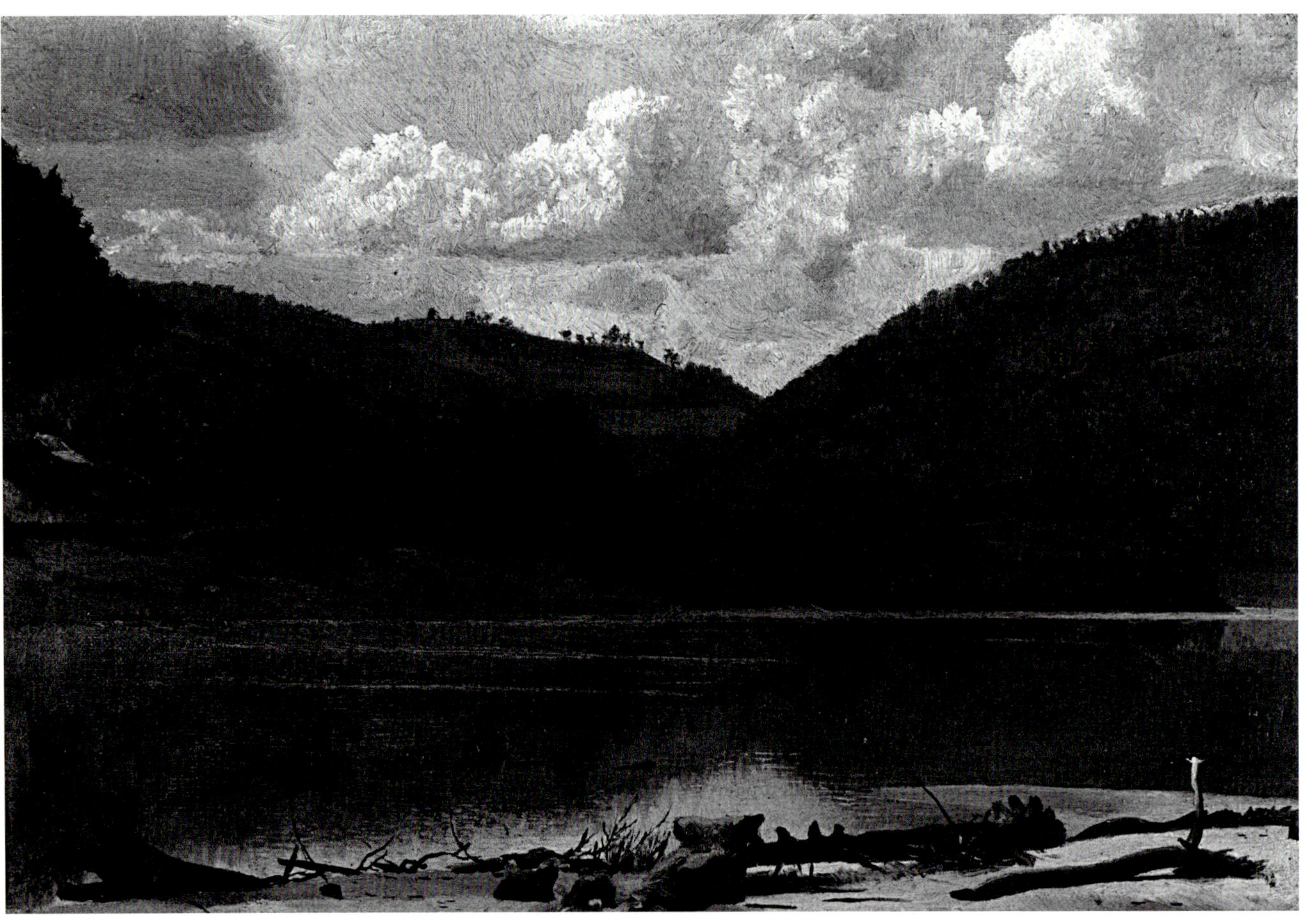

Charles Bregler, Eakins told his students always to "think in the third dimension," and Anshutz certainly sought this effect.[19] To facilitate the student's ability to learn the fundamentals of painting and to represent the basic sculptural substance of nature, Eakins required his pupils, including Anshutz, to depict in oil eggs, oranges, and pieces of chalk or sugar.[20]

Eakins also demanded that his students be able to understand and represent faithfully the movements of human and animal bodies. Anshutz later commented, "I learned [as a student at the Pennsylvania Academy of the Fine Arts] the difference between making a careful copy of lines and form which express some action, and trying to express the action itself."[21] Throughout his career, Anshutz returned to the artistic problem of representing the weight and movement of the human body, though his figures consistently look static. This is apparent in such early paintings as *The Ironworkers' Noontime* and *The Farmer and His Son at Harvesting,* in which he depicts the *contrapposto* of the workers' bodies (plates 1, 2). Regarding this subject, Anshutz wrote:

> The man whose work is real to him will plant a model on his feet, because unconsciously he feels the man's weight and where it is born[e]. While he who is governed by his eye will place the model's foot according to the angle of the leg with the trunk or by imagining a plum[b] line....[22]

Although Eakins' art and teaching affected Anshutz's approach to painting until the end of his (Anshutz's) life, the younger man more consistently and closely emulated his instructor's style of painting and drawing between 1878 and 1892. Yet even during this early "Eakins period," Anshutz produced images that sometimes differed from Eakins' art both thematically and stylistically.

During the years 1878-79, the majority of the paintings Anshutz produced were landscapes. Of these, most were river views, continuing his early interest in that subject. Of the seven paintings he exhibited at the Pennsylvania Academy in 1879, five were landscapes, of which four were river views.[23] This suggests that he initially considered becoming principally a landscape painter. In *On the Ohio* Anshutz employed a composition similar to those found in the Hudson River School (fig. 3).[24] Anshutz's strong horizontal emphasis (bands of shore, water, mountain, and sky), scarcity of human presence, and stillness are all reminiscent of works by John Frederick Kensett.

Anshutz's early paintings often contain simple, stark geometric forms. This is especially evident in his watercolor *Rooftop Scene, Philadelphia* (fig. 4). Eakins may have encouraged Anshutz to paint this, having himself produced rooftop studies years earlier in Spain, in which he was mainly concerned with a problem he considered extremely challenging, that of recording the changing effects of light.[25]. Anshutz, on the

Figure 4.
Rooftop Scene, Philadelphia,
ca. 1883
watercolor, 7 × 11"
Location unknown

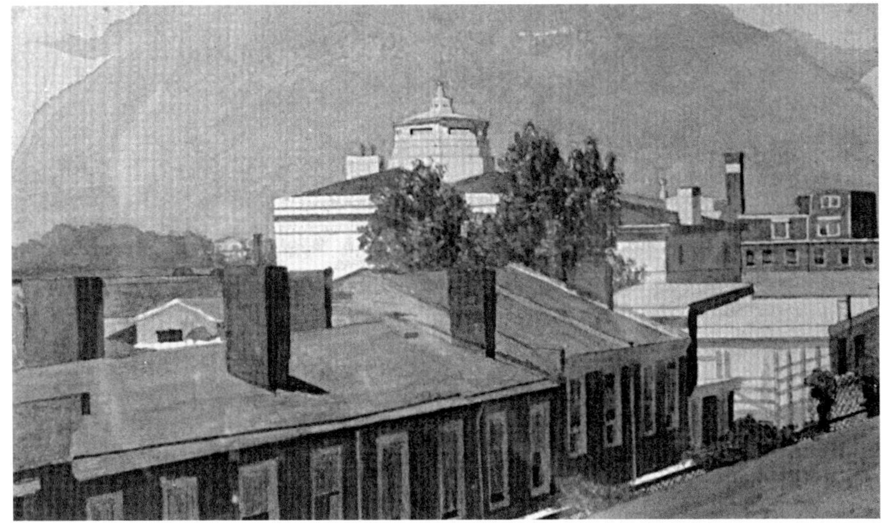

other hand, seems to have been equally interested in depicting the bold and rhythmic line of chimneys, so similar to those in his earlier painting *The Ironworkers' Noontime*. This Philadelphia watercolor's radical compositional cropping produces a feeling of modernity, foreshadowing later paintings by Edward Hopper and his contemporaries.

Many of Anshutz's paintings during the period 1878-82 were agrarian scenes. They reveal the painter's love for the countryside, as well as his affection for the nostalgic qualities of such scenes of rural society. He and other painters in the 1870s, like Eastman Johnson, Theodore Robinson, and Winslow Homer, produced scores of similar images of a rapidly disappearing American lifestyle. Never as saccharine or idealized as the scenes of Johnson or Jules Breton, Anshutz's high-keyed, agrarian images were especially inspired by the paintings of Winslow Homer, whose work Anshutz would have known from exhibitions at the Philadelphia Centennial and the National Academy of Design. Anshutz's rural imagery was also indebted to the realism of Eakins' art.

Anshutz's *The Farmer and His Son at Harvesting* is perhaps his strongest agrarian scene (plate 2). Set in the mountains of West Virginia, the picture shows two figures, under a deep blue sky, harvesting hay on a summer day. Anshutz never achieved a more masterful portrayal of natural light. Participating in a long tradition of rural imagery, his treatment is different from earlier American scenes of farmers by such artists as William Sidney Mount and George Henry Durrie. These latter two artists emphasized humor and narrative in their scenes; but Anshutz, following Homer, stressed instead the vibrant effects of light. The two figures stand out starkly in their white shirts and black trousers against the green and yellow background of foliage. *The Farmer and His Son at Harvesting* was loosely based on such paintings by Homer as *Crossing the Pasture*

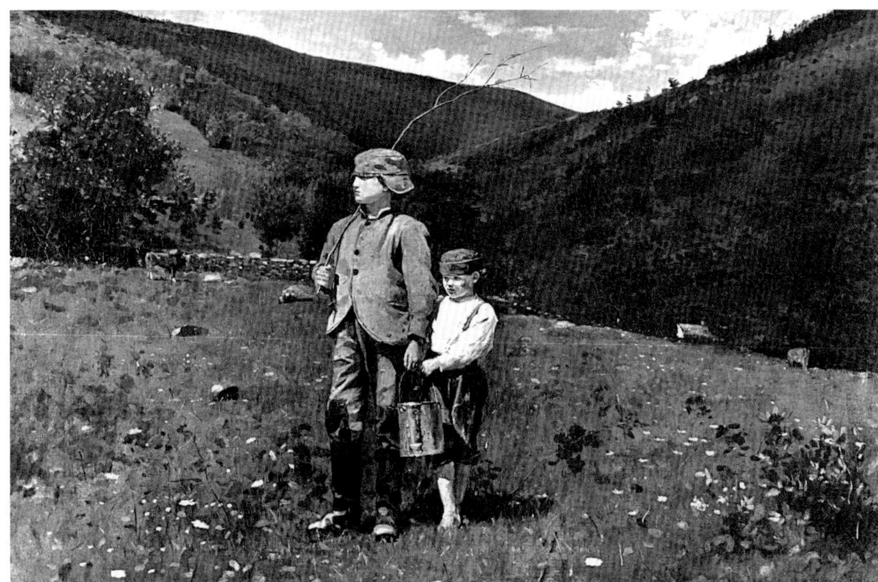

Figure 5.
Winslow Homer (1836-1910)
Crossing the Pasture, ca. 1872
oil on canvas, 26⅛ × 38⅛"
Amon Carter Museum, Fort Worth

(fig. 5). Yet even with its similar subject matter, mountain setting, quality of light, and palette, Anshutz's scene includes more detail and specificity. His use of a vertical format accentuates the mountain valley's feeling of remoteness and isolation. Perhaps an evocation of the artist's own pleasant memories of time spent on an uncle's farm in rural Ohio, it is a nostalgic image of rural harmony.[26] Arcadian and pre-industrial, Anshutz's farmer even wields an outdated type of scythe.[27] This arcadian quality is somewhat undercut by such carefully observed details as the boy's thirsty grip on the water pail and the father's back, bowed by hard labor.

Also in 1879 Anshutz produced *The Way They Live,* painted in a similar style to *The Farmer and His Son at Harvesting* (plates 3, 2).[28] Once again employing a vertical compositional format, Anshutz depicted the enclosing West Virginia hills and adopted similar greens, browns, and blues in shades that convey the heat of a summer afternoon. By nearly eliminating the cool blue sky and adding the foreground expanse of dry bare ground and a brilliant patch of red, the painter gave *The Way They Live* an arid, sweltering appearance. Unlike *The Farmer and His Son at Harvesting, The Way They Live* offers a gritty, though still decoratively presented, version of agrarian life. Illustrating the depths of rural poverty, it shows an African-American woman working a bleak plot. Her subsistence farm appears hardly productive or large enough to feed herself and her two children. The woman's body is stiff, her back bent, and her facial expression grim. Anshutz's dignified, relatively unpatronizing treatment of African-American figures is reminiscent of those by Homer. Anshutz's detailed, naturalistic treatment also owes an important debt to Eakins. He would have known Eakins' images of African-Americans, such as the watercolor *Whistling [for] Plover* (1874, The Brooklyn Museum), and *Negro Boy Dancing* (1878, The Metropolitan Museum of Art).

During the 1880s, Anshutz produced half-a-dozen additional oil and watercolor images of African-Americans, including, for example, *The Chore* (plate 4). *The Chore*, one of four paintings that portray the Anshutz family servant holding a broom, shows her as she pauses from sweeping a rug to tie up her bandanna.[29] The painting is overtly theatrical and contrived; yet, despite its staged appearance, *The Chore* conveys an impressive sense of monumentality. Although Anshutz must have been drawn to the theme's inherently picturesque character, in this painting he displays equal interest in conveying the illusion of sculptural form and in creating a visually complex assemblage of abstract shapes. The sinuous forms of the oriental rug, chair splats, and woman's contour contrast with that of the rigid, diagonal line of the broom. Even at their most Eakins-like, Anshutz's images always appear more concerned with abstract shapes and geometric forms, but lack the psychological force of Eakins' pictures.

In the summer of 1880 Anshutz painted *A Farmer Plowing* and *The Ironworkers' Noontime,* both of which closely emulate Eakins' work in style, though not subject (fig. 6, plate 1). In *A Farmer Plowing*, Anshutz chose to show the farmer and horses in profile, as Eakins had portrayed his subject in *John Biglin in a Single Scull* (1873-74, The Metropolitan Museum of Art). This compositional strategy objectifies the figures, and, as in many of Eakins' paintings, gives them a frozen appearance. One is

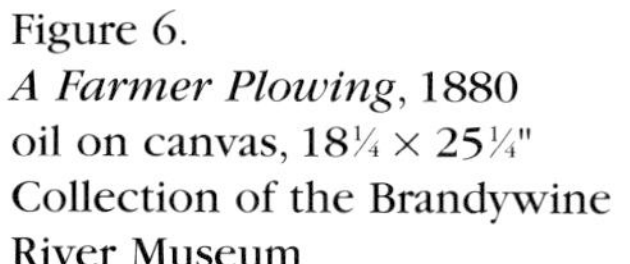

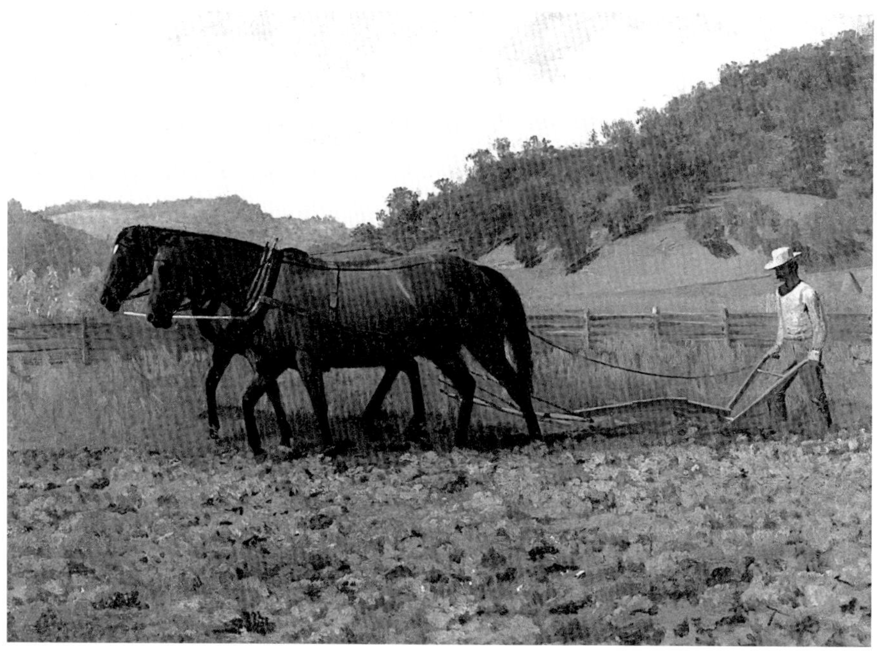

Figure 6.
A Farmer Plowing, 1880
oil on canvas, 18¼ × 25¼"
Collection of the Brandywine River Museum

struck by the scene's "documentary" look; nothing is prettified or overtly dramatic. It appears to be a straightforward recording.[30]

A Farmer Plowing may have been intended as a kind of homage to Eakins, referring obliquely to Eakins' painting *A May Morning in the Park (The Fairman Rogers Four-In-Hand)* (1879-80, Philadelphia Museum of Art). Anshutz's study of equine anatomy, conducted when he was Eakins' student, may also have encouraged him to include a prominent image of horses. As mentioned earlier, Anshutz had exhibited his *Plaster Cast from Original Model of a Horse* at the Pennsylvania Academy the previous year. Although Anshutz rarely produced preparatory drawings or oil studies until after 1905, for *A Farmer Plowing* he worked from pencil studies, which are included in the same Pennsylvania Academy sketchbook that contains anatomical studies of horses. These studies provide a clear record of his method for developing this painting, which consisted of a series of five drawings of the horses, ranging from simple outlines to fully modeled renderings.

That studies for *A Farmer Plowing* are interspersed in the sketchbook among preparatory drawings for *The Ironworkers' Noontime* indicates as well that Anshutz was simultaneously examining two sides of American life, one representing its agrarian past and the other its industrial present. In the industrial scene he also recast the nooning theme he had painted the previous year in *The Farmer and His Son at Harvesting. The Ironworkers' Noontime,* with its monumental, frieze-like grouping of figures, allowed Anshutz to display his skills in figure composition and his knowledge of anatomy and perspective in the service of realism (plate 1). Like *The Way They Live* and *A Farmer Plowing,* it is painted in a starkly Eakins-like, naturalistic manner. Of all Anshutz's paintings, it perhaps comes closest to his teacher's style. A distinctive and disconcerting image, it has commonly been regarded as Anshutz's most significant work, and thus, as noted in the introduction, merits lengthy exploration here.

In *The Ironworkers' Noontime* Anshutz created a new image of the American factory worker, one remarkably straightforward and unmelodramatic. Discarding the traditional representation of the ironworker as a Vulcan-at-the-forge figure, Anshutz instead focused on the men as human individuals. By compelling the viewer to meet these workers face to face, minus the veil of psychological distance common to genre scenes, in which figures exist in overtly self-contained worlds, Anshutz produced an image which transgressed conventional class-driven laws of decorum. The picture offered one of the first graphic views of the bleakness of American factory life.[31] Yet, despite the factual character of *The Ironworkers' Noontime*—an image that appears strikingly unmediated, authentic, and "real"—the painting is very much a construct circumscribed by widespread social concerns. A visual manifestation of the impact of industrialization on the American workplace, the painting also encodes late-Victorian notions about masculinity.

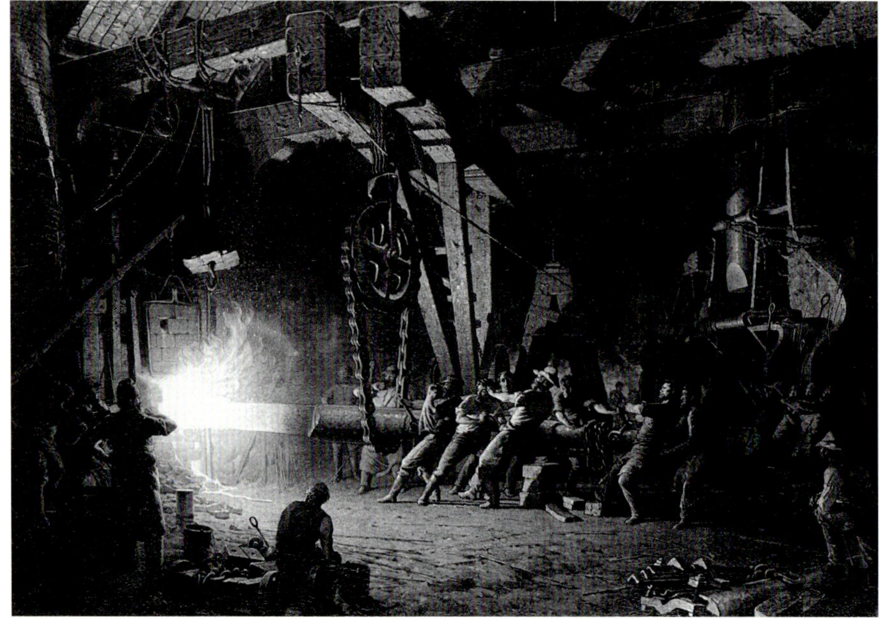

Figure 7.
John Ferguson Weir (1841-1926)
Forging the Shaft, 1877
oil on canvas, 52 × 73¼"
The Metropolitan Museum of Art, Purchase, Lyman G. Bloomingdale Gift, 1901 (01.7.1)

That Anshutz chose to paint the theme at all is somewhat puzzling in light of the fact that only a few American factory scenes precede his. One of those is John Ferguson Weir's *Forging the Shaft*, which, unlike *The Ironworkers' Noontime,* portrays men actually working (fig. 7). Moreover, Weir's scene emphasizes the fiery setting much more than the male figures; and, although many artists and authors included themes of technological progress in their work, which often contained representations of trains and steamboats, few undercut the preeminence of the natural landscape by focusing exclusively on the factory or the machine.[32] Since America was becoming a great industrial power and most Americans were proud of their nation's new technological prowess, the lack of prominent industrial themes in American art raises significant questions about the relationship of social change to art. Little patronage existed for this kind of painting; industrial themes were normally the province of popular illustration.[33]

What, then, explains Anshutz's decision, in 1880, to paint *The Ironworkers' Noontime*? Clearly the artist's own upbringing and family history encouraged his selection of an iron mill subject. The fact that many members of his father's family had actually owned and operated such mills earlier in the century, in Europe and America, suggests that a sense of family pride may have played a role.[34] Furthermore, as mentioned earlier, Anshutz spent much of his childhood in the industrial town of Wheeling, West Virginia, a major center for iron production, and the impressive row of iron mills dominating the town's Ohio riverfront would have been very familiar to him (fig. 8). Anshutz continued to make yearly trips to Wheeling throughout most of his adult life to visit his mother and his wife's family. While on one of these visits, in the summer of 1880, he began preparatory drawings for *The Ironworkers' Noontime*.[35] These drawings are in two small sketchbooks in the collection of the Pennsylvania Academy of the Fine Arts.

The sketchbooks also contain a group of riverfront drawings for *The Ironworkers' Noontime,* indicating that Anshutz had considered painting a broad river view of an iron mill, something he would later develop into *Steamboat on the Ohio* (fig. 9, plate 5).[36] Anshutz later stated that he had decided to focus instead on the ironworkers themselves because of the subject's picturesque possibilities.[37] By 1880 the word "picturesque" was commonly employed to describe scenes that juxtaposed untamed nature with the industrial landscape, as well as to describe factory images that evoked the hellish and the sublime.[38] Yet Anshutz's use of the word is somewhat idiosyncratic. Although he may well have considered the ironworkers to be exotic working-class figures and included the background chimney smoke as a "picturesque" ele-

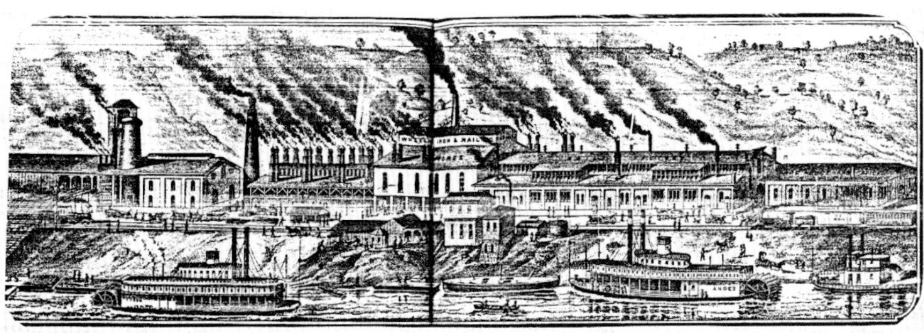

Figure 8.
Anonymous artist
Wheeling Iron and Nail Company, 1877
lithograph on paper
Illustration from Henry Dickerson Scott, *Iron and Steel in Wheeling*, 1929

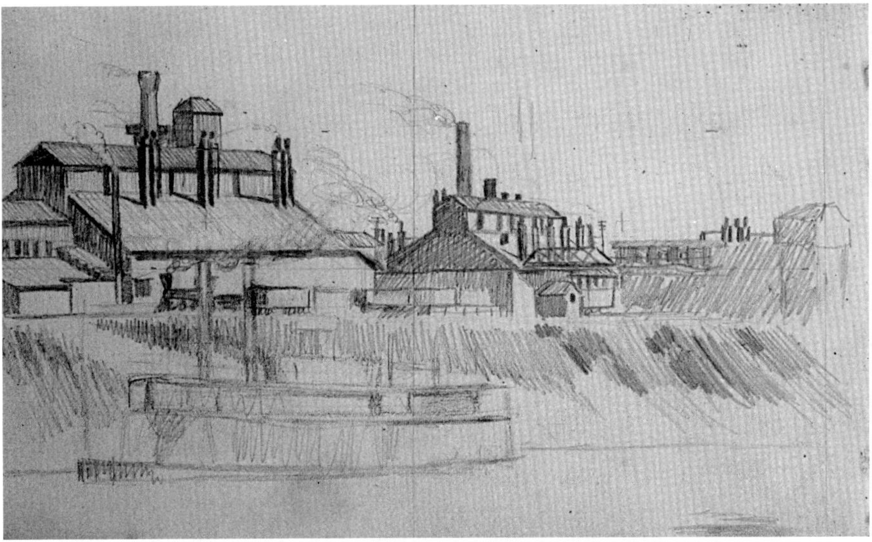

Figure 9.
Factory Study, 1880
Sketchbook #2, graphite on off-white wove leaves, 4¼ × 6½"
The Pennsylvania Academy of the Fine Arts, Philadelphia. Gift of Mr. and Mrs. Daniel W. Dietrich, II

ment—as Mark Twain does in his *Life on the Mississippi*—Anshutz employed the word—especially in letters to his artist friends—to signify, rather, the uniqueness of the subject matter among fine art imagery.[39] Although few nineteenth-century American painters chose factory themes, American illustrators began in the late 1870s to depict a wide range of industrial subjects, a proliferation that may have made Anshutz aware of the theme's currency.[40] Yet, unlike *The Ironworkers' Noontime,* most of these contemporary illustrations focus exclusively on the various stages of a worker's task; reminiscent of images in Diderot's *Encyclopédie,* they act as frame-by-frame narratives completely subservient to a written text.

The growing number of such images denotes profound changes in the nature of the American manufacturing system. Large-scale industrialization, which only became a widespread reality during the Civil War, brought with it more mechanization and a dramatic increase in the division of labor. This new increase in efficiency quickly made older workshop production, such as cabinet- and barrel-making, obsolete.[41] Factory workers lost the ability to advance towards self-employment, a common privilege of the workshop system. Moreover, industrialization sharply diminished the high levels of skill and craftsmanship previously common. John Morrison, a machinist, testifying about these changes in 1883 to a United States Senate committee, said:

> The trade has been subdivided and those subdivisions have been again subdivided, so that a man never learns the machinist trade now.... There is no system of apprenticeship.... You simply go in and learn whatever branch you are put at, and you stay at that unless you are changed to another....[42]

Owing to these widespread changes, long-held notions concerning worker independence and social mobility were becoming increasingly unrealistic in an industrializing America. As historian Daniel T. Rodgers has written, Americans were forced to reconcile traditional beliefs about the inherent dignity and sanctity of work with new working conditions where, in many cases, men were becoming mere assistants to machines.[43] Working skills associated with the workshop system had formerly been an essential defining characteristic of maleness.[44]

Americans were in the process of coming to terms with large-scale industrial production and its attendant consequences. It was unclear exactly where industrial workers fit into the fabric of American culture, and, from the perspective of artists, how they should be represented. Therefore, industrial imagery from this period, including *The Ironworkers' Noontime,* can be understood not only as a product of an American fascination with new technology and as hopeful symbols of America's economic growth and recovery from both the Civil War and the depression of 1873-77, but also as a manifestation of an American need to redefine traditional concepts of work.[45]

Just as Americans promoted the farmer as a national democratic hero, fictionalizing and gentrifying him to suit an urban audience, industrial workers assumed a more exotic and heroic role. American popular literature and illustration commonly romanticized and mythologized factory work, describing it in terms appropriated from Dante and Gothic horror.[46] For example, an article in *Harper's Weekly,* from 1883, about an industrial cotton mill reads:

> ...the machine assumes the aspect of a grand and solemn demon face, strangely human, recalling the famed genii of the Arabian Nights. Beside it are the furnaces, whose open doors glow with the fires supplying the vitality of the giant, while about them flit the half-naked forms of the firemen—attendant demons of this monster.[47]

Walter Shirlaw's powerful illustrations for an 1881 *Harper's New Monthly Magazine* article on Pittsburgh, offer an impressive contemporary visual example in this same tradition (fig. 10). Shirlaw, a Munich-trained painter, obviously owes a great debt to Adolf von Menzel's *The Iron Rolling Mill* (1869-75, Berlin-Dahlem, Staatliche Museen). Menzel himself was working in a tradition extending back to Peter Paul Rubens, Diego Velázquez, and Joseph Wright of Derby. Employing the theme of steel- and iron-making as a vehicle to create an infernal underworld, Shirlaw's scenes are demonstrably supernatural. The accompanying text explicitly identifies them as such, describing the factory interiors as "Satanic scenery [which] Dante, in conceiving his 'Inferno,' must have had in mind," and goes on to speak of the furnaces as "seething like miniature volcanoes in constant eruption."[48] The article also portrays the foundry workers as instinctual, demonic figures:

> In the men assigned this labor human endurance seems certainly to have reached its limit. The steel-melter, grasping such a pair of tongs as might have been used upon St. Dunstan, steps directly over the fiery pit below, seizes a crucible, and, with apparent ease, draws it, cherry red, to the surface. Man and glowing jar seem part and parcel, and equally impervious to the fearful heat. Salamander muscles come into graceful play as the melter beheads the sealed crucible.... In raiment the melter from his waist down is an Esquimau, from his waist up a Hottentot, a Zulu, or anything innocent of clothing.[49]

Such characterizations of laborers as animal-like, atavistic, and "primitive" closely echoed colonialist discourse. These types of representation manifested an imperialist fascination with race, and conveyed a message of the reader's superiority.[50]

Iron and steel workers may thus be understood as a type of demonized *other* in American late nineteenth-century culture. This otherness

Figure 10.
Walter Shirlaw (1838-1909)
Emptying the Crucible, 1880
Harper's New Monthly Magazine,
December 1880

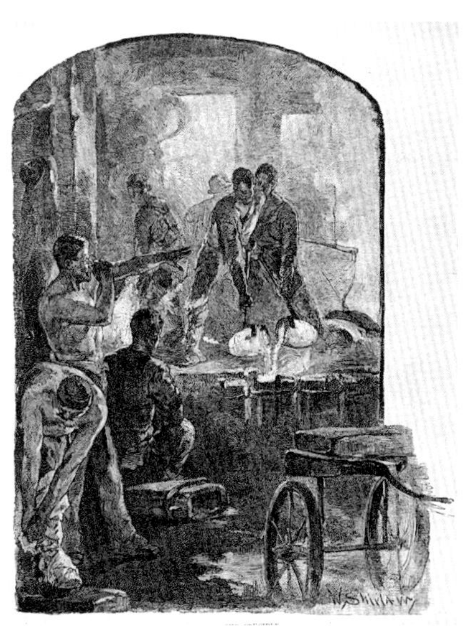

has to do with the workers' ethnicity (they were commonly Irish, Welsh, and German immigrants, or, in some cases, African-American), with the nature of their work (dangerous and dirty), and with the workers' resultant lower-class status. Associated visual and textual images naturalized racial and class stereotypes and virtually ignored the bleaker side of American industrialization. Few images alluded to worker exploitation or conveyed any sense of the workers as individuals. Instead, factory workers were depicted as cogs of a picturesque and sublime machine, fantastic and mythological, emphatically distancing the viewer from the worker's actual existence. By locating the men in spaces of sublimity—in inherently unfathomable places—artists and writers made even more emphatic the laborers' difference. What is omitted from these scenes of work is as important as what is included. The highly selective nature of such images played an important role in helping shape American public opinion concerning unions and factory workers. The use of traditional literary and pictorial conventions therefore functioned to make more acceptable changing technology and its consequent social transformations.[51]

By altering this popular characterization of the ironworker, and instead setting the workers in a "nooning scene," Anshutz undercut any sense of the exotic or the horrific and recast the worker as human hero rather than god or demigod. His interest in straightforwardly recording this most mundane activity in a manner that seems to emulate the camera's veracity further distances the scene from any preternatural associations.[52] The unidealized treatment of the workers acknowledges their humanity. Moreover, they are not dominated by their machinery, nor by the act of work itself and its accompanying stereotypical connotations—though their factory setting identifies them as industrial laborers.

The workers depicted in Anshutz's painting were puddlers. They held the majority of iron mill jobs in America in the 1870s and ran the mill's puddling furnaces, which were used to refine iron transported from the blast furnace (shown as the tall, grey cylindrical tower in the painting's background, plate 1).[53] The blast furnace converted raw iron ore into pig iron. The pig iron, in the form of "pigs," was then hauled to various puddling furnaces (whose small chimneys line the factory's facade), where it was reheated and refined into wrought iron.

Puddling work required high levels of knowledge, strength, and skill. No two "heatings" were alike because the metal always reacted in different ways. Two men, each on a separate shift, were assigned to each furnace. Children of the puddlers, such as the boys depicted in the painting, were hired to assist in this work.[54] Owing to the tremendous physical demands of the job, few puddlers ever stayed with furnace work past their thirties, which explains why all of Anshutz's laborers are so young.[55] One journalist described their work as being "so severe that they have to stop, now and then, in summer, take off their boots, and *pour the perspiration out of them.*"[56] *The Ironworkers' Noontime* depicts the men in the midst of a break between "heatings."[57]

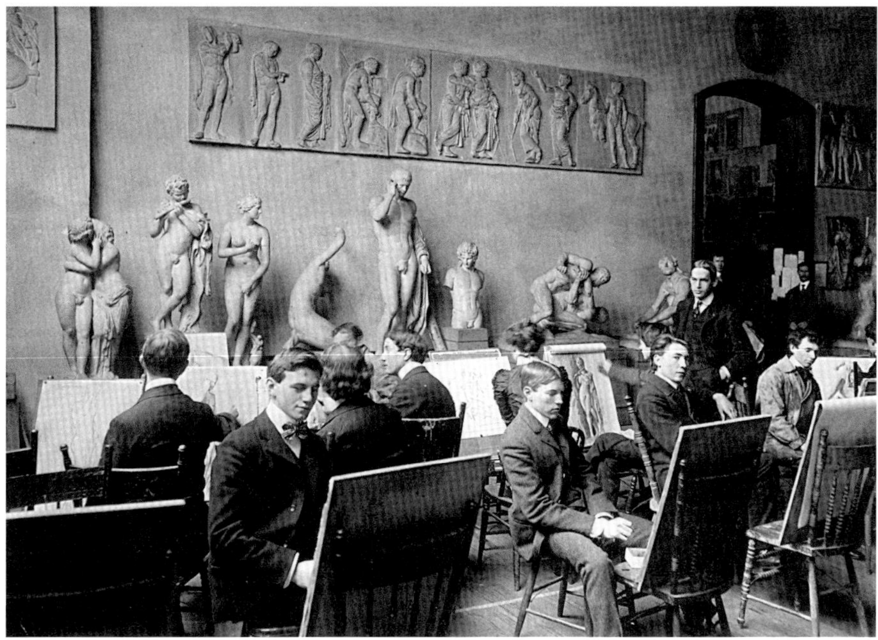

Figure 11.
J. Liberty Tadd (dated unknown)
Large Antique Class (#3), 1901
albumen print
The Pennsylvania Academy of the Fine Arts, Philadelphia. Archives

Judging from contemporary prints of Wheeling iron mills, produced for books on American iron production, yard activity was often very hectic, with an incessant stream of horses and carts full of supplies. Anshutz eliminated all of this, instead painting a monumental frieze of figures inhabiting a barren and blasted landscape, one entirely divorced from the "curative" forces of nature. Nothing detracts from the men. The workers' sunlit bodies stand out in bold relief against the dark factory facade. Arranged in a dramatic line, the figures form a series of rhythmic punctuation marks echoed in the factory facade's windows and chimneys. Although a few of the men and boys are depicted washing themselves after their hot work in the mill, none of them is shown eating, and most stand, distant from one another, perhaps from exhaustion. The disparately directed gazes of the various workers fracture an overall sense of pictorial unity.

All the preparatory drawings for the painting are cursory outline sketches that include no more than one or two figures. The use of these isolated pencil sketches helps explain why the workers in the painting appear slightly awkward and arranged. The effect achieved is that of a composite of separate figure studies. The tension and stiffness of the workers' bodies may reflect Anshutz's own struggle with the complex composition.[58] However, argument that Anshutz was inexperienced may be undercut by the fact that several of the painting's smaller background figures, as well as the playful boys, do convincingly interact with one another. This suggests that Anshutz may have consciously intended the painting's figural isolation, perhaps to depict the alienation of modern industrial life.

Figure 12.
J. Liberty Tadd
Large Antique Class (#3) (detail)
albumen print
The Pennsylvania Academy of the Fine Arts, Philadelphia. Archives

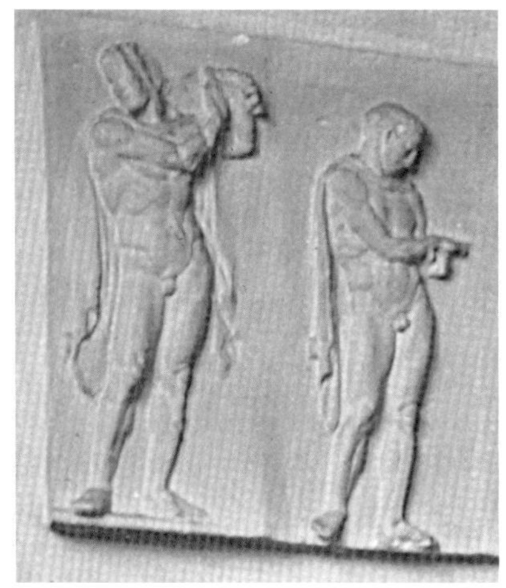

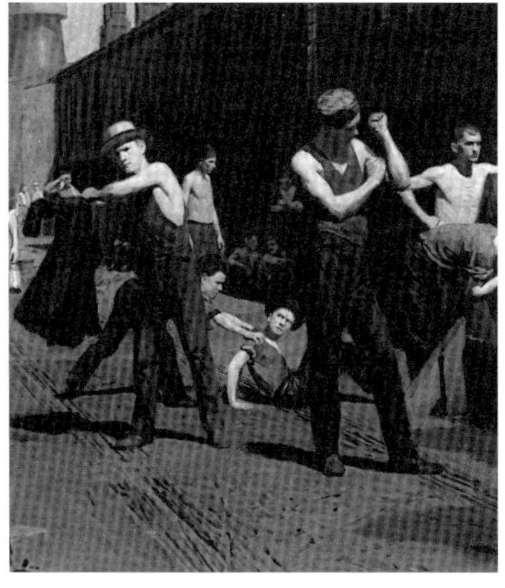

Figure 13.
The Ironworkers' Noontime (detail)
oil on canvas, 17⅛ × 24"
The Fine Arts Museums of San Francisco, Gift of Mr. and Mrs. John D. Rockefeller 3rd

Like much of Eakins' or Edgar Degas' subject matter, *The Ironworkers' Noontime* allowed Anshutz a vehicle for depicting the human body. This theme offered the opportunity to show a whole range of figural types and positions, in a tradition extending back to images such as Antonio del Pollaiuolo's *Battle of Ten Naked Men* (ca.1465, The Metropolitan Museum of Art). Even though realist in style, *The Ironworkers' Noontime* is informed by Anshutz's thorough academic training. The marriage worked well. Anshutz's evident knowledge of anatomy, perspective, and classical art did nothing to sap the image of its jarring sense of immediacy. Indeed, his indirect allusions to classical art helped transform what could have been banal into a form of modern history painting.

Anshutz clearly wanted his frieze of figures to convey monumentality. He achieved this by reducing narrative elements to a minimum and through use of an antique-inspired composition—like a classical frieze the group of figures even forms a half-pedimental shape. This was consistent with Anshutz's own love of antique sculpture: over his lifetime he produced hundreds of cast drawings. The two most prominent men in Anshutz's parade of workers—one with a jacket and the central preening figure—appear to be modern versions of two figures from Lord Elgin's Parthenon frieze that Anshutz would have studied in cast form at the Pennsylvania Academy (figs. 11, 12, 13). Eakins promulgated the idea of reappropriating and naturalizing Greek art to make it relevant for the present. In deciding not to idealize the workers' bodies, Anshutz was following the precepts of his mentor, who would have considered artistic inflation of the figures' muscles anathema. Therefore, *The Ironworkers' Noontime* is a kind of balancing act between the real and the ideal, the mundane and the heroic.

The painting was understood by contemporary reviewers as a nooning or midday break scene.[59] Although the noontime theme is not at all uncommon in nineteenth-century American art (some examples are by artists like Mount and Homer), such scenes are normally set in rural landscapes linking man to nature and the seasons. Anshutz's use of a nooning subject was probably due in part to his awareness of John George Brown's *The Longshoremen's Noon,* which had been exhibited in New York at the National Academy of Design in the spring of 1880 (fig. 15).[60] Brown's scene differs from Anshutz's in its inclusion of far more detail and in the overtly picturesque-anecdotal character of the various workers. Preserved and rendered with meticulous care, these quaintly passive figures seem meant for an historical or ethnological diorama, whereas Anshutz's workers appear vital and alive.[61] Moreover, the ironworkers take their midday break in the midst of a landscape that is insistently modern and urban, stark and monochromatic. A preparatory oil study for the painting emphasizes the starkness of the setting to an even greater extent (plate 6).

Some critics were startled by the bleakness of *The Ironworkers'*

Noontime. For instance, one wrote that Anshutz's "sympathetic" image verged on social critique:

> in the foundry yard, with its soil blasted and buried under the cinders, before you trends away the grim perspective of the foundry wall, with here and there a chimney belching forth its smoky malediction on the murky air. The gloomy place, and the air it renders gloomy; the grimed toilers wasted by their slavery of iron and flame; the dead earth buried under the refuse the fires cast out… [62]

Anticipating Anshutz's eventual conversion to socialism, the painting, to some eyes, depicted the enslavement of the factory worker.[63] Yet despite the picture's bleak setting and the evident exhaustion of the men, it is difficult to see the picture as strongly didactic, since it avoids any emphatic signs of worker exploitation. In fact, several of the most prominent figures appear formidable and confrontational.

The painting's sharply receding perspective acts effectively to draw the viewer into the workers' space. Anshutz's decision to place the audience in a position of social disadvantage and vulnerability, meeting these men on their own ground, as equals at best, probably reflects his own experience while sketching the workers, who at first mistrusted him.[64] Indeed, several of the men—described by critics as brawny giants—confront the viewer as outsider (fig. 13).[65] Potential buyers for the painting may have found this particularly disconcerting at a time when xenophobic feelings of nativism were on the rise and factory workers were often associated with radical politics.[66] A new contested arena of American conquest, the industrial landscape in post-Civil War America occupied an ambiguous site symbolic of both technological and economic prowess and political radicalism and social unrest. The image's psychological directness would have discouraged viewers from gawking comfortably at these exotic working-class figures. Anshutz's unidealized depiction of the workers must have upset viewers' expectations and preconceptions concerning the way factory workers should be represented. The only comic element, two pairs of wrestling boys reminiscent of those found in the work of Eastman Johnson and Winslow Homer, hardly alters the scene's overall harshness.

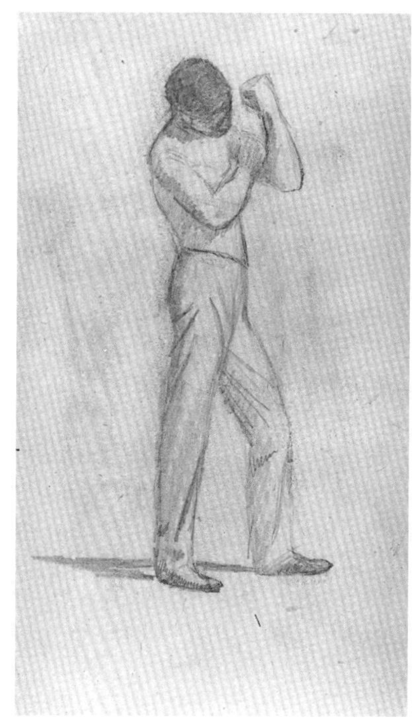

Figure 14.
Figure Study for The Ironworkers' Noontime, 1880
Sketchbook #1, graphite on buff wove leaves, 4 9/16 × 7 13/16"
The Pennsylvania Academy of the Fine Arts, Philadelphia. Gift of Mr. and Mrs. Daniel W. Dietrich, II

The above-mentioned considerations probably help explain the painting's failure to sell for over two years. It was ultimately purchased in August of 1883 by Thomas B. Clarke, one of the few wealthy Americans of his time to specialize in collecting American art.[67]

That Anshutz chose to produce so distinctive an image as *The Ironworkers' Noontime,* one certain to stand out in any exhibition, suggests that he thought of the painting as a kind of competition piece, proving his artistic abilities to the Pennsylvania Academy faculty. Although it measures only 17 x 24 inches (almost the same as *The Farmer and His*

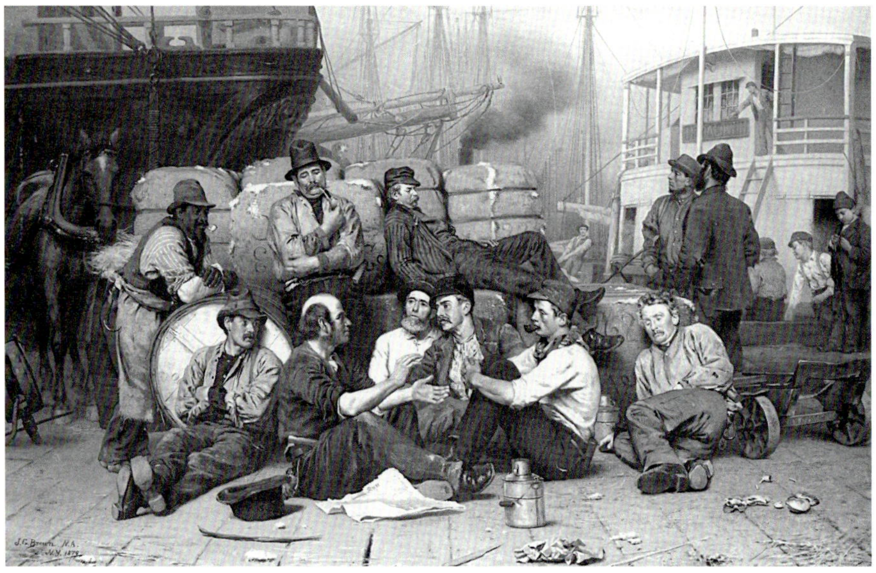

Figure 15.
John George Brown (1831-1913)
Longshoremen's Noon, 1879
oil on canvas, 33¼ × 50¼"
In the Collection of The Corcoran Gallery of Art, Washington, DC, Museum Purchase, Gallery Fund

Son at Harvesting and *The Way They Live*), its multi-figure groupings made it by far the most complex and ambitious painting he had yet attempted; and it was produced at a time when he was probably looking forward to a position on the Academy faculty, a post he obtained a little over a year later, in 1881. Anshutz, who had never previously worked on any larger-sized canvas, may have anticipated a possible commission for an expanded version of the scene. Whether or not he hoped the painting would influence the Academy faculty, Anshutz surely wanted to impress his favorite teacher and painter, Thomas Eakins.

In style and methodology the painting is an affirmation of Eakins' art and teaching, an homage to him. Indeed, when it was first exhibited, in January 1881 in the Philadelphia Sketch Club, it was even hung below an Eakins; and critics stated that it was patterned after his work.[68] From the painting's very inception, Anshutz proceeded in a manner that emulated his teacher's. Studies for *The Ironworkers' Noontime* include more than fifteen figure drawings, two oil sketches, and several perspectival diagrams (fig. 15, plate 6).[69] Eakins' teaching is also evident in the painting's focus on the male body; in the sculptural modeling of form and accurate anatomical construction, which were central to Eakins' art; and in the inclusion of half-dressed athletic figures (something quite unusual in Anshutz's work), which was a direct response to Eakins' sporting scenes, such as *The Biglin Brothers Turning the Stake-Boat* (fig. 16). Anshutz, like Eakins, was attempting a dispassionate objectification of the human body.

Yet these artists were not selecting such themes solely as a pretext to further their academic studies of the nude. According to Elizabeth

Johns, Eakins' sporting scenes manifest a growing American interest in organized athletics. Such post-Civil War interests were widespread in a culture which, for the first time, valued fitness programs, heroicized great outdoorsmen such as Theodore Roosevelt, and popularized such books as Thomas Hughes' *The Manliness of Christ*.[70] Even though this pervasive, sometimes obsessive, late-Victorian fascination with physical health and its association with masculinity rarely led artists to produce imagery as brawny as *The Ironworkers' Noontime,* it did have an important, virtually unacknowledged impact during the 1870s and early 1880s, on how certain artists and critics perceived the art profession, before the general acceptance of Whistler's work and "art for art's sake" aesthetics.

In the 1870s and 1880s art critics sometimes described the art profession in stereotypically masculine terms, defending it as a properly "manly" endeavor.[71] True artists were portrayed as men engaged in demanding forms of physical labor who embraced a strong work ethic. For instance, although the art critic G. W. Sheldon, in his survey book of contemporary American painting of 1878, referred to such painters as George Inness and Frederic Church as poetic interpreters of the landscape, he also made it clear that they worked long hours, were industrious, highly skilled, and disciplined; and in terms that could well describe a boxer's training method, he wrote that the act of painting itself demands not only excellent physical fitness but also a proper regimen of rest and careful diet. As an example, Sheldon stated, that before beginning a painting, the artist Sanford Gifford

> wishes to be in the best possible physical condition. He is careful about his food, he is careful to husband his resources. When the day comes, he begins work just after sunrise, and continues until just before sunset. Ten, eleven, twelve, consecutive hours, are occupied in the first great effort to put scene on canvas.... His luncheon, taken in his studio, consists of a cup of coffee and a piece of bread.[72]

Great artists were apparently never lazy. Sheldon wrote that "the manly persistence in toil...[is what characterizes] the most cultured of our painters."[73] He described the studio as a "battle-ground" for the artist. And, stressing the quintessentially "masculine" nature of his work, the American Barbizon school-inspired painter William Morris Hunt wrote, "It requires as much strength to paint well as to plough."[74] Many of the stereotypically male attributes associated with such avant-garde twentieth-century male artists as Pablo Picasso and Jackson Pollock were already established. Boldness, originality, and independence, prized in the entrepreneurial realm as well, were considered important for artists. Hunt wrote that "art is about the only occupation in which people can do what they please without consulting their neighbors."[75] Some American artists lambasted painters such as Edward Burne-Jones for not

Figure 16.
Thomas Eakins (1844-1916)
The Biglin Brothers Turning the Stake-Boat, 1873
oil on canvas, 40¼ × 60¼"
The Cleveland Museum of Art, Hinman B. Hurlbut Collection, 1984.27

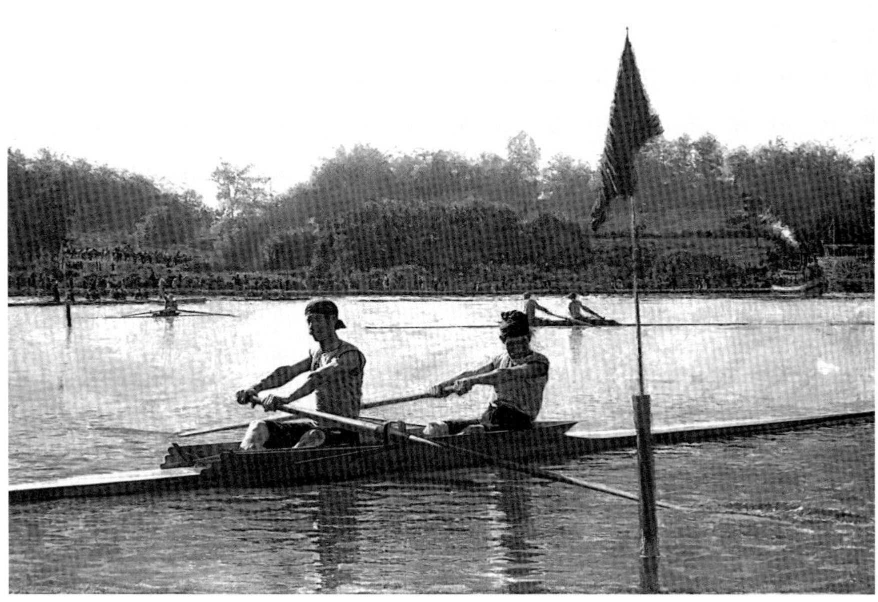

producing "a healthy or manly phase of art," and others, probably in reference to the growing number of female art students and to the recent visit of Oscar Wilde, longed for the days "before there were arty women and she-men."[76]

Such concerns about masculinity had a demonstrable (though probably half-conscious) impact on Eakins' and Anshutz's perceptions of their own work. As an example, Anshutz later wrote, regarding his summer art school at Fort Washington, Pennsylvania that, although he was "disgusted to find more women than men," he and his students were still producing "man's painting all straight."[77] This characterization reveals how certain members of the artistic community appropriated a commonly-shared definition of masculinity for a special purpose: to mitigate possible perception of their profession as effeminate. Traditional endeavors to be poetic and emotional interpreters of nature overlapped dangerously with accepted feminine attributes. Anshutz's description of his students' painting refers to one of his classes in portraiture, suggesting that his description had little to do with the subject matter of his students' art. Judging from his own approach to teaching, Anshutz was simply remarking that his students were turning out disciplined work founded on the conventions of academic training and demonstrating a thorough knowledge of figure construction and draftsmanship. Implicit in his statement was the common belief that professional painting was inherently a male pursuit, something still confronting many women artists today. Eakins held similar prejudicial views. In a contemporary letter, he wrote that he did not "believe that great painting or sculpture or surgery will ever be done by women . . . ."[78] His beliefs about women are reminiscent of so-called scientific studies from the 1880s which contended that giving women the right to vote might cause their brains to become artificially enlarged through over-analytical exertion.[79] As many scholars have noted, Eakins' intention was to pursue an analytical and empirical approach to art, one often verging on the scientific in its reliance on medical school-style dissection practices. This is not to argue that Eakins' and Anshutz's art was produced merely as a statement of masculine preeminence. Yet it is clear that they perceived their work, in its display of erudition and analytical reasoning, as an affirmation of the power of the male mind.

These attitudes inform *The Ironworkers' Noontime,* and its portrayal of working-class figures stretching and displaying their muscles makes it a scene no female artist would have been encouraged to paint. At a time when long-standing gender roles were become increasingly blurred and there was a growing mistrust of what T. J. Jackson Lears has called the "feminization" of American culture, *The Ironworkers' Noontime,* as well as Eakins' athletic scenes, presented clear-cut, reassuring icons of masculinity.[80] Simplified all-male worlds, free from any threat of emasculation or possible complications attendant on relationships with women, they are also Whitmanesque hymns to the male body.[81] Eakins' painting *The Swimming Hole* offers the most specific example of this (fig. 17). Both *The Swimming Hole* and *The Ironworkers' Noontime* raise questions about how manhood was defined and legitimated in late

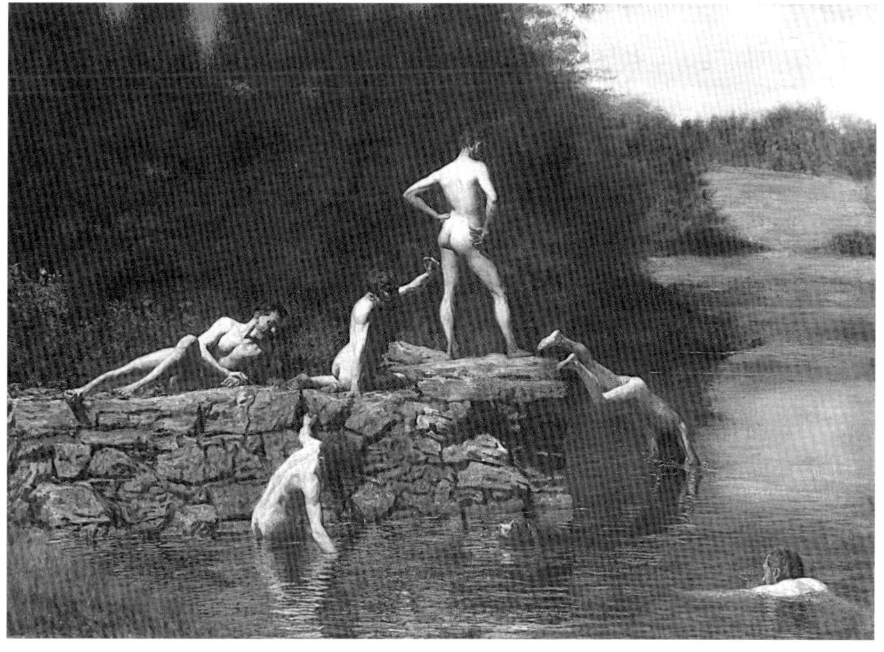

Figure 17.
Thomas Eakins
The Swimming Hole, ca. 1883-85
oil on canvas, $27\frac{5}{16} \times 36\frac{5}{16}$"
Purchased by the Friends of Art, Fort Worth Art Association, 1925; acquired by the Amon Carter Museum, 1990, from the Modern Art Museum of Fort Worth through grants and donations from the Amon G. Carter Foundation, the Sid W. Richardson Foundation, the Anne Burnett and Charles Tandy Foundation, Capital Cities/ABC Foundation, Fort Worth Star-Telegram, The R. D. and Joan Dale Hubbard Foundation and the people of Fort Worth.

nineteenth-century America. Yet, Anshutz's puddlers, with their "strongman" poses, contrast strikingly with Eakins' more elegantly posed, lithe swimmers, suggesting an intersection between the signification of class and the construction of the body. Although one painting evokes a cooling refuge and the other unremitting heat, it is possible that Anshutz's parade of half-naked men led Eakins, several years later, to produce his equally unusual homosocial scene.

Few other late nineteenth-century American artists produced similar scenes. Little demand existed for painting so exclusively focused on the male body, and sports and factory subjects were normally the exclusive province of popular imagery. Yet these deeply-ingrained definitions of gender must have had innumerable, sometimes subtle, effects on the way many American artists into the early twentieth century perceived and approached their work. Maxfield Parrish's humorous painting for a *Collier's* cover of 1909, entitled *The Artist, Sex, Male* illustrates a continuing public perception of the male artist as "unmanly," effete, and androgynous (fig. 18). Parrish, a former pupil of Anshutz's, probably intended it as a snide reference to the refined painters of the Boston School. Parodic though the image is, it points to an issue that must have worried certain male artists.

For Anshutz, then, *The Ironworkers' Noontime* functioned as a kind of assertive coming-of-age image, demonstrating both his mastery of academic technique and his ability to rethink traditional themes. Consciously updating the image of the ironworker, casting off accepted pictorial formulas, he ennobled the worker without resorting to romantic clichés. His image undermines an artistic tradition of depicting the ironworker as a god at the forge and re-mythologizes him as a doughty and highly-skilled embodiment of the American work ethic. Anshutz's scene is an attempt to redefine an appropriate image of the industrial worker. Consciously or not, Anshutz must have been attracted to this subject because it lent itself readily to a depiction of characteristics he and others deemed admirable in artists as well as ironworkers.

More pointedly than any of Anshutz's other paintings, *The Ironworkers' Noontime,* with its uncompromisingly direct vision of factory life, leans toward political critique. Yet, confounding any simple reading, the image purveys an open-ended mixture of interpretations: the figures can represent exploited victims of a Stygian factory system or the potential menace of labor radicalism. As well, the painting may be understood as part academic exercise, part idiosyncratic naturalism. Ultimately, what accounts for the image's continuing power is the way in which it offers a somewhat threatening confrontation between viewer and worker. Few nineteenth-century images produced as direct an encounter between disparate elements of culture. In presenting the ironworkers as ordinary men, instead of romanticized types, Anshutz compelled viewers to consider more objectively the changes engendered by industrialization that were sweeping the nation. Therefore, his accomplishment was,

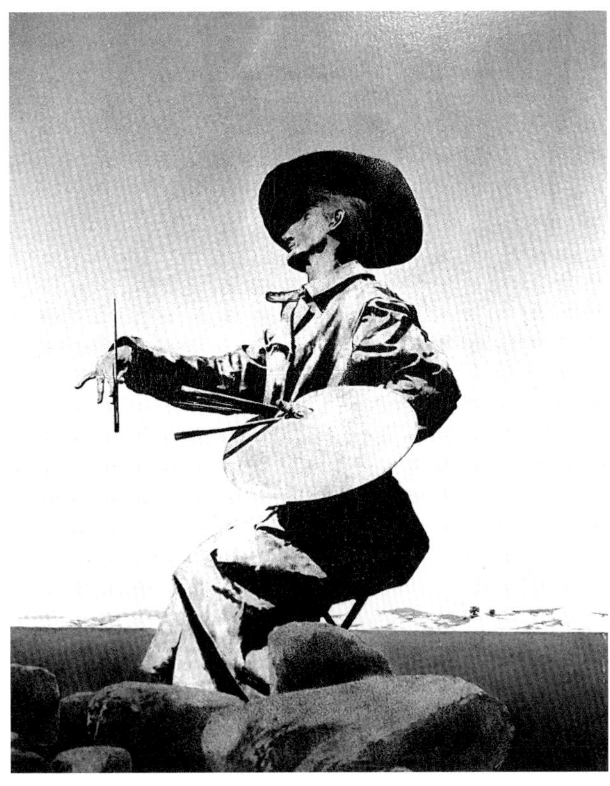

Figure 18.
Maxfield Parrish (1870-1966)
The Artist, Sex, Male, 1909
oil on stretched paper, 19¾ × 16"
Illustration for *Collier's,* May 1, 1909
Collection of the Brandywine River Museum. The Betsy James Wyeth Fund

above all, to make the factory worker seem strikingly human.

Perhaps the greatest irony of Anshutz's career is that he produced his most original and resonant work while still a student. He never again painted another scene of industrial workers, and although he showed the painting at the Philadelphia Society of Artists and at the Sketch Club, he never exhibited it at the Pennsylvania Academy of the Fine Arts or the National Academy of Design.[82] Several possibilities may account for his decision not to paint similar scenes again. First, although *The Ironworkers' Noontime* received an award from the Philadelphia Sketch Club in early 1881 and eventually was reproduced in *Harper's Weekly* in August, 1884, Anshutz experienced great difficulty finding a buyer. However, since no record of the artist's painting sales from that period survives, it is impossible to say whether or not this was unusual for him.[83] Secondly, and even more discouragingly, Proctor & Gamble appropriated the image for use as a soap advertisement (fig. 19).[84] Not surprisingly, Anshutz later mentioned that this upset and embarrassed him a great deal.[85] In addition, beginning in 1881, Anshutz painted less frequently and almost stopped exhibiting his work. By the time he started to paint more prolifically in the 1890s, his stylistic and thematic interests had begun to change, and he no longer adhered to Eakins' realism.

Figure 19.
Poster by Proctor & Gamble to introduce Ivory Soap, ca. 1883
lithograph on paper, 100 × 160"
Collection of The New-York Historical Society

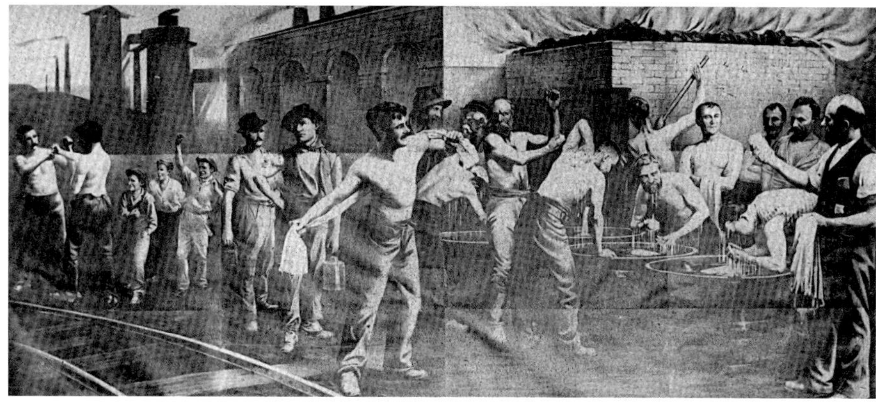

As mentioned earlier, Anshutz had been close to Eakins since 1878.[86] In 1884, Anshutz spent a great deal of time with his former instructor; he assisted Eakins with Eadweard Muybridge's photographic motion studies at the University of Pennsylvania, as well as with Eakins' own photographic studies there. Muybridge, who had become well known in 1878 for his photographically "stopped" records of a horse's and other animals' movements at Palo Alto, California, began working at the University of Pennsylvania in 1884.[87]

Eakins, who was a member of a University commission responsible for overseeing Muybridge's work, also carried out photographic motion studies of his own. In March 1885, a separate camera shed was constructed for Eakins' own use.[88] Anshutz helped develop the photographs and assisted Muybridge and Eakins in setting up equipment. Anshutz wrote several letters to his friend J. Laurie Wallace describing these experiments. In his first reference to them he wrote:

> M[uybridge] as you know is carrying on his scheme over at the University. He has...a machine for taking views on one plate, of moving objects, by opening and closing the camera rapidly at the rate of about 100 exposures per second. This shows...one clear view at every 2 or 3 inches of advance.... Eakins, Godley and I were out there yesterday trying a machine. Eakins had made [it] of the above design except he had only one wheel. We sewed some bright balls on Godley and ran him down the track. The result was not very good although you could see the position of the buttons at every step.[89]

The tone of Anshutz's letters concerning these experiments is often critical or even skeptical. Referring to Eakins only indirectly, the letters reflect Anshutz's unease about artists carrying out "scientific" studies. While he believed that mechanical aids, such as photography, were invaluable artistic tools, he also felt that they were only a starting point:

> The true artist, I think will call in mechanical methods to aid him. The former [someone merely competent, not inspired] sees nothing higher. And as his conscious efforts are all mechanical he credits all the good in his picture to those methods and he feels that without them he would have nothing. I do not belittle scientific methods for it is only by them that we can know nature. As in perspective we can blindly follow its rules or with clear sight we can use them to interpret the law or nature which governs them. I, too often, am dependent on the lower ways but still I think I can see beyond.[90]

In another letter to Wallace, Anshutz wrote:

> The study of movement is a good thing even by the aid of photography, but I have no desire to become an electrician in order to make my own photographs, and so I do not feel a very lively interest in the matter.[91]

These passages, with their implicit criticism of Eakins' teaching and art, illustrate the growing differences between Anshutz and Eakins. Anshutz's pejorative use of the words "mechanical" and "electrician" indicated an indictment of his former instructor's emphatically empirical and analytical approach to picture-making, and his belief that such reliance on scientific methods would lead to a literal-minded and "lower" form of art. Anshutz felt that artists should interpret nature poetically and convey their own feelings, or "sentiment" (the word perhaps most often used by contemporary critics), of what they were representing.[92] An artist's ultimate goal, according to Anshutz, was to produce images of nature that would reveal what he called a "higher truth."[93] In November 1885 he wrote that students "must be governed in their work by a higher principle than the reproduction of the light and shade and line of the model."[94]

Anshutz's notion of a dichotomy between a strictly empirical understanding of the world and an artist's poetic interpretation offers a microcosm of a general shift in late nineteenth-century American art and art criticism away from naturalism and its frequent ally, science. It became increasingly less common for American artists to borrow from scientific inquiry. Perhaps one fundamental reason for this change in the American artist's relationship to science was the new, popular presence of photography. Its ability to capture nature with great detail and precision threatened to undermine the function of the artist. Critics generally felt that artists should consciously distance their imagery from that of photographs, and, indeed, Eakins' paintings were often criticized for emulating photographs. His "factual" realism implicitly undermined the artist's interpretive position by openly appropriating a photographic-scientific syntax. Much of Eakins' imagery and approach to teaching was directly at odds with late nineteenth-century notions of the role of the artist as poetic interpreter and "improver" of nature, and were also out of tune with the newly popular European styles, such as the Barbizon school of painting.

Although Anshutz disliked Eakins' attempt to marry art and science, he never thoroughly abandoned his former teacher's ideas. Both felt that an artist's personal interpretation must be based on a conscientious study of nature, especially of the human body and on the mastery of technical skills, such as draftsmanship. Moreover, Anshutz's Eakins-inspired painting style did not change dramatically until the 1890s.

Between 1883 and 1892, Anshutz's artistic production diminished significantly. He seems to have lacked a certain artistic confidence, drive, and ambition; and, he may have felt that his painting would never equal that of his primary artistic model, Eakins. Up until the final years of his life, Anshutz lacked confidence as a painter.[95] He later stated that he had "accomplished little in his chosen field...and that he...[was still] learning how to paint."[96] During these years (1883-92) he exhibited nothing at the Pennsylvania Academy of the Fine Arts annual exhibitions.[97] In 1884, Anshutz again began, or possibly continued, the practice of open-air sketching. Although he had produced such sketches as early as 1873, and may have continued open-air work through the 1870s and early 1880s, none of the painter's letters mention it, and no Anshutz landscape oil sketches or watercolors seem to have survived from this period. In spring 1884 Anshutz took students on *plein-air* painting trips, something not otherwise offered by the Pennsylvania Academy. Eakins, suggesting that Anshutz enthusiastically organized this excursion, wrote in May 1884 to his young friend Harry Barnitz:

> As for sunlight studies that is new too for you & I regret for a good many older fellows in the life school....When you get back you will hear a lot about sunlight from Tommy Anshutz & the crowd that [went] sketching with him & you will see their work & that of others in the exhibition.[98]

Eakins may have encouraged Anshutz's efforts in this direction, since he considered *plein-air* work to be one of the most difficult challenges an artist could face, offering a way to improve skills in the study of color and light.[99] Eakins' own Schuylkill River rowing scenes from the early 1870s, especially the high-keyed watercolors, are, in part, careful studies of the effects of natural light. In 1884, Anshutz wrote that painters should attempt to capture a natural quality of light:

> He whose work is real to him feels light in his picture as light and shade. The light and shadow of his palette and so in his picture may be weak compared to nature but if they be real to him each slight step becomes correspondingly great, and things which the mechanical copyist would paint cautiously after the most careful

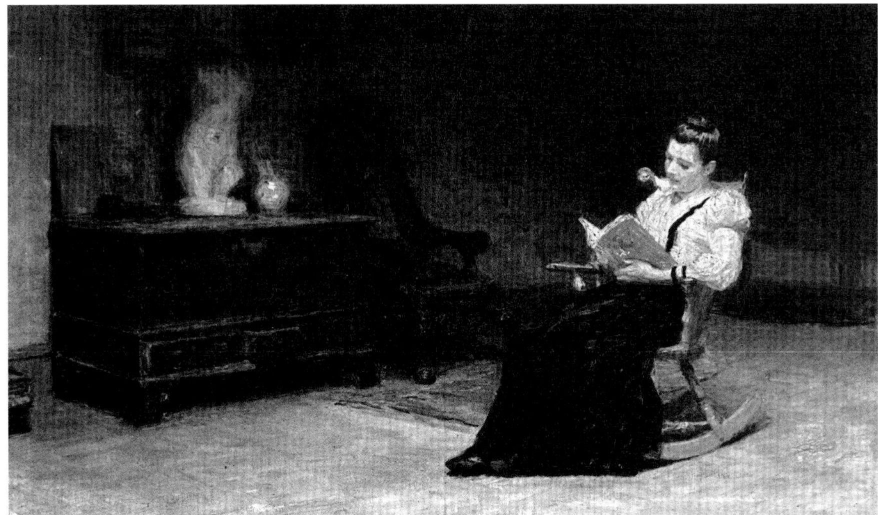

Figure 20.
A Studio Study, ca. 1891
oil on canvas, 22 1/16 × 36 1/8"
The Pennsylvania Academy of the Fine Arts, Philadelphia. Bequest of Helen W. Henderson

comparison would be placed by him almost without thought. And truthfully, for his aim would be definite.[100]

Given Anshutz's apparent interest in evoking or reproducing the effects of light, it is not surprising that he was later "electrified" by his first exposure to French Impressionist painting, in 1886, at the Earle's Galleries in Philadelphia.[101] Impressionism must have seemed radically new to him, but it had little or no effect on his painting until the early 1890s.

After a ten-year hiatus, Anshutz began to exhibit more extensively, beginning in 1892, at the Pennsylvania Academy's annual exhibitions, suggesting a renewed sense of artistic purpose and ambition. In that year he showed three paintings, one of which was *A Studio Study* (fig. 20). It depicts a woman reading, set in an austere interior. Seated in a rocking chair, she is balanced on the left by the wooden chest supporting the torso cast and vase. With subject matter similar to that treated by dozens of late nineteenth-century European and American artists, *A Studio Study* recalls especially some of Eastman Johnson's images of women reading. Anshutz's painting also bears a resemblance to some of Eakins' interior genre scenes, like *Elizabeth Crowell and Her Dog* (1871, San Diego Museum of Art) and *Seventy Years Ago* (1877, The Art Museum, Princeton). *A Studio Study* similarly includes a convincingly modeled, illuminated, seated figure set against a dark background.[102] Anshutz's deep shadows are also common in Eakins' imagery. The younger artist's representation differs from those of his teacher in its inclusion of a smaller figure, its asymmetrical composition, and its lack of painstakingly completed detail.

During this same period, the early 1890s, Anshutz became especially interested in portraiture, and focused on improving his skills in that genre. In November of 1891, he wrote:

> The time not taken up by my teachings I am putting in at portrait painting from all the sitters I can get and when no sitters [are] to be had I [employ] live models. I have good training and think I can, from life, do a better piece of work than the common place. But I intend to push my style to a high class of portraiture.[103]

In the spring of 1892, after having taught at the Pennsylvania Academy of the Fine Arts for eleven years, Anshutz decided to return to art school, this time in Paris. Feeling frustrated as a teacher and inadequate as a painter, he had watched his brightest students, such as Robert Henri, leave for the center of the contemporary art world. Insecure about his own artistic abilities, he hoped that training in Paris would provide him with a more well-rounded education, new enthusiasm and ideas, and added professional credibility. Moreover, Eakins had always encouraged his students to study in Europe and many prominent contemporary American artists had been trained there—including the majority of Anshutz's former teachers at the National Academy of Design and the Pennsylvania Academy of the Fine Arts.[104]

In 1892 Anshutz wrote to the Board of Directors that he was leaving the Academy in order to study abroad:

> I would not be justified in accepting my position for another year, knowing that it would be as bad for the school as for me. I will follow the plan I spoke to you about and as soon as I am able will go abroad, where I hope to gain the experience necessary to anyone who properly fills the positions I am leaving. The future teaching in this school may not be different from what mine has been, but it must have something back of it that I only know well enough to desire.[105]

Anshutz's trip to Europe formed a watershed in his artistic career. His experiences there encouraged him to begin a series of bright watercolor landscapes in the 1890s. More importantly, Anshutz's Parisian exposure to the work of the Nabis and other Post-Impressionists later (after 1900) engendered a fruitful and diverse period of artistic experimentation, entirely unlike his Eakins-inspired beginnings.

Chapter 2

1892-1912: A Period of Continual Change

On September 1, 1892, Anshutz married Effie Shriver Russell. They spent the next several months preparing for their trip to France. Arriving in Paris in December 1892, he immediately enrolled at the Académie Julian.[1] The Académie was immensely popular with Americans because it was a respected art institution that required no entrance examinations and English was commonly spoken there. Anshutz took classes from Lucien Doucet and Adolphe William Bouguereau.

Anshutz's initial impressions of the school were positive. Excited by the international character of the place, he wrote to his brother that his fellow students were "Frenchmen, Italians, Hungarians, Poles, Americans, South Americans, Canadians, Turks, Germans, English, Australians, Swiss, Russian, Romanian, Egyptians, Serbians, Spaniards."[2] He went on to describe how large the school was and how various artistic styles were being practiced:

> It is a big place (Julian Academy). About 400 men and new ones coming all the time. I am working with plenty of interest but am not paralyzing Paris with the results. However we all seem to be in the same boat and it will take a very big fish indeed to make much stir. My own work remains careful but Academic. Which in Artist lingo means uninteresting. However I am glad that I came over. It has settled many ideas for me and has been an eye opener in some directions. The one thing settled to my full satisfaction is that there is no one correct style of painting or sculpture. But that any style is correct if the man is master of it.[3]

That he felt there was "no one correct style of painting or sculpture" shows the seeds were apparently sown at the Académie for his own future ventures in artistic experimentation.

Anshutz attended life drawing classes, in which charcoal was the primary medium. He wrote that the drawing technique required of the students was very "mechanical," but that it was appropriate and understandable for beginning students.[4] One of Anshutz's few extant life drawings was produced at the Académie Julian (fig. 21). An accomplished

Figure 21.
Nude Model, ca. 1892-93
charcoal, 24¾ × 18¾"
Location unknown

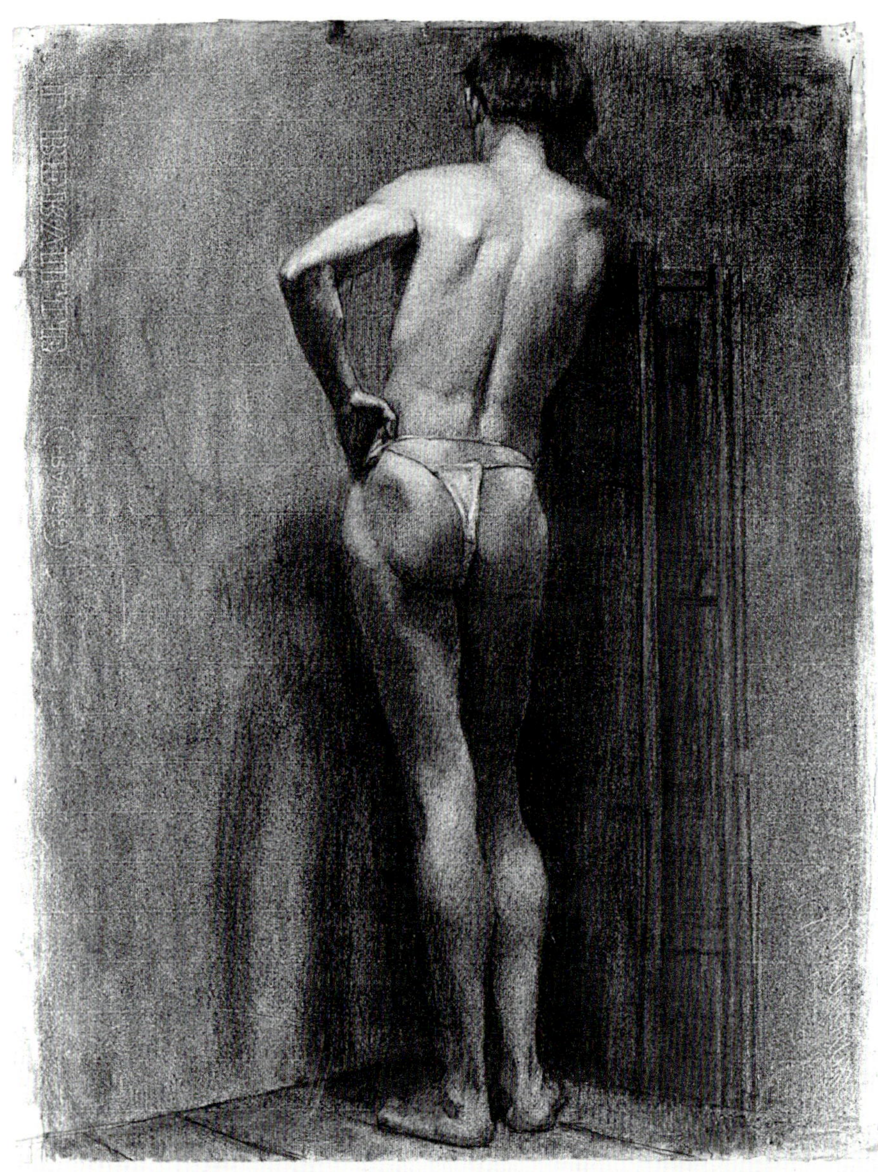

work, it describes a male model in the kind of academic detail typical of student work at the Parisian institution. Matisse recalled bitterly that, when he was attending the Académie Julian, Bouguereau had insisted on a meticulous drawing style. Bouguereau had instructed him not to "rub out the charcoal with your fingers—that denotes a careless man."[5]

Within three months Anshutz had become dissatisfied with the Académie. In February 1893 he wrote, "I do not know how long I will keep at the school but not a day longer than necessary."[6] Late that spring he wrote to his brother that, after the third week of April, he had stopped going to classes.[7] Although his letters never explain why he became unhappy there or why he decided to leave, his correspondence shows that he spent the next four months producing watercolor sketches of the city and visiting Parisian museums, exhibitions, and art galleries.

For the first time Anshutz was exposed to a wide array of styles, from Old Masters at the Louvre to the paintings of the Nabis at the Salon des Indépendants. This contact with stylistic diversity had an important impact on his subsequent work, showing him numerous artistic routes he might pursue. Apparently Anshutz greeted the newer French art he saw somewhat skeptically, noting that "the great mass of modern work seems somewhat uninteresting after the old masters.... I suppose that only one in a thousand of the old masters lived and it is just so today."[8] Although it is impossible to know exactly what sort of avant-garde art Anshutz saw in Paris, it is clear that he visited the Salon des Indépendants in 1893, where he could have viewed the work of Pierre Bonnard, Henri-Edmond Cross, Maurice Denis, Gustave Loiseau, Maximilien Luce, and Henri de Toulouse-Lautrec.[9]

Robert Henri, whom Anshutz respected, may have conveyed his enthusiasm for the single "modern" painter praised by Anshutz, Paul Albert Besnard, the conservative Impressionist. Anshutz wrote that, "The most interesting of all the men of today to me is Besnard," and Henri exclaimed, similarly, that Besnard "is a very great man."[10] Besnard's pastels, it should be noted, had an impact on Anshutz's late pastel portraits.

Anshutz's concern about finances and further employment may help to explain why he did not stay in Paris longer than nine months. As he wrote to his brother Edward,

> I was on the point of writing to you to send the rest of the money to me as I had run down to $50.... However, if I don't go back there [the Pennsylvania Academy of the Fine Arts], it will not be entirely a case of unmixed sorrow. I feel very anxious to make a living outside of teaching. And see no better scheme than to go to Holly Beach [New Jersey] and turn out a lot of water color pictures of the sea shore etc. And taking them to the dealers and sending to all the exhibitions. If this succeeded teaching would be much more easily and profitably done.[11]

Anshutz's comments suggest that at this point in his life he was considering the possibility of giving up teaching for full-time painting. His letter also indicates that he still held very modest ideas about his own artistic abilities. Instead of envisioning ambitious genre scenes like those of Homer or Eastman Johnson, or full-length society portraits like those of John Singer Sargent or William Merritt Chase, he was instead thinking in the more limited terms of picturesque seashore watercolors. That Anshutz soon accepted the offer of a teaching position at the Pennsylvania Academy of the Fine Arts, however, suggests that financial stability was ultimately his greatest concern.

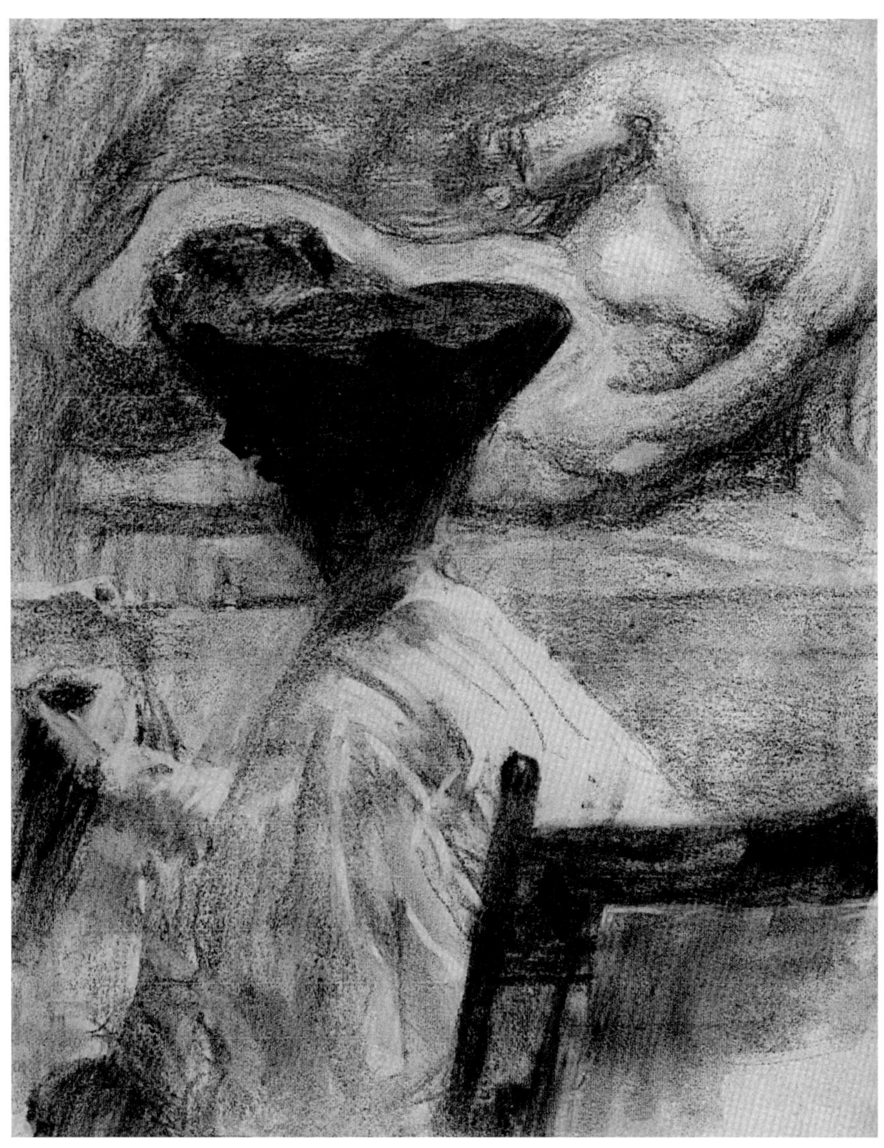

Figure 22.
Cast Drawing with Woman Student Drawing, ca. 1895
charcoal on paper, 24 × 18½"
Collection of Mr. and Mrs. Raymond J. Horowitz

While in Paris Anshutz continued to practice open-air painting:

> I have been working every day of late at watercolor sketching and will be able to show you our surroundings.... It is very difficult stuff to paint with for me, but I am improving.... Around the outskirts [of Paris] are some very picturesque old moss covered buildings. Many of them deserted. I made...five sketches which are better than any I have yet made.[12]

Employing a wide range of yellows, greens, and browns, Anshutz generally painted these scenes of rooftops and building facades with a quickly applied brush (plate 7). Few details are included. Compared with his earlier watercolors, such as *Rooftop Scene, Philadelphia,* the Paris work is looser and more spontaneous, and in these examples he demonstrates a growing mastery of the medium. Moreover, these watercolors are brighter than anything he had previously painted, suggesting that he may have been inspired by Impressionism. Yet the hues in Anshutz's Paris scenes are never as intense and the brushstrokes never as loose as those of the French painters. Also, unlike French Impressionist works, his scenes do not include larger city views, rarely people, and never humanity "in motion." Buildings and vegetation dominate, still subjects more easily studied than shifting crowds. At their best, these Paris images contain striking graphic complexities, and they reveal the artist's fascination with the city's many juxtapositions of geometric buildings and irregularly-shaped vegetation.

In August 1893, the Pennsylvania Academy of the Fine Arts' Board asked Anshutz to rejoin the Academy faculty. He accepted the position and then spent several weeks touring Venice, Florence, Bologna, Padua, and London, prior to returning to Philadelphia in the middle of September.[13]

After he returned from Paris, Anshutz produced a series of charcoal drawings: "I am getting a corn on the end of my finger like a violinist from rubbing charcoal."[14] Owing to the fact that, with the exception of his earlier Paris drawings, none of his extant charcoals is dated, it is impossible to trace his stylistic development in this medium. However, because it is likely that the bulk of these approximately two hundred charcoal drawings were produced while Anshutz was supervising cast-drawing

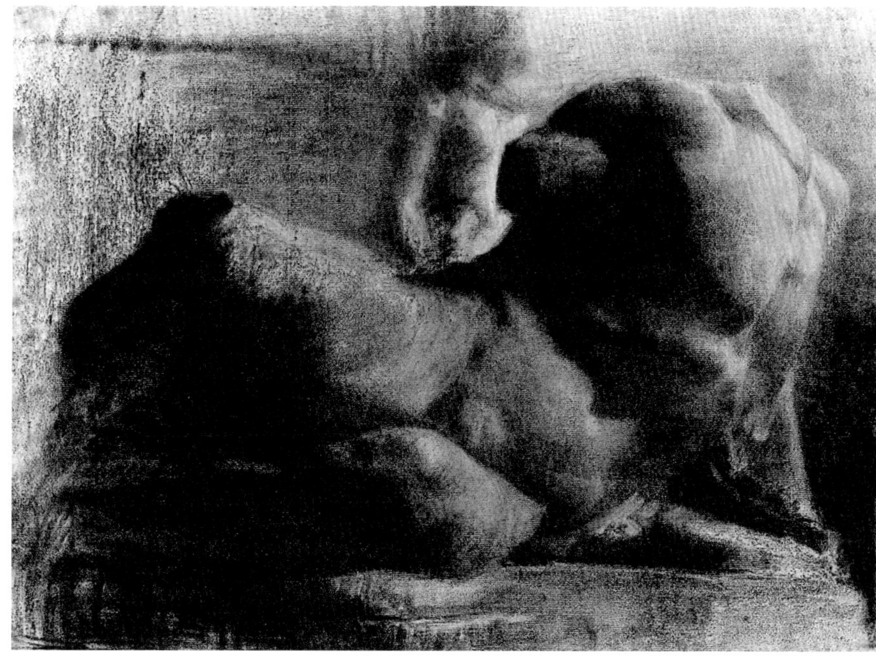

Figure 23.
Cast Study: Reclining Torso, ca. 1895
charcoal on paper, 18¾ × 24½"
The Hon. Joseph P. Carroll and Mrs. Carroll, New York

Figure 24.
Cast Drawing of Milo of Croton,
ca. 1895
charcoal, 24¼ × 18¾"
Private Collection

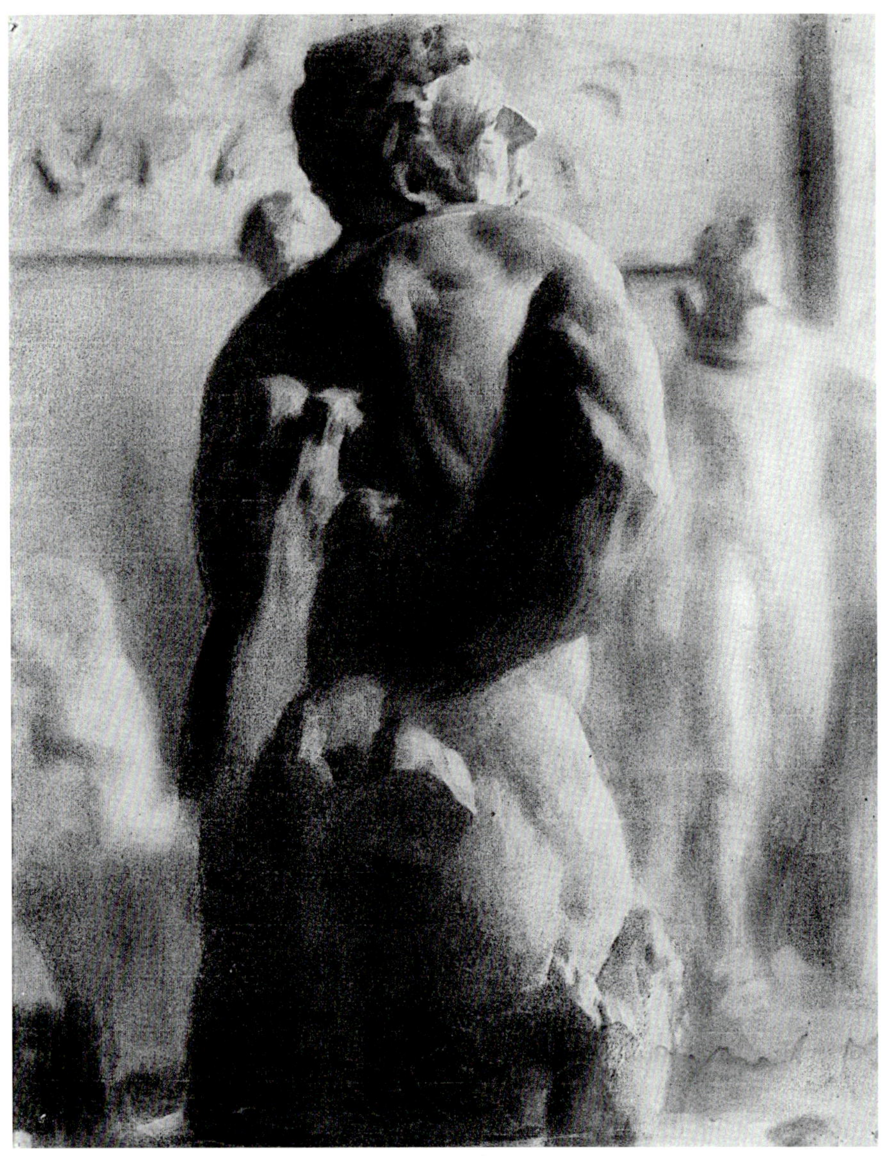

classes at the Pennsylvania Academy, most of which he taught after 1893, it is reasonable to assume that the majority postdate his Paris trip.[15] Such drawings served primarily as demonstration pieces for his cast drawing classes. Anshutz stated that "it [was] his custom to spend considerable time with paper and charcoal in the midst of such of his academy students as are wrestling with the beautiful difficulties of the antique."[16] Recording this process of learning to draw, his charcoals sometimes include renderings of his students (fig. 22). They often appear compositionally fused with their antique model, suggesting intense concentration and an effacing of boundaries between art and life.

The strength and power of Anshutz's charcoal drawings are evidence of his genuine interest in the genre. It is as though they were produced partially in an attempt to refute Eakins' objections to drawing ancient sculptures. Anshutz practiced an inventive revivification of the antique, the casts in his drawings animated and coursing with life, with a sensuousness verging on the erotic. In a remarkable way, Anshutz was able to transform a genre generally considered repetitive and elementary into something challenging and creative. Many of his charcoal drawings reveal bold, abstract massing of light and dark, little detail or suggestion of texture, a soft raking light, and a centrality of figure placement (fig. 23). Among the finest American charcoals of the late nineteenth century, the drawings reveal an adventurousness and experimentation rare in American academic drawing from this period. None of Anshutz's cast drawings was ever exhibited during his lifetime, but three were illustrated in a *Brush and Pencil* article about the artist in 1899.[17]

Anshutz's best charcoals, such as *Milo of Croton,* have considerable emotional and aesthetic power (fig. 24). This work could not be more convincingly expressive of pain or struggle. The drawing reveals an inner darkness. By depicting Pierre Puget's tortured figure from the back and below and emphasizing, through the use of strong highlights and deep velvety shadow, the lion's deadly paw on Milo's bound arm and the Greek wrestler's anguished facial expression, Anshutz effectively conveyed the sculpture's drama and pathos, and in the process made the sculptor's vision his very own.

In the fall of 1893 Anshutz began arranging for the purchase of a summer house in Holly Beach, New Jersey, where his family had vaca-

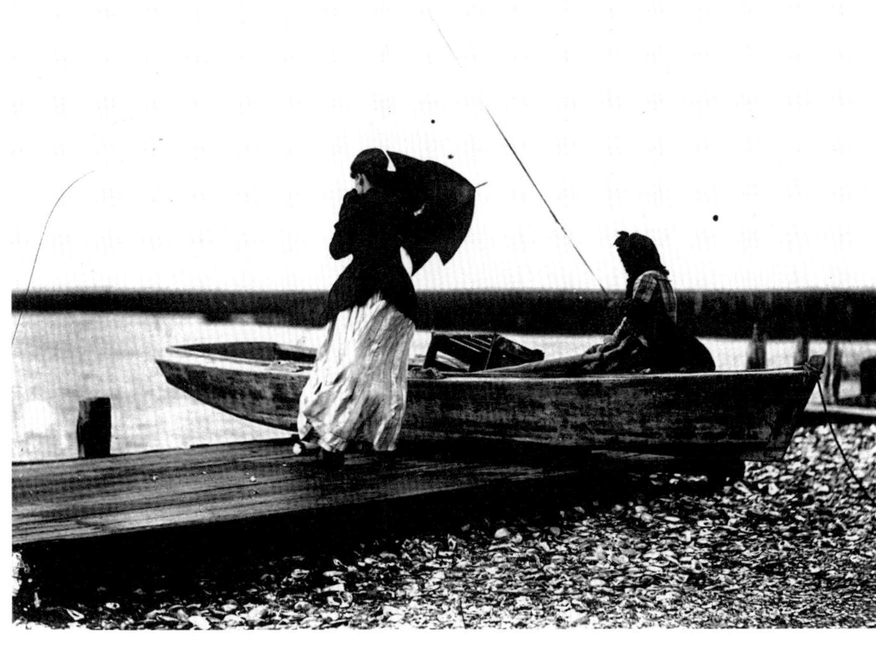

Figure 25.
Women by a Boat, ca. 1893
photograph
Thomas Anshutz Papers, Archives of American Art, Smithsonian Institution

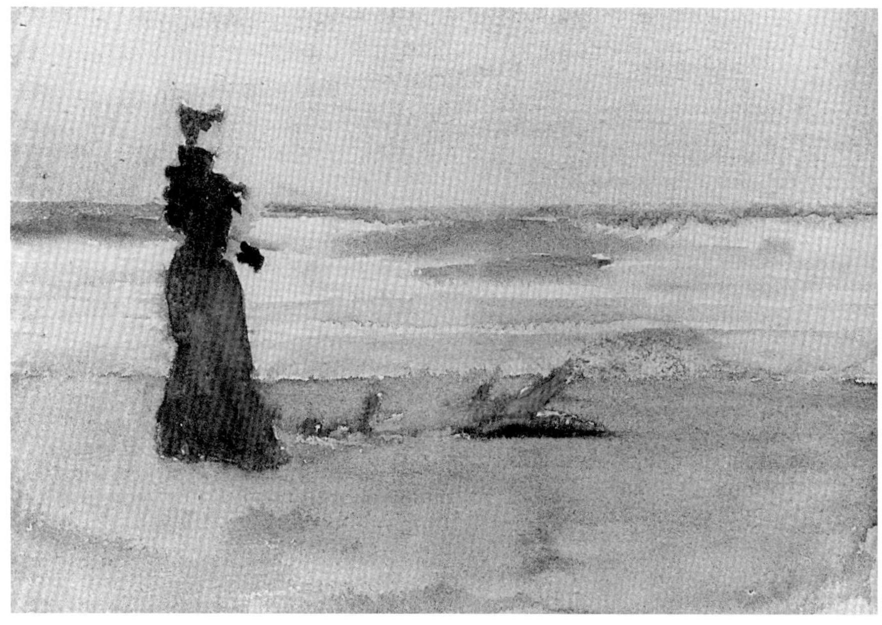

Figure 26.
Woman on Beach, ca. 1894
watercolor on paper,
$8\frac{5}{8} \times 12\frac{1}{2}$" (sight)
Yale University Art Gallery,
Collection of Mary C. and
James W. Fosburgh, B.A. 1933,
M.A. 1935.

tioned for years.[18] His letters of November 1893 to his wife Effie state that the Holly Beach lighting would be much better than in his Philadelphia studio.[19] That fall, he produced a small number of simple watercolor renderings of women in boats, several being taken from photographs he had made at the time (plate 8, fig. 25). Starting the following year, Anshutz and Effie spent part of many of their remaining summers at Holly Beach. From 1894 to about 1900, he produced numerous small watercolors and photographs of life near the shore, including scenes of women, fishermen, children, and landscapes (figs. 26, 27). These Holly Beach scenes form the beginning of a new phase of his work (1894-1900), one dominated by landscapes and marine images. Although he had produced landscapes as early as 1878, Anshutz had never, until this period, been as prolific or as wide-ranging a painter. This group of watercolors, pastels, and oils, many of which were never exhibited during his lifetime, represents some of his finest work; he seemed to be at his surest and least concerned about the opinions of others.[20]

Late in the summer of 1894 the painter wrote that he had "been making some pictures of kids lately and as they all have to start to school next week my occupation is gone."[21] These pictures constitute a small series of approximately fifteen watercolors showing boys along the New Jersey coast near Holly Beach.[22] Most of the paintings include a small sailboat or dory and two or three standing or sitting boys.[23] Many are only quickly sketched vignettes. The more finished watercolors, such as *Two Boys by a Boat* and *Boys Playing with Crabs,* convey an impressive monumentality and simplicity (plates 9,10).[24] Anshutz's Holly Beach scenes contain nothing superfluous—only the boys and a few minimal props. Working with high-keyed colors and taking advantage of the inherent luminosity of the watercolor paint, Anshutz was able to achieve a greater feeling of natural light than he ever had with oils. Apparently proud of the New Jersey watercolors, he exhibited many of them over the next several years at the Pennsylvania Academy, the Art Institute of Chicago, and the Boston Art Club.[25]

Anshutz based several of these pictures directly on photographs he had taken in the summer of 1894, sometimes virtually copying poses from the photographs, following a method he had learned from Eakins (fig.27).[26] Yet the watercolors include little of the photographs' detail or textural elements and retain only the larger shapes and dominant areas of light and dark. For instance, Anshutz's watercolor *Two Boys by a Boat* represents, with slight alterations, the photographic source's same dory and boys, but none of its spindly weeds, lines of cracked paint on the boat, or posts in the background. By effacing those details, as well as the standing boy's laughing face, and by emphasizing the simple mass of the children and boat, Anshutz transformed the photograph's design into something simpler, bolder, and more monumental.

Influenced by Winslow Homer's watercolors from 1880, especially those of boys sitting on beached dories, the Holly Beach watercolors also may have been stimulated by the French Impressionist paintings Anshutz had seen in Paris.[27] A direct source for Anshutz's scenes of boys and boats may also have been several photographs owned by Anshutz, probably taken under Eakins' supervision in the early 1880s, showing Eakins

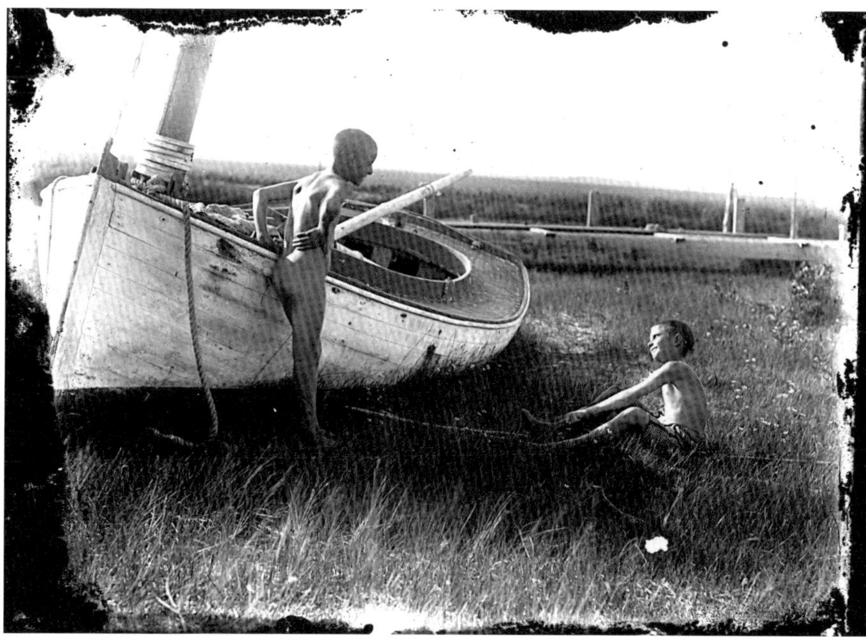

Figure 27.
Two Boys by a Boat, ca. 1894
photograph
Thomas Anshutz Papers, Archives of American Art, Smithsonian Institution

and J. Laurie Wallace standing nude in front of a beached boat (fig. 28). Both Eakins' and Anshutz's imagery participates in the popular theme of nude swimming, but Anshutz transformed Eakins' potentially controversial photographs of nude adult men into conventional images of nude prepubescent children. Anshutz was probably also thinking of Eakins' arcadian scenes, such as *Arcadia* (ca. 1883, The Metropolitan Museum of Art, New York). Both Anshutz's and Eakins' images show static figures of nude children in the landscape, and both represented the idyllic pleasures of a summer day. However, Anshutz's more simplified and apparently spontaneous scenes contain none of Eakins' references to classical art.

As William Innes Homer has argued, these Holly Beach watercolors

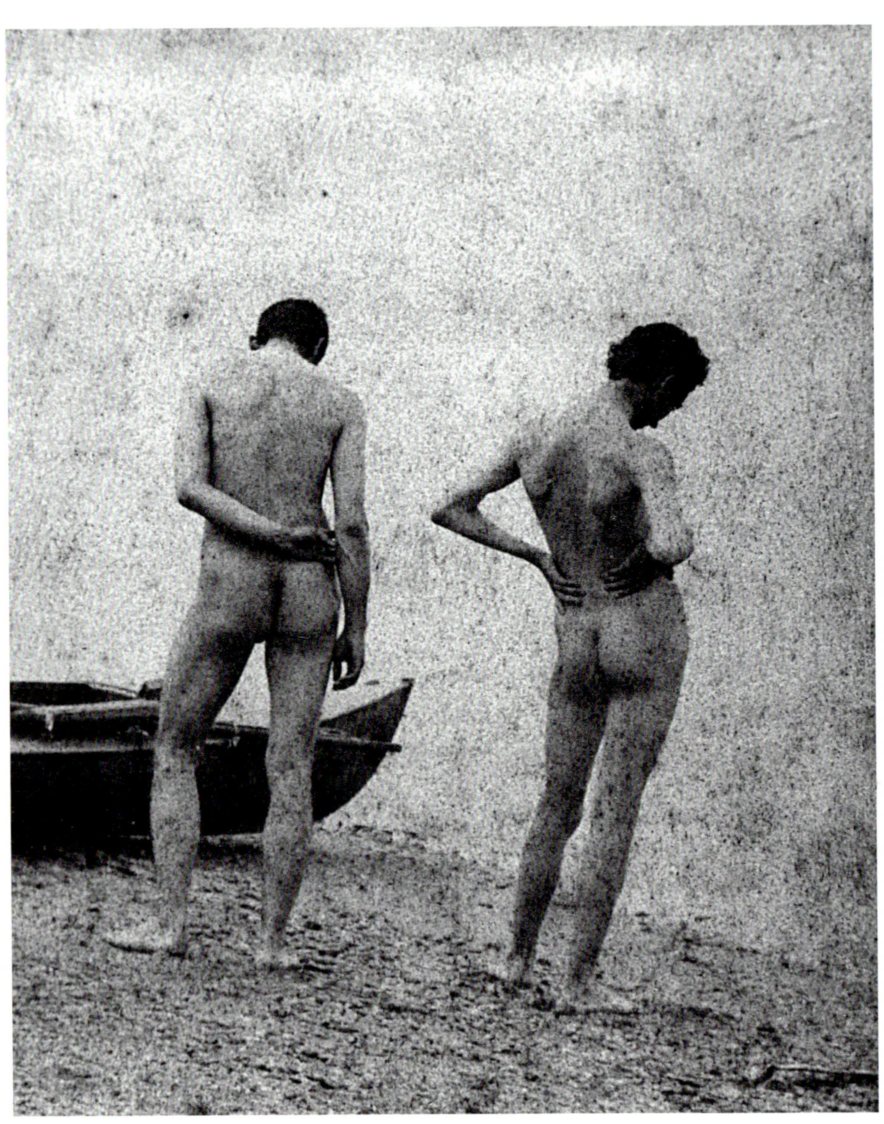

Figure 28.
Thomas Eakins and J. Laurie Wallace, ca. 1883
photograph
Thomas Anshutz Papers,
Archives of American Art,
Smithsonian Institution

constituted Anshutz's first decisive break from Eakins.[28] Although they represent the artist's Parisian-period interest in the medium of watercolor, the Holly Beach scenes also convey a new feeling of spontaneity, confidence, boldness, and directness (plate 11). In addition, the painting technique is looser than in most of the earlier work from Paris, and the palette brighter and more varied, including a whole range of greens, purples, and browns, and, occasionally, blues. In places, Anshutz thoroughly soaked areas of the paper, allowing colors to bleed together to form flat iridescent passages displaying chromatic vibrancy. Rarely throughout his career did he employ such a high-keyed palette. They exhibit a new level of luminosity that convincingly conveys a sense of warming sunshine and brilliant light. This is due largely to the areas of unpainted white paper. Yet the carefully modeled, emphatically three-dimensional boats and boys and the lack of any broken brushwork reveal Anshutz's unwillingness or inability to entirely jettison his academic training.

The Holly Beach scenes epitomize late-nineteenth-century concepts of rural innocence, the relaxed and unself-conscious boys seemingly stepping directly out of the pages of a Mark Twain novel. The theme of the boy in nature was ubiquitous in American late-Victorian culture; it represented a nostalgia for a supposed earlier, simpler American culture. Boats, too, were an appropriate prop sometimes signifying male prowess and freedom: Twain, Herman Melville, Homer, Eakins, and various popular illustrations frequently presented images of boys or men with boats.

In the summer of 1897, accompanied by the Pennsylvania Academy's president, James L. Claghorn, Anshutz made a two-and-a-half-month trip down the Delaware River. They began in Millville, New Jersey, and proceeded south into Delaware. Anshutz painted and took many photographs along the way.[29] This river trip testifies to Anshutz's long-standing love of river life and river boats.[30] It was an adventure for him, an opportunity to escape his teaching responsibilities and return to subjects he had drawn and painted in his youth, of a simpler, arcadian America. The 1897 excursion offered him an ever-changing selection of subjects to paint in the open air, for, during this trip, he—like many contemporary artists—used the boat as a kind of outdoor studio and painted oils and watercolors of other boats along the river.[31] His photographs from the Delaware River trip record scenes of dories, schooners, shipyards, and farmers. To a present-day viewer, the photographs provide a poignant record; for Anshutz, the images preserved visual memories of the trip for future paintings (fig. 29).[32]

In a letter to Effie, which includes a watercolor and pencil sketch of a boat out of water Anshutz wrote, "Tell Neddie [their three-year-old son] that the following is a sketch of a schooner's hull pulled out on the marine rail-way. She is going to have her main deck raised to give her a deeper hold."[33] Anshutz's oil painting of that site, *Down the Delaware Bay*, which is based on a photograph, evocatively contrasts three boats of varying sizes with the jagged lines of trees in the background (plate 12).

The boating theme, soft brushwork and flattened, silhouetted vegetation suggest the painting of the American Impressionist Theodore Robinson.

Anshutz's numerous letters to his wife written on this trip provide an invaluable record of a late nineteenth-century American artist's views about what constituted appropriate artistic subject matter. While in Delaware, concerning this very subject, Anshutz wrote:

> This river is navigable for twenty-five miles up country and there is not a settlement on it I suppose because it runs through marshes all the way. There is consequently nothing picturesque here but the haying. That however is the most excellent subject. And all yesterday morning the rude broad tired hay wagons with their ox teams and the men with high boots[,] flannel shirts[,] broad brimmed hats kept forming composition after composition each one perfect. The subject reminds me of Millet—except that it is thoroughly American.[34]

This and other comments from the river trip illustrate Anshutz's preference for recording nostalgic "American" themes of man and nature in harmony. One of the few times he complained about available subject matter was when nothing in sight looked old. He wrote: "The river here is full of rather uninteresting boats nearly all with a brand new coat of white paint."[35]

Based on this river trip in 1897, Anshutz produced perhaps a dozen oils of river vessels between 1897 and 1900. Unlike his Holly Beach watercolors and unlike the work of many of his contemporaries who were influenced by Impressionism, Anshutz's ship scenes contain few bright colors. Yet his choice of theme echoes that of many contemporary artists in America and Europe, such as Eakins, John Henry Twachtman, Robinson, Whistler, and Monet. Similar in appearance to Monet's pre-Impressionist oils from the mid 1860s, *The Lumber Boat* offers a good example of how painterly Anshutz's work had become by the late 1890s (plate 13). Unconcerned about the inclusion of small details, he made broken cobweb-like marks to represent the ship's ropes, quick comma-shaped brushstrokes for waves, and several cursory black and white lines to portray the seated figure in the small dory. The artist employed this technique effectively in capturing the atmospheric effects of a rainy, breezy day and in conveying the sense of the boat's weight and mass. Owing to the repetition of dull yellows, browns, reds, and greys throughout the image, and the opposition of the horizontal shoreline to the prominent vertical forms of the ship's masts, the cropping of which adds further stability to the design, Anshutz was able to create a unified and harmonious composition.

Working in a similar style, Anshutz painted *On the Delaware at Tacony,* which shows a majestic four-masted schooner anchored in the Delaware River several miles north of Philadelphia (plate 14). By depicting the ship from a low position, just above the waterline, Anshutz made

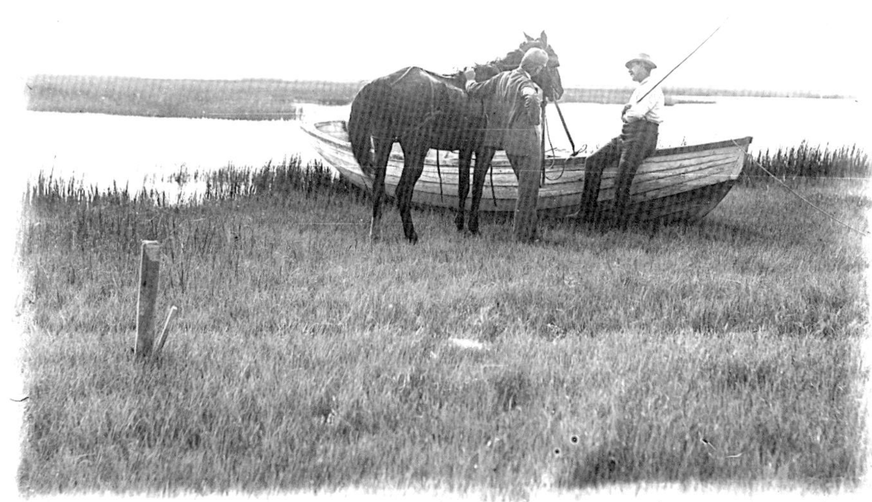

Figure 29.
Two Men by a Boat, ca. 1897
photograph
Thomas Anshutz Papers,
Archives of American Art,
Smithsonian Institution

it imposing: surrounded by sky and water, the vessel dominates the composition. The scene conveys the reduced light of an overcast day and contrasts—Turner-like—the older style of sailing ship to the more modern steam-powered tugboat.

What makes some of Anshutz's ship scenes different from others of their era is the inclusion of industrial shorelines dominating the backgrounds. The majority of American painters during this period avoided "ugly" urban and industrial subjects, considering them suitable for popular illustration but not for fine art. Although *On the Delaware at Tacony* contains only distant buildings and smoke plumes, other paintings in this group include backgrounds dotted with oil tanks, factories, smokestacks, and warehouses. In several smaller oils, painted from a perspective much closer to the shore, Anshutz made the industrial landscape far more prominent: large oil tanks and smokestacks loom above the ships. It is never clear whether he intended such scenes as celebration, criticism, or neutral reportage. The inclusion of such factory imagery foreshadows the later harbor scenes of George Bellows and John Sloan and anticipates the interest among early twentieth-century painters and photographers in urban themes.[36] Anshutz's upbringing in Wheeling and his work on *The Ironworkers' Noontime* must have made him aware of the industrial subject's distinct pictorial possibilities.

Anshutz's *Steamboat on the Ohio* is another example of his juxtaposition of older ships with industrial settings (plate 5). However, unlike the artist's other boat paintings, *Steamboat on the Ohio* contains passages of non-naturalistic bright oranges and reds, areas of mosaic-like

Figure 30.
Figures by the Ohio River, Wheeling, West Virginia, ca. 1890
photograph
Thomas Anshutz Papers,
Archives of American Art,
Smithsonian Institution

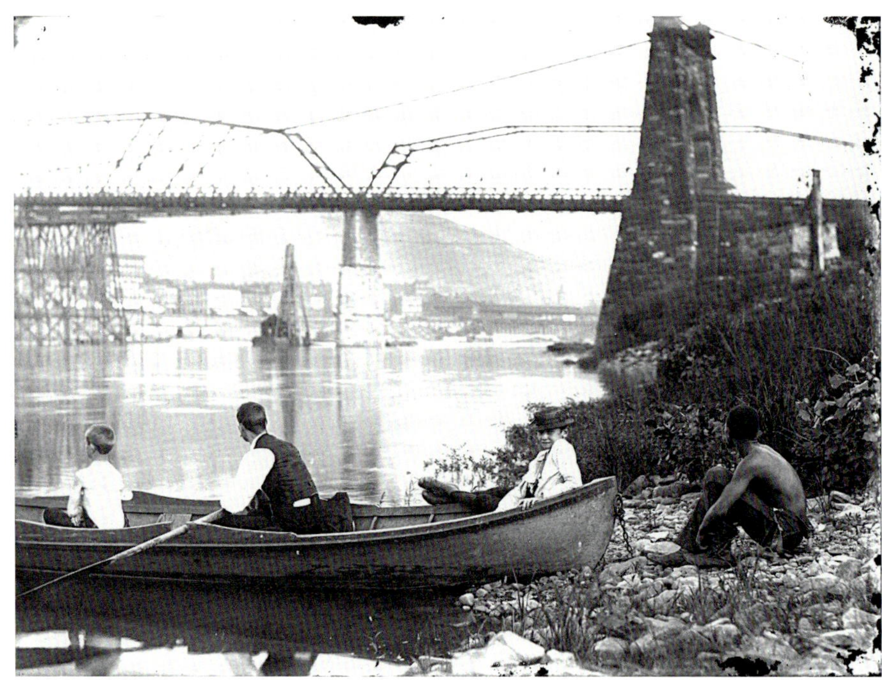

brushstrokes, and a flattened, abstracted background. With its Nabis-inspired color scheme, prominent ship, and nude boys in the foreground, the Carnegie Museum of Art's painting summarizes better than any other oil Anshutz's artistic interests and development, outside of portraiture, after 1890. Furthermore, because of its large number of human figures, ambitious scale, and the artist's unusual use of preparatory sketches, no painting in Anshutz's *oeuvre,* with the exception of *The Ironworkers' Noontime,* was more ambitious. *Steamboat on the Ohio* actually represents a conflation of two different sources. Whereas the painting's background derives from one of Anshutz's earlier Ohio River sketches from 1880 (fig. 9), the foreground is based on several Anshutz photographs from around 1890 of the same Wheeling area (figs. 30, 31). From one photograph Anshutz closely adopted the foreground figures of the man sitting in the boat and the boy seated on the rocks, and from another he reconfigured a group of nude boys looking out across the water.

These photographs provide a temporal benchmark for dating the painting. They could not have been taken before 1886, the year a steamboat shown in one of the photographs was commissioned.[37] Additional evidence moves the painting's earliest date of origin to around 1895: the poses of the two nude boys standing in the image's foreground derive from the artist's summer Holly Beach watercolors from 1894, and the boat theme itself, as discussed earlier, was common in Anshutz's work from the late 1890s. In addition, an undated preparatory pastel drawing for the painting is stylistically similar to pastels from the 1890s by American Impressionists such as J. Alden Weir and John Twachtman

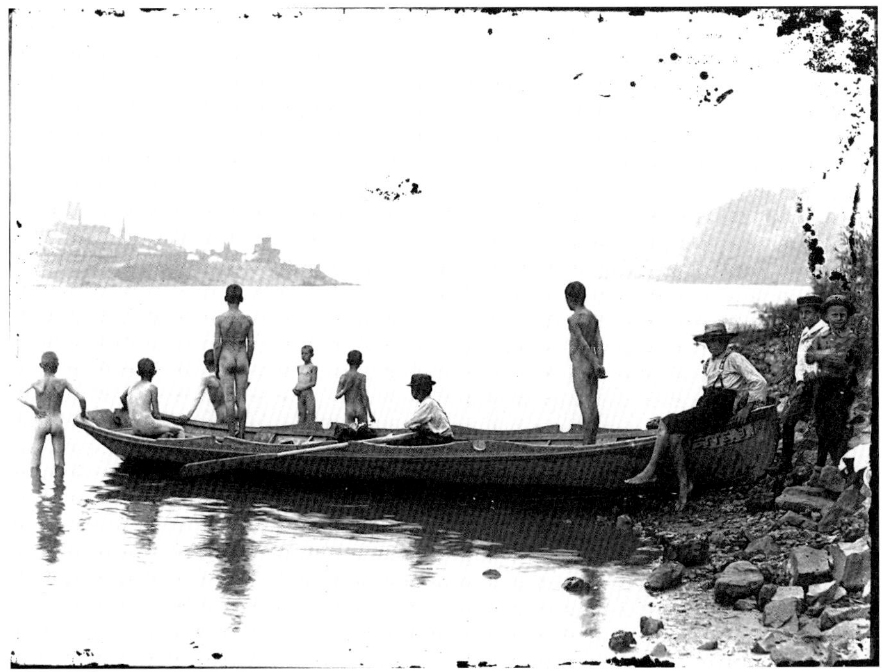

Figure 31.
Figures by the Ohio River, Wheeling, West Virginia, ca. 1890
photograph
Thomas Anshutz Papers,
Archives of American Art,
Smithsonian Institution

(fig.32).[38] The study lacks only the finished painting's adult figures, enlarged smoke plumes, and patches of bright color. About the same time, Anshutz produced an undated oil study for *Steamboat on the Ohio* (plate 15). With the exception of the seated adult foreground figure and the brighter palette, the study is very similar to the pastel. That it was highly unusual for Anshutz to have made preparatory images at all suggests he considered *Steamboat on the Ohio* important.

But even with this information, *Steamboat on the Ohio* remains one of the artist's most difficult paintings to date accurately.[39] On the basis of the theme and the style of the preparatory pastel drawing and oil study, it seems reasonable to date *Steamboat on the Ohio* from the 1890s. However, it was probably painted sometime after 1900, perhaps as late as 1911. This argument is based on stylistic grounds alone, specifically the passages of bright oranges, blues, and reds not included in the artist's other boat scenes. Indeed, *Steamboat on the Ohio* looks unlike anything else Anshutz produced until after 1900, when he first began experimenting with brighter colors. Thus, after producing the studies in the late 1890s, Anshutz may well have set aside the theme for several years before going on to paint the larger oil. He had, after all, waited over a decade between the initial pencil drawing and the pastel study. Such a five- or ten-year gap would help to account for the stylistic discrepancy.

It is probable that *Steamboat on the Ohio* is an unfinished painting. With its darker and more detailed foreground against an abstracted, illuminated background, the scene appears almost a composite of two entirely different works. Both stylistic and technical variances help

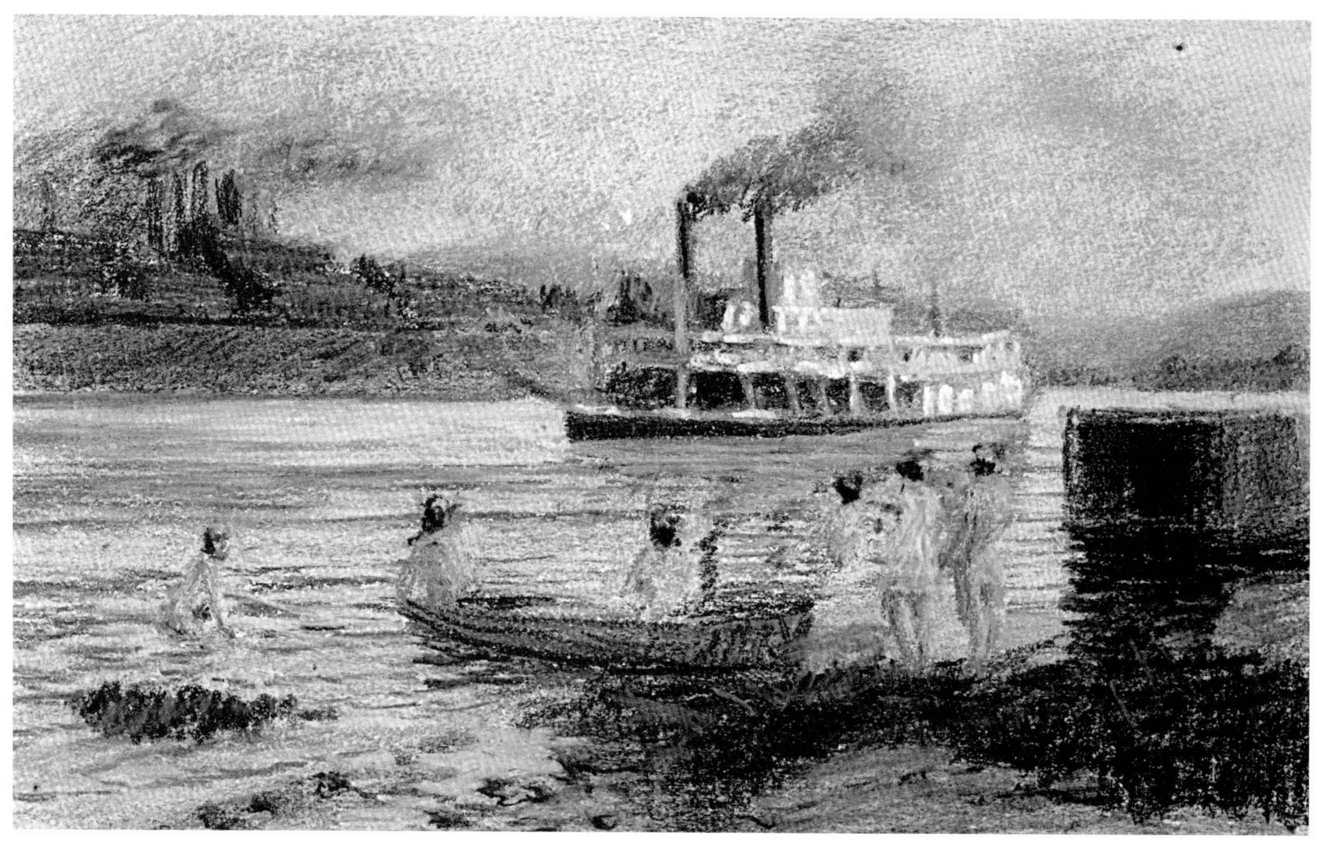

Figure 32.
Steamboat on the Ohio, ca. 1897
pastel on paper, 7¼ × 11½"
Westmoreland Museum of Art,
Greensburg, Pennsylvania,
Gift of William A. Coulter Fund, 59.73

explain this dichotomy. In the background the artist employed what he may have meant as a preparatory underpainting technique, quickly painting in areas of smoke, sky, hills, and factory in tonal contrasts of light and dark. The brushwork in these background sections is reminiscent of pastel and charcoal drawings. That those passages of pigment were applied so thinly, allowing the luminous white of the canvas to emerge throughout, further supports the underpainting thesis. There is even an incongruous patch of green in the sky on the upper right, left entirely unresolved. Yet, in one important respect, these sections are not typical of Anshutz's underpainting, which in other paintings was consistently dominated by dark browns and rarely included such bright colors.

The artist's unconventional combination of bright colors and the probable underpainting technique suggest that *Steamboat on the Ohio* could have been produced as a way of coming to terms with the Post-Impressionist—principally Nabis—painting Anshutz had seen in Paris ten years or more previously. However, even in its unfinished state, its colors generally lack the high-keyed intensity of paintings by Maurice Denis or Paul Sérusier; its objects retain the illusion of sculptural mass;

and its space is broken into legible fore-, middle-, and background segments. Yet, seen in an early twentieth-century American artistic context, *Steamboat on the Ohio* is a daring and experimental image. The scene abstracts the factory and sky and is dominated by heightened sunset oranges, reds, and blues, much in the manner of a toned-down Nabis work. Indeed, the image afforded Anshutz the opportunity to explore fully his abilities as a colorist and contains numerous inventive and unexpected juxtapositions of color. For instance, he represented the distant shoreline by using a daring band of blue, green, yellow, violet, and red patches, and then audaciously sandwiched these between the brightly saturated colors of the water below and the muted palette of the sky above. He also included the patch of brilliant red on the shore in the foreground, which seems to be there only to create color harmony and compositional unity. That same red is repeated in the water, smoke, and factory façade, and the rest of the painting similarly repeats mauves, greens, browns, and blues.

Even with its mildly Nabis-inspired style, *Steamboat on the Ohio* was a variant of a long tradition in American art: the theme of contrast between America's rural arcadian past and its urban future.[40] Yet, in depicting this collision between two symbolic spaces, Anshutz recast it idiosyncratically. By pairing a traditional theme with an unorthodox style, he both rethought an accepted American typology and transformed a French stylistic model (Nabis painting) into something the painter probably considered distinctly American. Anshutz's style and theme were ideally matched. The more conservatively rendered foreground figures, representing America's innocent, timeless, and "natural" rural past, stare across the river at the nation's industrial-capitalist future, with all its attendant violent transformations of nature and temporal constrictions. Thus, the picture implies the inevitable demise of rural America in the face of expanding industrialization. Appropriately, Anshutz depicted the factory in a more abstract style, connoting modernity and change. The men and boys thus witness a dramatic meeting of two emblems of change and progress. The majestic white steamboat and the red-orange factory appear to be engaged in a counterpoint of activity, competing to see which can belch out the most ostentatious plumes of smoke.[41]

Steamboat on the Ohio may also be read as a deeply personal, self-referential statement, a projection of the painter's own upbringing and artistic career. The image's foreground figures, shown staring across the river, function as surrogates for the artist himself, looking into his own past. Indeed, a figure seated in the boat even resembles the artist. The figures' combined gazes and the emphatic compositional line formed by the group of boys in the river effectively draw the viewer to the background scene of industrial Wheeling, where Anshutz had been reared. That Anshutz chose to return to the site and time of his earlier, best-known painting, *The Ironworkers' Noontime,* suggests that he may have intended *Steamboat on the Ohio* as a summary of his own artistic journey, the river being a traditional symbol for a voyage through life, and as a kind of competition piece with his own earlier industrial scene. Presenting the factory theme from an entirely new perspective, *Steamboat on the Ohio* illustrates how much he felt he had achieved since his Eakins-dominated early years. No longer was he intent on producing an "objective" rendering of nature.

Anshutz's new openness to modern styles is somewhat surprising. After all, as discussed earlier, the painter had seemingly been unimpressed by the Post-Impressionist painting he had seen in Paris in 1892-93. It is unlikely that he experienced an overnight conversion; he instead began a period of artistic exploration with the Paris and Holly Beach watercolors in 1893 and 1894, and from these years through the end of his life worked his way through many different artistic styles, predominantly via oil and watercolor landscape sketches. He apparently took to heart his realization in Paris that "there is no one correct style of painting."[42] The American Impressionist paintings he saw in New York and Philadelphia in the 1890s and the late nineteenth-century Nabis-inspired imagery of Robert Henri may have also helped move his painting style in a new direction.

Anshutz's art was also influenced by the imagery and opinions of his former student and co-founder of the Darby Summer Art School, Hugh Breckenridge, who had become very enthusiastic about Impressionism by the late 1890s. After the two men established the Darby school in 1898, they spent the next ten summers together, most of that time in Fort Washington, Pennsylvania.[43] Anshutz would have had many opportunities to study Breckenridge's canvases, which displayed high-keyed yellows, reds, and oranges; and these paintings seemed to have inspired Anshutz to experiment with such vivid hues. Anshutz's close friend Helen Henderson later mentioned that his association with Breckenridge provided, late in his career, a "new impetus" for working with a brighter palette.[44]

Some evidence suggests that Anshutz's use of brighter colors may have been influenced indirectly by his awareness of color theory. Although nothing indicates that he ever set his palette according to the tenets of color theorists and practitioners such as Hardesty Maratta, as did Sloan and Henri, it is clear that Anshutz had been somewhat interested in the subject of color theory at least as early as 1895. At that time, and several years later, he had considered its application for classes at the Pennsylvania Academy of the Fine Arts. The records of the Pennsylvania Academy's Committee on Instruction show that Anshutz played a role in bringing color theorists to speak there.[45] In the 1890s Anshutz felt that color theory might offer students another valuable tool. At some point after 1907, Anshutz acquired color charts by the American theorist Denman Waldo Ross.[46] A lecturer at Harvard and one of America's most influential writers on color theory, Ross was an amateur painter who set out to educate artists through his writings. Among other things, he attempted to help painters make their palettes more controlled and calibrated.[47] Yet despite the fact that Anshutz owned several of Ross' color charts, none of Anshutz's late paintings suggests any strong debt to Ross.

On occasion, Anshutz discussed color somewhat in the manner of the art-for-arts-sake movement, that is, in synesthetic terms. For instance, in 1902, he wrote his friend Cresson Schell, "When you can play them [colors] like that in chords of color you will be in it . . . . True colors form into chords and the shadows are [the] bass notes."[48] His statement shows a clear awareness of contemporary European and American associations of color and music.

During the same period of Anshutz's sporadic interests in color theory (1895-1911), much of the painter's artistic production consisted of small-scale, quickly-produced landscape sketches—most of which were watercolors and oils, with a few pastels—of the rural countryside in southeastern Pennsylvania. Few if any of the approximately fifty landscapes were ever exhibited during the artist's lifetime, nor were they employed as preparatory studies for other paintings. What is surprising is that these sketches form the bulk of Anshutz's output as a painter from around 1895 to 1902, at which time he once more returned to portraiture. During the period just described it was as though he had returned to the year 1878, when the majority of his artistic production had also taken the form of landscapes. Anshutz's letters from around 1900 reveal the pleasure he gained from walking excursions into the rural countryside and the great artistic challenge that he found in *plein-air* sketching.

All of the painter's landscapes from this period (1895-1911) can be viewed as attempts to solve what Anshutz saw as fundamental problems of painting. As he wrote:

> It is still an unsolved problem to me how to paint a landscape and also what makes a picture subject. Most subjects that you see have something that you don't want or lack something you do. And when you take the something out and put the something in where you want it the result looks so much like a pretty pretty picture that it makes you sick. And that's the hell of it. . . . [The] problem to me [is] how to paint a landscape and also what makes a picture subject. I have an idea that we seldom or never find a subject ready made. If we did the camera would handle it better than the artist generally.[49]

This conundrum of reconciling realism with "improving" nature was a driving force behind Anshutz's sketches. In 1900, he wrote, "Details are essential to good work but full unity and truth of effect are only gotten by showing the details that nature shows and hiding those that are hidden."[50]

In addition to allowing Anshutz to grapple with questions of artistic judgment, his landscape sketches gave him the opportunity to try out various styles. In a letter to his former student, Cresson Schell, written in 1900, he stated that the Pennsylvania countryside around Fort

Washington was a "place to knock the scales off of your eyes."[51] In that same note, he mentioned that it was good to free oneself "from local color."[52] His letters from this time convey the impression that he was delighted at the opportunity to paint without catering to public expectations and at being able to move beyond the confines of his own academic training.

Albert Boime, in his book *The Academy and French Painting in the Nineteenth Century,* argues convincingly that the oil sketch has traditionally embodied notions of modernity and originality.[53] By employing the sketch, an artist could set aside concerns with finish, illusionism, and artistic convention. As an inherently personal form of image-making, the sketch provided the artist an opportunity to experiment with new ideas and take chances he or she could not afford in the public arena. Once transformed into a finished composition, it inevitably lost its sense of spontaneity. As Anshutz wrote concerning one of his sketches, "I could not help thinking however that it would be the easiest thing in the world to lose its charm in putting it on canvas."[54]

He continued to produce landscape sketches from about 1894 until around 1911, the year before his death. Because virtually none of his landscapes is dated, it is extremely difficult to trace convincingly any stylistic progression among them. However, they can be grouped according to style.

One group of approximately ten oil sketches, judging by Anshutz's

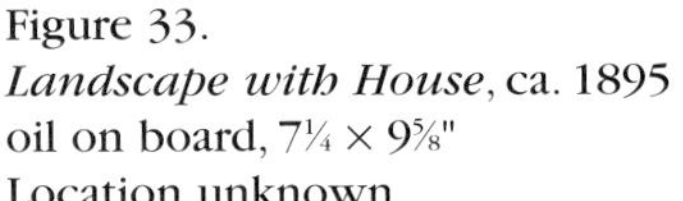
Figure 33.
Landscape with House, ca. 1895
oil on board, 7¼ × 9⅝"
Location unknown

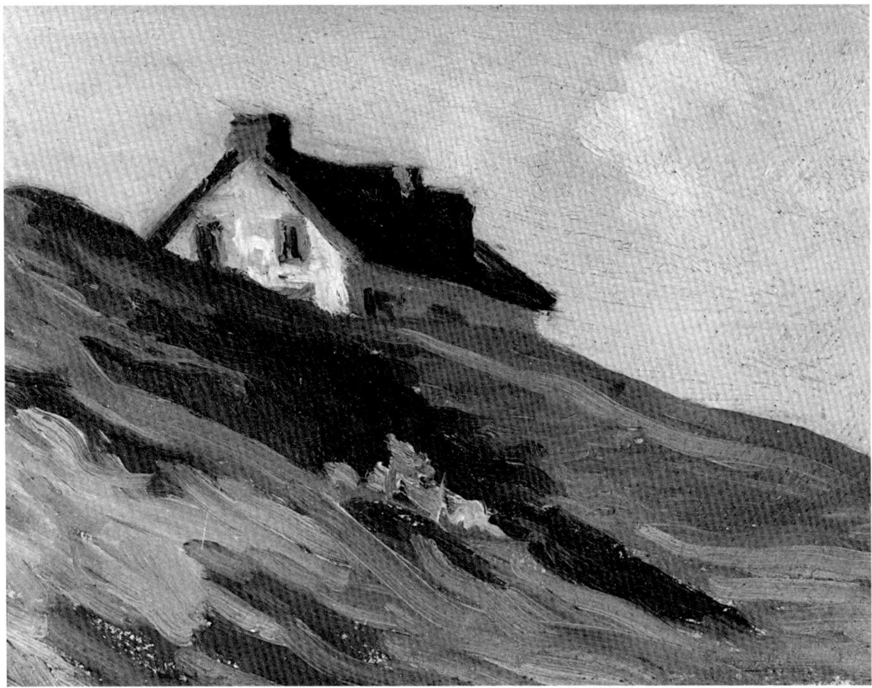

handling of light and application of pigment, resembles images of such Barbizon school painters as Theodore Rousseau, an artist Anshutz had praised in the 1880s (plate 16).[55] The dark palette suggests that these undated sketches may have been painted in the early or middle 1890s. Like many other nineteenth-century landscape oil sketches by artists such as John Constable and Frederic Church, all scenes focus solely on the the larger features of sky, earth, and trees and are dominated by simple blocks of tone and color. Following in this tradition, Anshutz's best *plein-air* sketches convey a feeling of genuine natural light, movement, and color, with monumental simplicity (plate 17).

A related group of oil landscapes, which may, with their brighter palette, have been executed several years later, also differs from the previous scenes in their wider and more heavily coated brushstrokes and in the inclusion of prominent buildings, which add an emphatically sculptural element to the landscape.[56] The buildings' volumetric, compact masses, austerely set against flat expanses of field and sky, appear as natural outgrowths of the land. Among this group of rural scenes, none is more impressive than *Landscape with House* (fig. 33). Painted with a superb combination of spontaneity and control, the scene's design is one of the painter's most immediate and direct. By reducing everything to basic components of land, sky, and house, Anshutz created a vision of the strength of the rural home; crowning a hill, rooted in the earth, and set apart from the rest of society, the edifice embodies an American ideal of self-reliance and independence.

The artist's architectonic, pictorial construction produces strong underlying visual tensions: the house seems squeezed between land and sky, and thick buttery brushstrokes continually reassert the presence of the picture plane, creating constant shifts between flatness and depth. The scene's dominant, sharply-uptilted foreground recalls some of Homer's late coastal scenes. Yet, *Landscape with House* also looks forward, in its reduction of form and its paint application, to canvases by such early twentieth-century American artists as George Bellows and Rockwell Kent, and to images Edward Hopper would create several decades later.

A third group of the artist's landscapes can loosely be described as Impressionist, because of their high-keyed colors and loose brushwork. These scenes of trees, houses, and streams are mainly watercolors, although the painter also occasionally worked with pastels in a similar style. *House by a Pond,* from around 1900-05, is representative of this group and is one of his most iridescent watercolors as well (plate 18). Anshutz painted the two-story stone farmhouse, set by the edge of a pond, as a luminous, rich, and layered tapestry of greens and blues. He exploited the reflective surface of the pond and included a wide range of brushstrokes, from small and delicate to extremely bold. The water's fluidity was convincingly rendered by thoroughly soaking the paper before application of pigment.

Anshutz also executed several related landscapes, in watercolor and oil, with a series of short brushstrokes, many of which form crossed vertical and horizontal lines (plate 19). These crosshatchings create a mosaic-like effect, with dozens of small points of white interspersed throughout, which increase the luminosity and vibrancy of the half-muted greens and browns and the passages of bright yellow. This watercolor style was quite distinctive, in an American context, and betrays the influence of the oil landscapes of late French Impressionist painter Gustave Loiseau, an artist whose work had been exhibited in Paris at the time of Anshutz's first visit.[57] Several of Anshutz's Loiseau-inspired landscapes, probably produced several years later in oil, are darker, flatter, and much more abstracted, with larger crosshatchings and a palette dominated by greens, browns, and lavenders (plate 20).

Anshutz produced, as well, a small number of Whistlerian landscapes. Their haziness makes them reminiscent of contemporary Tonalist work and the landscapes of Thomas Dewing and John Twachtman, an artist whose imagery Anshutz particularly admired.[58] Anshutz's *Seated Figure in a Landscape,* for example, shows a barely-defined person seated in a meadow and facing a stand of trees (fig. 34). In this highly simplified, abstracted image, Anshutz eliminated surface detail, contour lines, and uncharacteristically, even the slightest suggestion of mass. Everything in the picture is suspended in a penumbral haze of diffused light. Perhaps these somewhat otherworldly scenes reflect Anshutz's experience of being raised in the New Church. It is possible, although not verifiable, that, as a result of Swedenborgian influence, Anshutz—like George Inness and Paul Sérusier—may have considered the physical world a reflection of a higher spiritual realm. However, Anshutz's extant writings never include mention of Swedenborg or his ideas.[59]

Of all Anshutz's landscapes, only two combine bright non-naturalistic color and a high level of abstraction. Probably dating from the fall of 1911 or the spring of 1912, both are likely to have been inspired by the painter's second trip to Paris, which occurred in the summer of 1911.[60] Already suffering the effects of terminal heart disease and bronchial illness by December 1910, Anshutz was forced to stop teaching at the Pennsylvania Academy of the Fine Arts in the following spring.[61] That summer he visited London, Paris, and Bad Neuheim, Germany, where, for six weeks, he was hospitalized for an unknown type of "curative treatment."[62] While in Paris, the artist's friend and former student, Lyman Saÿen, who had himself begun to paint Fauve-like images, conducted Anshutz on gallery tours to view the latest developments in Parisian avant-garde art.

Of the two images probably inspired by this Paris trip, both titled simply *Landscape,* one is a watercolor and the other an oil (plates 21, 22). The watercolor is the less adventurous of the two. It shows a river backed by a grass-covered bank and forest. This painting resembles both Anshutz's *Steamboat on the Ohio,* which, although much more conserv-

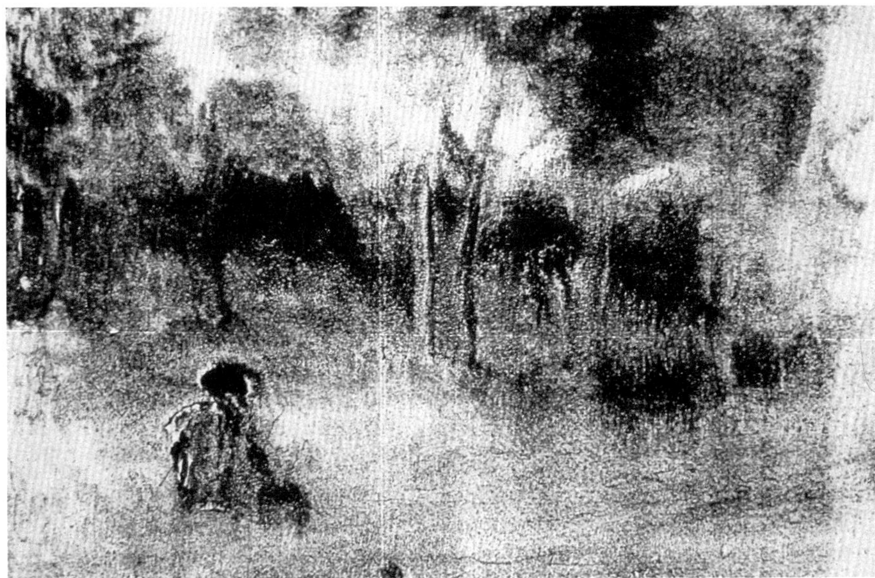

Figure 34.
Seated Figure in Landscape,
ca. 1904
watercolor, 7 × 10"
Location unknown

ative, offers similarly flattened passages of oranges, reds, greens, and blues, and his Nabis-inspired *Woman in Interior Reading* (plate 23). However, the hues in the watercolor are higher keyed, and the scene is much more abstracted in its overall flatness and lack of detail. The incandescent forest canopy in glowing yellows and oranges, the tree trunks in red, and the stream in bright blue was a radical departure from his previous landscape sketches. The watercolor's non-naturalistic style transforms the Pennsylvania landscape into something visionary and mysterious.

If the watercolor suggests Paul Gauguin or the Nabis, the oil landscape, which is unequalled within Anshutz's production for its abstraction and brilliant palette, is reminiscent of Vincent Van Gogh or Maurice Vlaminck. This painting represents the culmination of Anshutz's interest in the European avant-garde. With its prominent tall tree to one side and its vigorous impasto brushwork, it must have been painted after Anshutz saw one of Van Gogh's or Vlaminck's images. He exaggerated Van Gogh's characteristic style, employing larger and bolder brushstrokes and more non-naturalistic and dissonant colors. Yellows and blues, greens and reds, and pinks and violets are juxtaposed in the manner of a Fauve work by Vlaminck.[63]

The comments of contemporary critics indicate that the painter's interest in avant-garde art was becoming publicly known at the time of his death. For example, one of Anshutz's obituaries from 1912 included the phrase "Champion of 'Post-Impressionism'" in the headline.[64] The same article mentioned that his recent trip to Paris had made Anshutz "profoundly and actively interested" in the "post-impressionists."[65] And a contemporary essay by John Cournos noted that Anshutz was struggling in his studio with the ever-shifting nature of modern painting, believing that no "one truth" existed in art.[66] Later, Helen Henderson wrote that Anshutz's

> curiosity in art was insatiable. With open mind and unflagging zeal, he never wearied of analyzing, speculating, examining new movements as they came along. [He spent the] last months of his life... grappling with the tenets of the so-called modern movement just lifting its head about this time.[67]

During the period from 1894 to 1911, Anshutz not only painted landscapes and boating scenes, but also portraits and genre pictures, which, not unexpectedly, differ from those types of images among his earlier work in their subject matter and style. Whereas most of his paintings from the 1870s and early 1880s show outdoor activities, for example, *The Ironworkers' Noontime* and *Farmer and His Son at Harvesting,* works from the 1890s include larger numbers of dark interior scenes with women reading. After the middle 1890s, when Anshutz painted his Holly Beach watercolors, these interiors dominate his genre production. The only two outdoor figural scenes he painted after 1900 were *Steamboat on the Ohio* and the brightly colored *Two Indians on the Ohio* (ca. 1905, location unknown).

An image that typifies Anshutz's later genre painting is *A Studio Study,* from 1892 (fig. 20). Unlike his earlier interior paintings, such as *The Chore,* which were mainly of standing figures, *A Studio Study* presents the single seated figure of a woman reading. Another interior, *In a Garret,* offers a rare example of an American treatment of the theme of death and the woman, with its human skull prominently perched atop a spinning wheel, leering menacingly down at the seated figure (fig. 35). The woman, who has paused in rummaging through a chest of old letters, seems unaware of the skull's presence. In the context of Anshutz's scene, the skull signifies not only the brevity of life, as in Dutch seventeenth-century art and in some contemporary American paintings such as those of William Harnett, but also the otherness and unattainability of what is past. The spinning wheel itself, which here seems to suggest the traditional theme of the cycle of life, was a standard Colonial Revival motif, sometimes also used by Eakins.[68]

In addition to producing five or six paintings of women reading, Anshutz painted a range of genre subjects, including several Colonial Revival costume pieces. A good example of this type of painting is his undated *Woman Writing at a Table* (plate 24). One of Anshutz's most accomplished genre scenes, it displays an exquisite Vermeer-like rendering of diffused light.[69] The canvas also bears a strong affinity to contemporary paintings of the Boston School. Yet the image's cluttered assortment of antique props overlaid with a patina of stillness and velvety

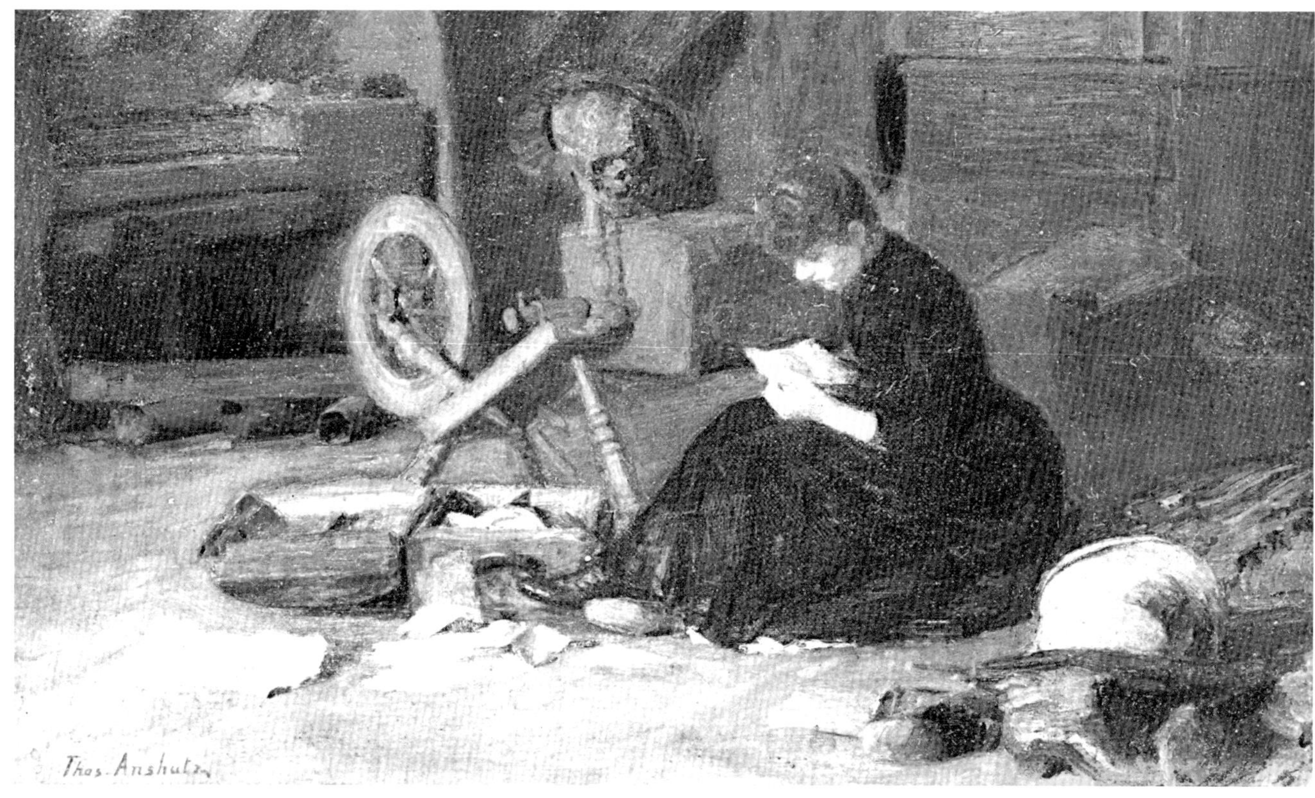

Figure 35.
In a Garret, 1891
oil on canvas, 10 1/16 × 16 1/16"
The Pennsylvania Academy of the Fine Arts, Philadelphia.
Gift of pupils of the artist in the Pennsylvania Academy School

Thomas Dewing's austere Whistler-inspired moodpieces. Anshutz was more interested in achieving a look of naturalism than meditative elegance.

Beginning in 1898, after a three-year hiatus, Anshutz once more began to exhibit his work at the Pennsylvania Academy annuals, as well as at the Art Institute of Chicago. This renewed interest in public exposure stemmed from his increasing confidence, ambition, and excitement about portraiture. Indeed, portraiture dominates the public side of Anshutz's late work; with few exceptions, every painting he exhibited between 1898 and 1911 was a portrait or a clothed figure study. This genre provided Anshutz with his first widespread recognition and a slightly larger income, while on a personal level his letters indicate that he found portrait painting challenging. During much of this period after 1898, he also taught portrait classes in the summers at Fort Washington.[70]

Between 1880 and 1900 Anshutz's portrait style changed as did the style of the rest of his other work, albeit in a different direction. Whereas early portraits, such as *Portrait of the Artist's Mother* (1882, Westmoreland Museum of Art), were detailed and somewhat wooden, his later portrait style, beginning around 1893, assumed greater verve. This is especially evident in a series of painterly portraits of Philadelphia Sketch especially evident in a series of painterly portraits of Philadelphia Sketch Club members, the majority of which were painted between 1894 and 1896.[71] At the same time, Anshutz also executed a number of painterly pastel renderings of women. His interest in pastel dated at least as far back as the spring of 1892, when he exhibited a pastel entitled *Study* (ca. 1892, location unknown) at the Pennsylvania Academy. After returning from Paris, where he had been captivated by the pastels of Besnard, Anshutz produced occasional landscapes, genre scenes, and portraits using that technique through the remainder of the 1890s.[72] One early example of his pastel portraiture is *Portrait of Mrs. Anshutz* (plate 25). Created in 1893, it is a *tour de force* of pastel work from the period. Composed of a series of short, controlled strokes, it features a sharp juxtaposition between the background's palette of dark browns and yellows and Mrs. Anshutz's bright turquoise dress. The sweeping dress dominates the picture field and conveys a dramatic and successful illusion of sculptural mass. The picture presents a wonderful contrast between the monumental sitter and the small teacup she is holding.

The styles of the approximately thirty portraits painted after 1900 vary, from Eakins-like naturalism to bright Impressionist-inspired pastels. Anshutz therefore used portraiture, as he did landscape painting, as a vehicle for coming to terms with various artistic styles. Several of Anshutz's portraits from 1900-08 closely resemble those of Eakins. One of Anshutz's former students, Dr. David Wilson, commented on the similarity of their methods:

> Anshutz taught me to begin my portrait with an outline on the canvas in burnt sienna and turpentine, and to put in burnt sienna shadows all over before doing the flesh parts in vermilion, yellow ochre and white. Eakins also used these for his flesh colors![73]

Several of Anshutz's unfinished portraits confirm the accuracy of Dr. Wilson's description. Anshutz first painted the face in some detail, leaving the sitter's body loosely delineated with bold dark brown outlines. Typically, he also made preparatory oil sketches in which the forms of the body and surrounding objects were, Eakins-like, quickly blocked into areas of light and dark. Pastel or oil preparatory drawings for these late portraits were common, whereas previously Anshutz had employed preparatory sketches for only a handful of pictures, such as *The Ironworkers' Noontime.*[74]

A number of Anshutz's late portraits, for instance *Portrait of Emily Fairchild Pollock,* painted around 1905, manifest his assimilation of Eakins' portrait style (plate 26).[75] Displaying Anshutz's consummate skills in this genre, this three-quarter-length image depicts the artist's maternal aunt, wearing a black and pink floral dress, and seated before the austere, richly-modeled maroon backdrop that unifies the composition. The freely brushed, decorative gown sets off the sitter's magnetic face, which, appearing intelligent and strong-willed, commands our attention. The forthright portrayal is comparable to the best of Eakins' psychological portraits. Typically, the unprettified face is highlighted and is the painting's most sculptural element. The curve of her head is answered in the illuminated joined hands at the bottom of the picture, which creates a second focal point.

This portrait of the artist's aunt is similar to approximately ten other Anshutz paintings. In all of these, seated figures illuminated by a raking light gaze directly at the viewer. Most of the subjects wear somber expressions, and all are shown in a contextless space. This generic studio setting and the lack of genre-like activity on the part of the subject differentiate these works from many of Eakins' portraits, which often included objects meant to elucidate the subject's interests and personality. But the realism, lighting, and sculptural quality of many of Anshutz's portraits illustrate his debt to Eakins. Also, like Eakins, Anshutz strove to present the sitter's personality. One interviewer wrote:

> Mr. Anshutz declares that he inclines towards portrait work, because he finds humanity so interesting, and one line of work is enough to occupy anyone, although he likes to paint landscapes. "Life is too short for more than one issue," he says. "But when one succeeds, as Sargent so often does in seeing and producing on canvas even more of the mental calibre of the subject than the friend or acquaintance may have seen, and yet convincing that person that you have rightly judged the friend, how interesting it is! That is no mere reproduction of form and coloring.[76]

Another critic remarked, in 1910, that Anshutz favored portraiture over all other genres because it allowed him to explore the temperament and intellect of the sitter.[77] As Anshutz told his class in portraiture,

> [Of] the millions of [human] beings, no two . . . are alike. [They] are even more different internally than externally, and . . . the duty of the artist is to record these temperamental shades of difference.[78]

Anshutz wrote that good portraits should include "a mental temperament manifest in the features."[79] Many of his best portraits, including *Portrait of Emily Fairchild Pollock* and *Self-Portrait,* illustrate this attempt to examine the subject's mind. Anshutz painted the romantic *Self-Portrait* as an entrance piece for the National Academy of Design (frontispiece, fig. 36).[80]

One of Anshutz's most masterful portraits is his *Portrait of Margaret Perot* (plate 27).[81] Executed around 1908, in a painterly style similar to that of his aunt, this full-length image of twelve-year-old Margaret Morris Perot is remarkable for its sensitive depiction of the transitional state between youth and adulthood. The white-clothed figure,

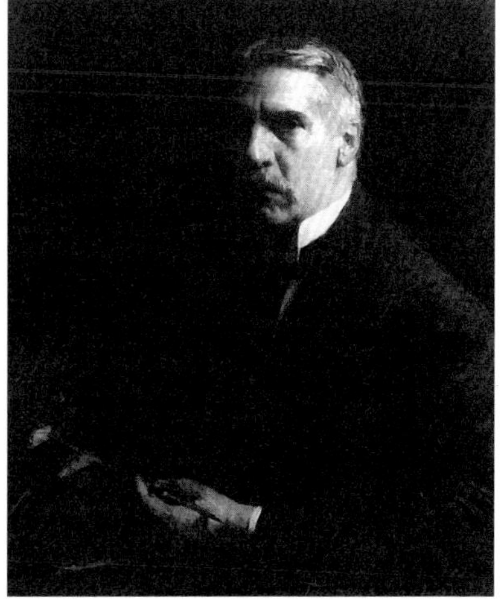

Figure 36.
Self-Portrait, ca. 1909
oil on canvas, 30 × 25"
National Academy of Design, New York

with its blue hairbow and sash, is set strikingly against the dark red and brown background. The figure's introspective profile establishes the face as the painting's focal point. That Anshutz pictured the figure in profile before a nearly featureless dark background, and modeled her form with strong *chiaroscuro* suggests that this work was inspired by such Eakins portraits as *The Pathetic Song* (fig. 37). Yet for all their similarities, Anshutz's portrait seems more to record a lasting stillness than Eakins' capture of a fleeting moment, and it discards Eakins' intensive observation. Anshutz's bravura treatment of the girl's clothing is more reminiscent of the contemporary painting style of Robert Henri, an artist whose imagery Anshutz especially admired at the time. However, even at their most painterly, Anshutz's oil portraits are never as freely or sensuously painted as works by artists such as Henri or Sargent.[82]

Along with this group of oil portraits, Anshutz also executed, after 1900, many pastel renderings of figures.[83] He was one of the finest pastelists of the period. For example, one which was probably exhibited as *A 'Cello Player* at the Art Institute of Chicago in 1902, is his portrait of Edwin S. Clymer, a Pennsylvania Academy of the Fine Arts student (fig. 38).[84] The brooding portrait, in which the subject stares intently out of darkness, offers another example of Anshutz's interest in conveying the sitter's state of mind. It may have been the dark, atmospheric oil paintings of John White Alexander that provided the most immediate inspiration for Anshutz's hazy, penumbral portraits. The well-known Alexander, whose work was often included in Pennsylvania Academy of the Fine Arts annual exhibitions at this time, had painted images like *A Ray of Sunlight (The Cellist)* (1898, location unknown), which shows a female cello player in a smoky half-light.[85] However, Anshutz's sitters never appear as stylized as Alexander's. Subsequently, from 1902 to 1910, Anshutz produced approximately ten portraits and symbolically-titled pastels of women. Many of the works he exhibited the last three years of his life, including *The Iris, A Passing Glance* (locations unknown), and *A Bird* (known today as *The Parrot,* Hirschl & Adler Galleries, New York), were pastels.

In contrast to the dark and monochromatic Clymer portrait, Anshutz, beginning around 1908, produced in both pastel and oil, more brightly-colored and detailed works in that genre, for example *A Rose,* which was probably painted in 1908 (plate 28). Rebecca Whelan, daughter of the President of the Pennsylvania Academy of the Fine Arts and one of Anshutz's students, served as the model for many of his late figure pieces, including that picture.[86] Certainly indicative of the artist's growing confidence and ambition, *A Rose* provides further evidence of Anshutz's abilities as a colorist. The brilliant reds of the model's dress, which are repeated in the rug, cut roses, flesh tones, and even the artist's signature, contrast emphatically with the dark background. Unlike those in some of Anshutz's later paintings, the dress and figure are not overtly stylized, and the sitter's strongly modeled face, with its introspective

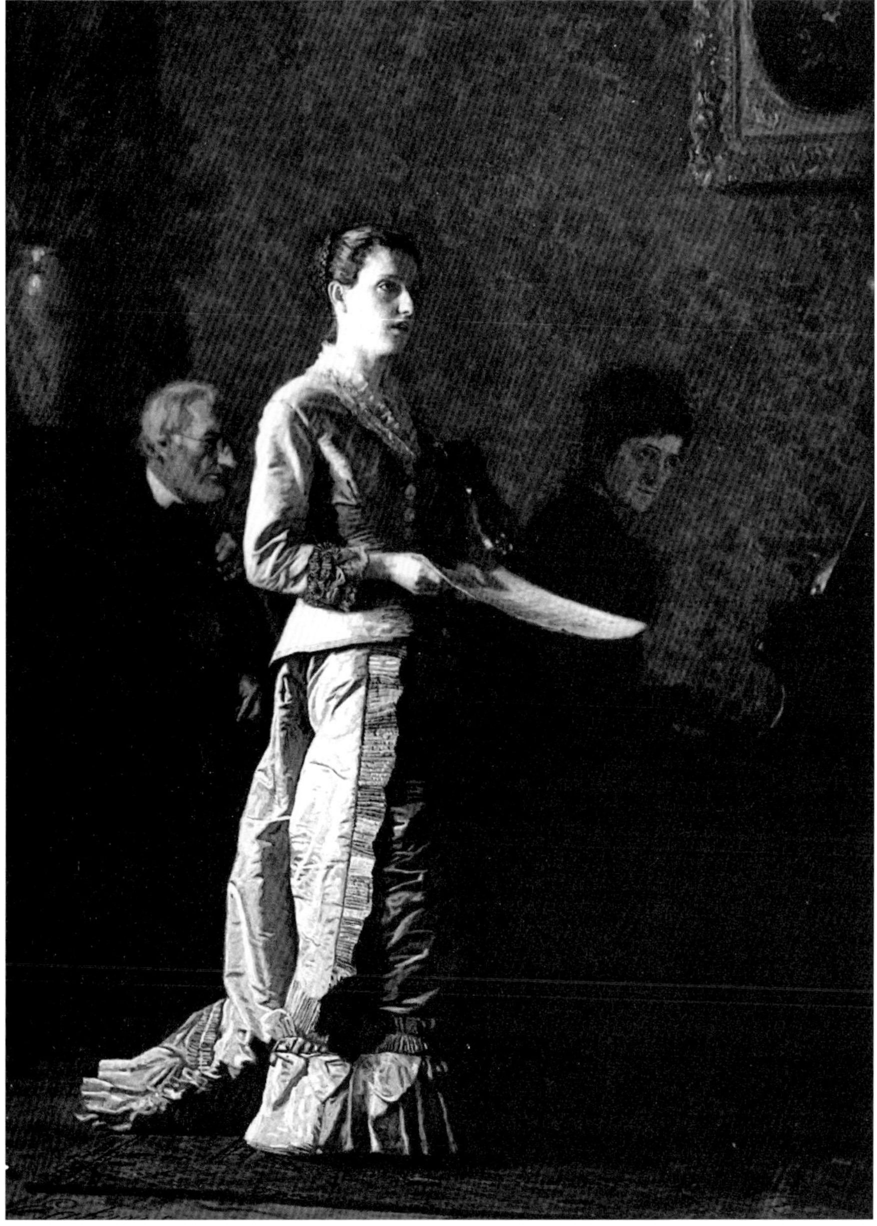

Figure 37.
Thomas Eakins
The Pathetic Song, 1881
oil on canvas, 45 × 32½"
In the Collection of The Corcoran Gallery of Art, Washington, DC, Museum Purchase, Gallery Fund

countenance, still retains its place as compositional focal point. When it was exhibited at the Pennsylvania Academy of the Fine Arts in 1908 critics compared this painting favorably to John Singer Sargent's *The Lady with the Rose* (1882, The Metropolitan Museum of Art). One reviewer wrote, "Surely there isn't a portrait in the exhibition, save only the 1882 Sargent which touches Mr. Anshutz's Miss Whelan."[87]

By emphasizing the attractiveness of Rebecca Whelan's figure in this manner, Anshutz may have betrayed his own emotional attachment to a woman with whom he spent a great deal of time between 1905 and

Figure 38.
Portrait of Edwin S. Clymer, ca. 1900
pastel on paper, 48 × 39"
Courtesy of the Reading Public Museum, Reading, Pennsylvania

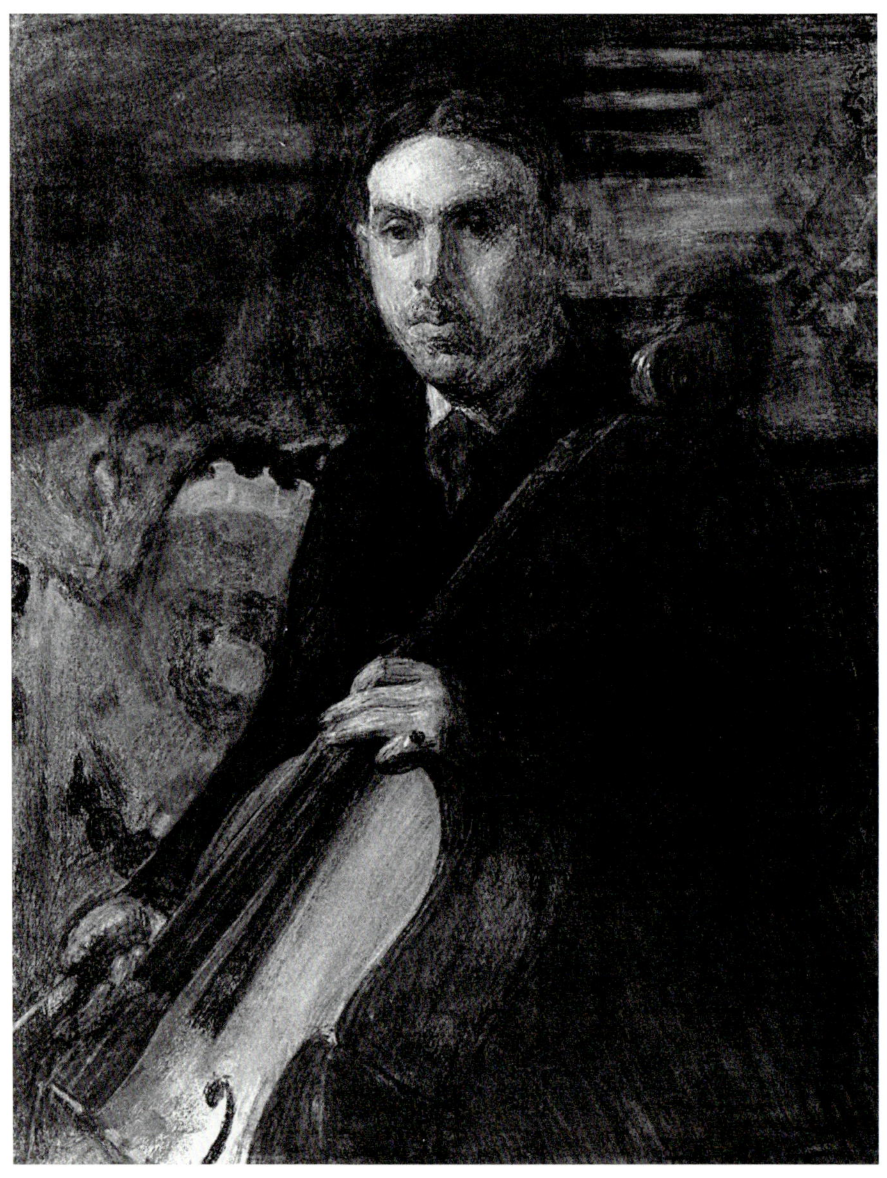

1910. His vibrant pastel study for *A Rose*, entitled *A Challange*, is much more overtly sensuous (plate 29). A year later, when he exhibited his scarlet-dominated pastel of Miss Whelan, entitled *A Bird,* one reviewer's mention of her "daring scarlet" dress and "coquettish" hat indicate that he found the depiction flirtatious. His surprise over the "audacity" of Anshutz's palette illustrates how relatively bold the artist's color choices had become.[88]

A Rose, late pastels such as *A Bird* and *A Challenge*, and the still more brightly colored contemporary landscapes suggest he was embarking on a new coloristic phase in his art. Yet, these stronger colors do not characterize the majority of his late oil paintings of women. Images such as *Figure Piece,* which was painted around 1909, are dominated by dull greens, blues, or reds (plate 30). The languorous and self-absorbed woman in this work, shown reposing in an armchair and wearing a long flowing, wave-like green dress, could almost be mistaken for a figure in a work by John White Alexander.[89] With the face in shadow, it is the sumptuous dress that dominates the picture. Even so, despite her elegance and reverie, Anshutz's figure lacks the ethereal quality of Alexander's or Dewing's figures. Anshutz's subject remains corporeal. Almost constant in his work was a concern for representing weight and mass.

The Tanagra, for which he received in 1909 the Pennsylvania Academy of the Fine Arts's highest award, the Gold Medal of Honor, offers a similar combination of decorative stylization and materiality (fig. 39). An example of Anshutz's continuing interest in antique art, evident earlier in *The Ironworkers' Noontime* and in his cast drawings, *The Tanagra*—with its dark background and the model's classically-inspired pose—is reminiscent of Sargent's famous *Madame X* (1884, The Metropolitan Museum of Art). The pose of the model, again Rebecca Whelan, mirroring the stance of the small Greek figure she studies, embodies a widespread American interest in antiquity. As well, it speaks of an intersection between notions of contemporary and past femininity.

The artist's figure pieces and portraiture brought him his first widespread recognition as a painter.[90] Some of Anshutz's awards included a silver medal at the Saint Louis World's Fair in 1904 for his portrait of John E.D. Trask, Pennsylvania Academy of the Fine Arts Secretary and Manager, and a gold medal at the Buenos Aires International Exposition in 1910. As his artistic reputation grew, so did his stature in art organizations. In 1909 he became head instructor of the Pennsylvania Academy of the Fine Arts and, a year later, President of the Philadelphia Sketch Club. Also in 1910, he was made an associate member of the National Academy of Design.[91]

However, by the time Anshutz finally began to receive national and international recognition, he was also becoming increasingly ill. His 1911 trip to Europe had made him feel healthier, and, upon his return to Philadelphia, he attempted to teach a life class in the fall of 1911 at the Pennsylvania Academy.[92] By the end of October his condition had worsened to the point that he was ordered by his doctor to stop teaching and rest at home. In November, the painter was confined to Philadelphia's Hahnemann Hospital, his stay there lasting until several days before Christmas, when he returned home. There, in Fort Washington, he remained until his death from heart disease and bronchial problems on June 16, 1912.[93]

Figure 39.
The Tanagra, ca. 1908
oil on canvas, 80 × 40"
The Pennsylvania Academy of the Fine Arts, Philadelphia. Gift of Friends and Admirers of the Artist

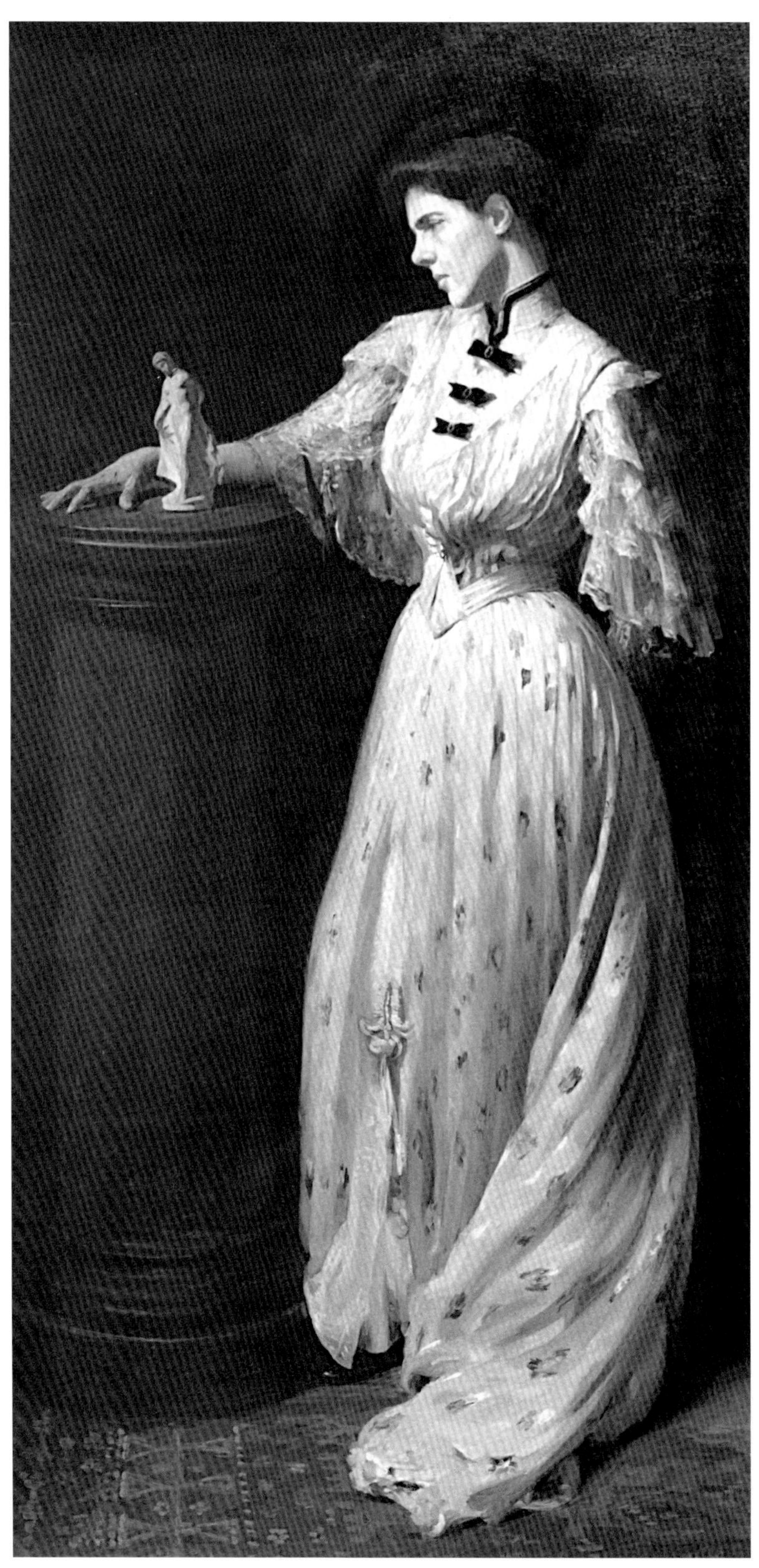

CHAPTER 3

Anshutz as Instructor

For nearly three decades Anshutz taught courses at the Pennsylvania Academy of the Fine Arts. These were varied, including cast and life drawing, costume sketching, and still-life painting. Significantly, his teaching formed a nexus between Eakins and "The Eight" and indirectly encouraged the beginnings of early American modernism in Philadelphia. Among his now-noted pupils (including some who were not to become modernists) were Robert Henri, John Sloan, William Glackens, Maxfield Parrish, Edward Redfield, Charles Demuth, Hugh Breckenridge, Arthur B. Carles, Lyman Saÿen, and John Marin, to whom Anshutz promoted artistic experimentation and openness to newer styles. His performance as a teacher led Henri to characterize him as "our nation's greatest art instructor."[1] Toward the end of Anshutz's life, art critics consistently wrote that, although they felt he was not a painter of the caliber of Homer or Chase, he had, nonetheless, been a master instructor and wielded great influence on a whole generation of Pennsylvania Academy of the Fine Arts students. An obituary in the *Philadelphia Inquirer* read:

> It would be difficult to point out an individual who has done more for art, especially American art. It is said that over one third of living American artists who have achieved fame were his pupils and every one of them speaks of him in the very highest terms. It is likely that if Anshutz had devoted himself exclusively to his own easel he might have achieved a higher fame and much fortune, but he loved to teach; nothing was more pleasing to him than to help develop young talent, to guide it aright.[2]

Anshutz's early years (1876-81) at the Pennsylvania Academy conditioned his approach to teaching. During that time, as discussed in chapter one, Anshutz became extremely knowledgeable about human and animal anatomy. Although he later, in and after the 1890s, considered dissection unnecessary and even somewhat detrimental for art students, he continued to stress that they learn about the body's dominant muscle and bone structures.[3] Anshutz taught this not, however, by dissection, but

Figure 2.
John Sloan (1871-1951)
Anshutz on Anatomy, 1912
etching, 8th state, 12¾ × 14½" (sheet)
The Pennsylvania Academy of the Fine Arts, Philadelphia. Gift of Helen Farr Sloan

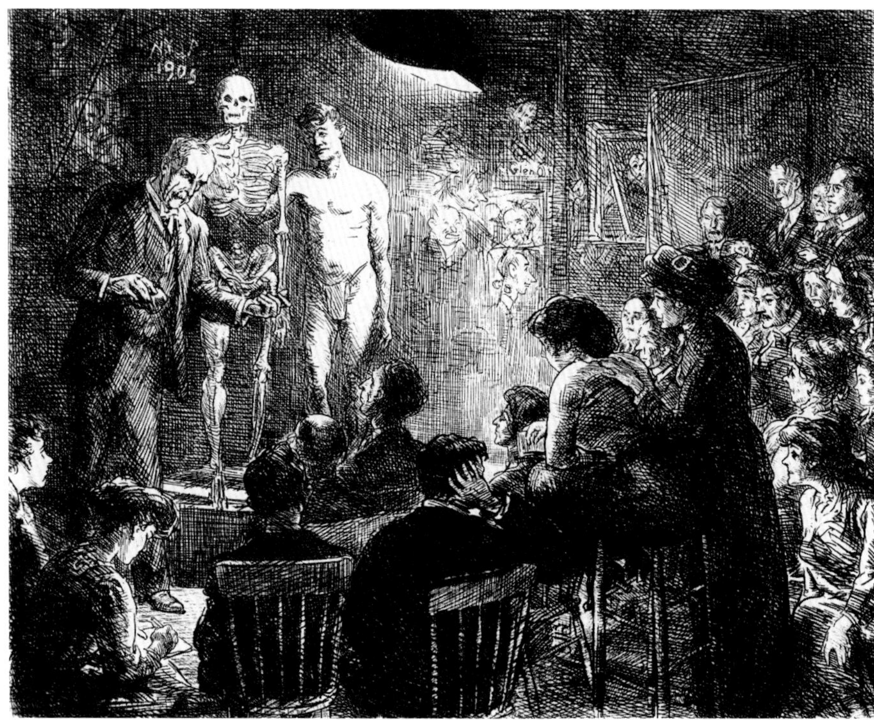

by applying clay to skeletons, as shown in John Sloan's etching *Anshutz on Anatomy* (fig. 2).[4] Anshutz's continuing emphasis on anatomy was intended to reveal the body's "grand construction."[5] Another technique that he considered essential for instilling this kind of perception, and which he employed throughout his career, required students to model the human figure in wax.[6] Anshutz learned this technique from Eakins, who had himself borrowed it from his teacher, Gérôme.[7] Capturing in paint the solid sculptural mass of the figure was a central tenet in both Eakins' and Anshutz's teaching.[8] As Eakins asked his students to "think in the third dimension," Anshutz similarly told his students that they would someday "learn in the third dimension" and would be able to "plant a model on his feet, because unconsciously... [the student would feel] the man's weight and where it is born[e]."[9]

In Eakins' life class, students were encouraged to employ the brush, rather than pencil or charcoal, and were told to work quickly and to emphasize prominent forms. Anshutz, in his drawing and painting classes, similarly encouraged students to block in figures quickly. He also followed Eakins' lead in insisting that his students employ broad, general areas of light and dark when drawing or painting. Thus, both men discouraged their students, in rendering the human form, from placing too much emphasis on outline or contour.[10]

Anshutz, again like Eakins, believed that at first artists could benefit from what he called "mechanical" or "scientific methods," such as the study of anatomy and perspective.[11] Yet, as discussed in chapter one, even during the years 1879-84 in which Anshutz most admired Eakins, he never fully embraced the older man's belief in wedding art to scientific methodologies. Anshutz always placed as much emphasis on imagination as on empirical observation. He believed that students could not be taught to recognize what he called "higher truth," by which he meant a selective and "poetic" perception of nature, "improved" through the artist's deletion of certain visual details. Nevertheless, Anshutz did attempt to encourage his students to discover this process of aesthetically editing nature.[12]

For example, Anshutz, unlike Eakins, assigned memory exercises to his students. Henri reported that Anshutz had told him:

> Draw what you see, finish by memory. When at leisure notice a man—his position[,] draw him he will move but you go on and finish from memory. Try to draw what you saw. This will be hard but keep it up for a while—two years or more, you will gain great results from it.[13]

Judging from Henri's comments, Anshutz apparently intended this sort of exercise to sharpen student powers of observation to the point where they could record unposed scenes of everyday life. He may have thought, as well, that such assignments would compel students to develop their "impressions" of nature, something William Morris Hunt had discussed earlier in his well-known book *Talks on Art:*

> It's the impression of the thing that you want to get. You want to make people receive the same impression that you have received from nature. Then you can make things beautiful and exact so long as they don't interfere with the impression. Do things from memory, because in that way you remember only the picture.[14]

Hunt, and perhaps Anshutz, found memory exercises a useful tool for teaching artists to communicate their personal impressions without drawing too literally upon their immediate perceptions of nature.

In 1887, according to Henri, Anshutz also required students constantly, outside of class, to sketch from observation as a method of improving visual acuity.[15] He encouraged this throughout his career as a teacher.

Both Eakins and Anshutz were intolerant of what they saw as affectation, technical tricks like *trompe l'oeil* polish or ostentatious brushwork; and both perceived painting as a disciplined craft, not something intended to sway a viewer through stylistic virtuosity. Both equated a "realist" artistic style with sincerity and individuality, i.e., an artist's record of his or her personal experience of nature.

As instructors, both men attempted to inculcate artistic individuality and independence by allowing their students to work through problems without much guidance. As Eakins wrote, "A good teacher can do very little for a pupil and should only be thankful if he don't [sic] hinder him, and the greater master, mostly the less he can say."[16] Anshutz similarly told his students to "look for [them]selves."[17] He wanted to encourage pupils to do their own thinking and also believed that a class would "always learn more from its own [older] members than from its teacher."[18]

However much Anshutz and Eakins believed they were fostering student self-knowledge and "individuality," both men demanded that their students conform to certain tradition-bound stylistic and methodological expectations of what constituted art. Both considered teaching basic tools, such as anatomy and perspective, to be an art school's preeminent function.[19] In 1884, Anshutz wrote, "The greatest and most lasting good comes from making clear to [the students] the great principles of technical art so that they may stand on their own feet."[20] At that time, as a young teacher, Anshutz was apparently able to reconcile in his teaching the seemingly opposite goals of conformity and independence. Beginning in 1884, Anshutz's letters—reflecting his interest in newer art—frequently included complaints and snide remarks about the Academy's Eakins-influenced conservatism. For instance, in 1884, writing about a Pennsylvania Academy life class, he noted:

> We have seen many life studies, and painted some (I speak of myself) which were moderately good pictures of the model, of his character, color, roundness, solidity...but which were made almost without one grain of true art. Except conscientiousness. They were the result of following the eye mechanically. Where true art, appreciating the character and quality of the model and the light in which he stood, would endeavor to create them in a picture using the natural sense of sight as an instrument.[21]

By 1884, Anshutz and other junior faculty members felt increasing resentment toward Eakins, whose autocratic and dogmatic style of running classes left little room for more current approaches to art, such as teaching classes in landscape painting.[22] Many younger members of the faculty, including Anshutz, belonged to the Philadelphia Sketch Club, an organization that encouraged artistic exploration.[23] For Anshutz and other junior faculty, Eakins' old-fashioned, Gérôme-inspired conception of art, with its overriding emphasis on the human figure, seemed hidebound.

In 1886, the faculty became increasingly intolerant of Eakins' teaching methods. They were especially incensed over his use of student models. As such scholars as Kathleen Foster and William Innes Homer have noted, Eakins employed students of both sexes to pose nude in front of classes, as well as for his own private painting sessions. Both of these practices were considered unacceptable, and were formally prohibited by the Pennsylvania Academy's Board of Directors.[24] In addition to employing nude student models, Eakins had also exposed his own genitals to at least one student while illustrating the "movement of the pelvis," again indicating his lack of concern for common propriety.[25]

In response to criticism that the junior faculty had spread vicious and unfounded rumors, a group of instructors, including Anshutz, wrote this letter to the Board:

> In the absence of any official statement as to the cause of Mr. Eakins' resignation from the Academy rumors have spread...resulting in the general belief that he has suffered without cause. This is unjust to those who have brought Mr. Eakins' offenses to the notice of your Board and still more to those who come under his influences now, or may hereafter, believing that he is, as he claims, the innocent victim of a conspiracy. We who are acquainted with the case cannot defend ourselves except by detailing the facts and that being in every other sense undesirable we bring the matter to the attention of your Honorable body & appeal, most earnestly, for an official statement from your Board to the effect that Mr. Eakins' dismissal was due to the abuse of his authority and not of the malice of his personal or professional enemies.
>
> Respectfully,
>
> James P. Kelly
> Colin Campbell Cooper, Jr.
> Charles H. Stephens
> T. P. Anshutz
> Geo. Frank Stephens[26]

Forced to resign on February 8, 1886, Eakins felt betrayed by his younger colleagues, especially by Anshutz. Yet as Maria Chamberlin-Hellman and others have argued, a complex series of events led to Eakins' ouster from the Pennsylvania Academy of the Fine Arts. Tensions between Eakins and the Board of Directors dated back to 1876. The Board, composed principally of businessmen, was anxious to maintain a public image for the Academy free from any taint of controversy.[27] Members feared that Eakins' unconventional approach to teaching, with its emphasis on the nude, would offend some students and parents, causing women students to leave and discouraging future enrollment.[28] By 1886, over half of the Academy's students were women, and the Board wanted to keep enrollment figures high.[29] Although the well-known incident of Eakins' having removed a male model's loincloth in front of a women's class was only one in a series of disputes between Eakins and the Board, it provided Board members with a specific reason for asking Eakins to resign. His action had been a direct provocation, violating a stated ruling of the Board. As Secretary George Corliss wrote,

> Professor Eakins' resignation was the result of complaints from several students of the life class regarding his methods of instruction. They were unsatisfactory. The trouble is not a recent one. It has been brewing for some time, and the action of the Board of Directors in requesting the Professor's resignation was not decided upon without long and careful consideration.[30]

Yet it was not just a matter of the Board's contesting Eakins' belief that "art knows no sex." Board members had resented Eakins' recalcitrant and independent attitude for years and disliked his demands for higher pay at a time when the Pennsylvania Academy was not in the black financially.[31]

Immediately following the older artist's departure from the Academy, Anshutz expressed willingness to take over Eakins' classes temporarily, which he initially did.[32] That Anshutz had benefited from Eakins' resignation suggests he may indeed have conspired against his former instructor at least in part to gain a higher salary and more prestige. In May 1886 Thomas Hovenden was hired to replace Eakins and teach painting classes.[33]

After Eakins left the Pennsylvania Academy of the Fine Arts in 1886, Anshutz was freer to become a more conceptually oriented teacher. Although the younger man continued to stress the importance of depicting the human figure in its essential forms as Eakins had, he also emphasized to a greater extent an intuitive approach.

Anshutz's time at the Académie Julian in 1892-93 reinforced the views he shared with Eakins that instruction in artistic fundamentals and the nourishment of individuality were not mutually exclusive tasks, at least for the better students. Anshutz thought that the instructors at the Académie Julian accomplished this well, writing that their "hands-off" approach encouraged a healthy "plucky...struggle [in students]."[34] Noting that the Parisian school gave its students much more freedom than did the Pennsylvania Academy, Anshutz felt that "in a sense it is hardly a school at all, but a place for the hundreds of men following art to practice in."[35] However, he wrote that this lack of structure would be inappropriate in Philadelphia due to the poorer quality of students at the Pennsylvania Academy. As a group, he saw the Académie Julian's students as more advanced, more varied in their approaches, and more inclined to question authority.

After returning to his teaching position at the Pennsylvania Academy in the fall of 1893, Anshutz became increasingly concerned with how best to facilitate the development of student individuality and become more open to student experimentation in the classroom. In a note penned to a friend in 1893, Anshutz wrote that as a teacher he approved of almost anything that would facilitate student individuality and discourage pupils from "falling into a rut."[36]

Two articles written by John Cournos, published in 1910 and 1912 and based on an interview with the painter in 1910, provide the most detailed picture of his teaching practices and philosophy. According to Cournos, Anshutz considered his teaching a foundation for change, did not encourage students to copy an instructor's style or follow fashionable trends in art, and like Eakins believed that art awards and prizes perpetuated accepted artistic conventions and thus stifled invention:

> It is a temptation to the student to win a prize rather than to develop his mentality; also it creates a great distinction between the man who has and the man who has not the prize, while there may be little or no distinction in their work; aside from the fact that human judgment is as fallible in awarding art prizes as in other things.[37]

Probably Anshutz's greatest legacy was in conveying Eakins' teachings to the artists who later formed the core of the Ashcan School. One of those painters, John Sloan, wrote that he "got the Eakins' influence through Anshutz in a very good way."[38] Among "The Eight," Anshutz's influence was felt most strongly by Henri and Sloan, the two painters of the group who had been closest personally to Anshutz. When Sloan heard about Anshutz's death, he expressed his belief that Anshutz had played a part in shaping the artistic production of many artists of his generation:

> the teacher of all of us—Henri, Glackens, Shinn and all the rest—Schofield, Redfield. About thirty years of service, splendid manly service as instructor in the Pennsylvania Academy of Fine Arts. We have heard recently that his highest wages [were] twenty-five dollars a week. This is less than an organized bricklayer gets![39]

Sloan, Henri, and George Luks admired their former teacher both as an individual and as an ideal instructor.[40] Anshutz's modesty, erudition, open-mindedness, and general lack of interference with students' work received high praise from many former students.

Anshutz's own painting seems to have had little direct impact on members of the Ashcan School or on other artists. Critics and artists universally praised his teaching far more than his painting. Large numbers of his students never knew what his work looked like, and those who did, through his portraits at the Philadelphia Sketch Club or through images he exhibited in the Pennsylvania Academy annuals, seldom mentioned it in their letters.[41] This was equally the case with critics, who rarely reviewed his paintings until he first began to receive a measure of publicity around 1908.[42] There is no evidence to suggest that any members of "The Eight" were influenced by Anshutz's *The Ironworkers' Noontime.* They would, in fact, have had only a single opportunity to see the painting. It stayed in private collections during this entire period and, with the exception of early showings in 1881 and 1883, was exhibited publicly prior to World War II only at the Clarke sale in New York in 1899.[43] In 1912, none of Anshutz's many obituaries even mentioned *The Ironworkers' Noontime.*

Instead of emulating his painting, members of the Ashcan School absorbed Anshutz's general philosophy of art. The major ideas he emphasized in his classroom and in outside discussions, including his belief in the rejection of older artistic conventions, the repudiation of fashion-driven painting, the primacy of cultivating artistic individuality, and the importance of recording the everyday world, later became standard concerns of Henri, Sloan, Glackens, Luks, and Shinn. Anshutz's Eakins-inspired belief that artists should try to attain a level of observation as free as possible from accepted formulas and conventions was something many members of the Ashcan School would adopt. Anshutz had often asked his students to always carry a sketchbook in which to record scenes of everyday life, in an effort to sharpen visual acuity.[44] He believed such sketching, along with memory exercises, would lead students to develop perceptive and interpretive skills—their own artistic visions.

The sketching assignments may have led John Cournos to write of Anshutz, "His Americanism is another of his distinct characteristics. He is thoroughly imbued with the necessity of the student's entering the life of his own people and their needs."[45] Cournos' description of Anshutz evokes Eakins' own comment that "American art students and painters [should] study their own country and portray its life and types."[46] Both Eakins and Anshutz felt that it was unhealthy for art students to undertake lengthy periods of study abroad.[47] Anshutz stated:

> The right thing for the student is to work out his own salvation in his own country.... For a student to be artificially supported in a foreign country for two, or three, or even five years, is not long enough to make a successful development of his art, but is long enough to cause him to sink the roots of his art into foreign soil and their transplanting to his own soil is a check to his growth.[48]

John Sloan was the member of "The Eight" who grew closest to Anshutz, becoming quite fond of the older man over the years. Despite Sloan's early bitterness towards his former teacher over an incident in a cast-drawing class, by 1905 he and Anshutz were close friends, often spending evenings together discussing art at Anshutz's Fort Washington home.[49] In 1909, after Chase decided to retire, Sloan wrote,

> Hear that Chase has retired from the schools of the Penn. Academy of Fine Arts. Anshutz is now the head instructor—good! Now and then we read in the papers articles which give Chase the honor of

> being an instructor of Henri at the P.A.F.A. This is ridiculous as Henri left the school years before Chase started to teach there. The same error has been made in my case at times. Anshutz is the only teacher I had at the Academy of Fine Arts, Philadelphia.[50]

Sloan particularly respected Anshutz's knowledge of anatomy. The younger man's etching *Anshutz on Anatomy* was produced as a tribute to his former instructor, just after the latter's death in 1912 (fig. 2).[51] It depicts Anshutz presenting one of his six lectures on anatomy at the New York School of Art. Sloan wrote:

> He [Anshutz] used to demonstrate anatomy by building muscles on a skeleton with plasticine.... He had the same things as Eakins to say to his students about observation of life, the character of forms, striving for solidity and plain painting without bravura.[52]

The other member of "The Eight" who was strongly influenced by Anshutz was Henri. After Anshutz's death in 1912, Henri wrote, "He was a man of the very greatest value. A simple straight big man. The best influence to art students and artists I have known."[53] Henri, in fact partially modeled his famous approach to teaching after Anshutz's.[54] Nathaniel Pousette-Dart thought Henri's teaching style was quite similar to Anshutz's:

> I first met [Anshutz] in 1903 at the Pennsylvania Academy of Fine Arts. The first week I attended the life class...and had the following experience. Toward the end of the class I heard a man enter the back of the class room and when he started speaking I said to my self, "I didn't know that Henri was teaching here." It was Anshutz of course, but their voices were identical...[Anshutz's] methods of teaching were very similar to those of Henri...[55]

This last may have referred to a whole range of similarities. For instance, both Henri and Anshutz disliked *trompe l'oeil* effects and bravura brushwork. Henri, for instance, wrote that he did not "like the flash of Sargent portraits...."[56] He also felt antipathy toward showy displays by art instructors and emulated Anshutz's forthright, down-to-earth style of criticism. He considered Anshutz an ideal critic in class.[57] Henri later wrote that "the beauty of form & color [is] to be obtained from the largest masses only."[58] Again, this notion of emphasizing the most prominent masses had been a central component of both Eakins' and Anshutz's teaching. To assist students in achieving this effect, Henri, like Anshutz, assigned memory exercises. Henri himself noted:

> The special order has to be retained in memory—that special look, and that order which was its expression. Memory must hold it. All

> work done from the subject thereafter must be no more than data gathering.... All good work is done from memory whether the model is still present or not."[59]

Henri also, like Anshutz and Eakins, believed a teacher's major responsibility to be facilitating a student's idiosyncratic artistic development. They all felt that art instructors should try not to impose their own ideas. Henri wrote:

> It seems to me that before a man tries to express anything to the world he must recognize in himself an individual, a new one, very distinct from others. Walt Whitman did this, and that is why I think his name so often comes to me.[60]

Eakins had also admired Whitman; and Henri, Eakins, Anshutz, and Whitman all produced imagery recording or celebrating the American scene.

During the last decade of his life, Anshutz's own interests in modernism and his philosophy of teaching coincided and reinforced one another. After 1900, he became more than ever devoted to nourishing student individuality and experimentation. During these years he taught the future modernists Arthur B. Carles, John Marin, Charles Demuth, and Lyman Saÿen.[61] However, again, Anshutz's impact on these artists was probably oblique. He acted mostly as a catalyst encouraging their future experimentation. Of all the early Philadelphia modernists, Anshutz probably had the closest friendship with Lyman Saÿen. He and Anshutz had been close friends and had conducted color experiments together. Nevertheless, it was Saÿen's exposure to the museums and galleries of Paris and his experiences in Matisse's classes that proved much more important influences on the development of his modernist style.[62]

Over the late years of his teaching, Anshutz struggled to balance teaching standard art knowledge with preparing students for the continual onslaught of new styles of art. He told one critic that, given all the emerging trends in painting, it was hard to know what should be taught anymore and that there were "no hard and fast universal rules" remaining.[63] For Anshutz, and presumably many other American artists, this early twentieth-century collision between old and new, academic and modern, undermined much of what he himself had been taught. To speak of art without rules raised specters of an ever-changing artistic canon and the complete relativity of taste. This clash of ideologies forced him to question the basic function of art instruction. Anshutz stated, "The subject of art is so full of subtle distinctions and seeming contradictions that there is not a statement one may not controvert."[64] The critic John Cournos wrote that Anshutz was opposed to imposing any "one formula—any one truth" and that he believed students were more receptive than more mature artists to newer styles and ideas in art.[65] Many stu-

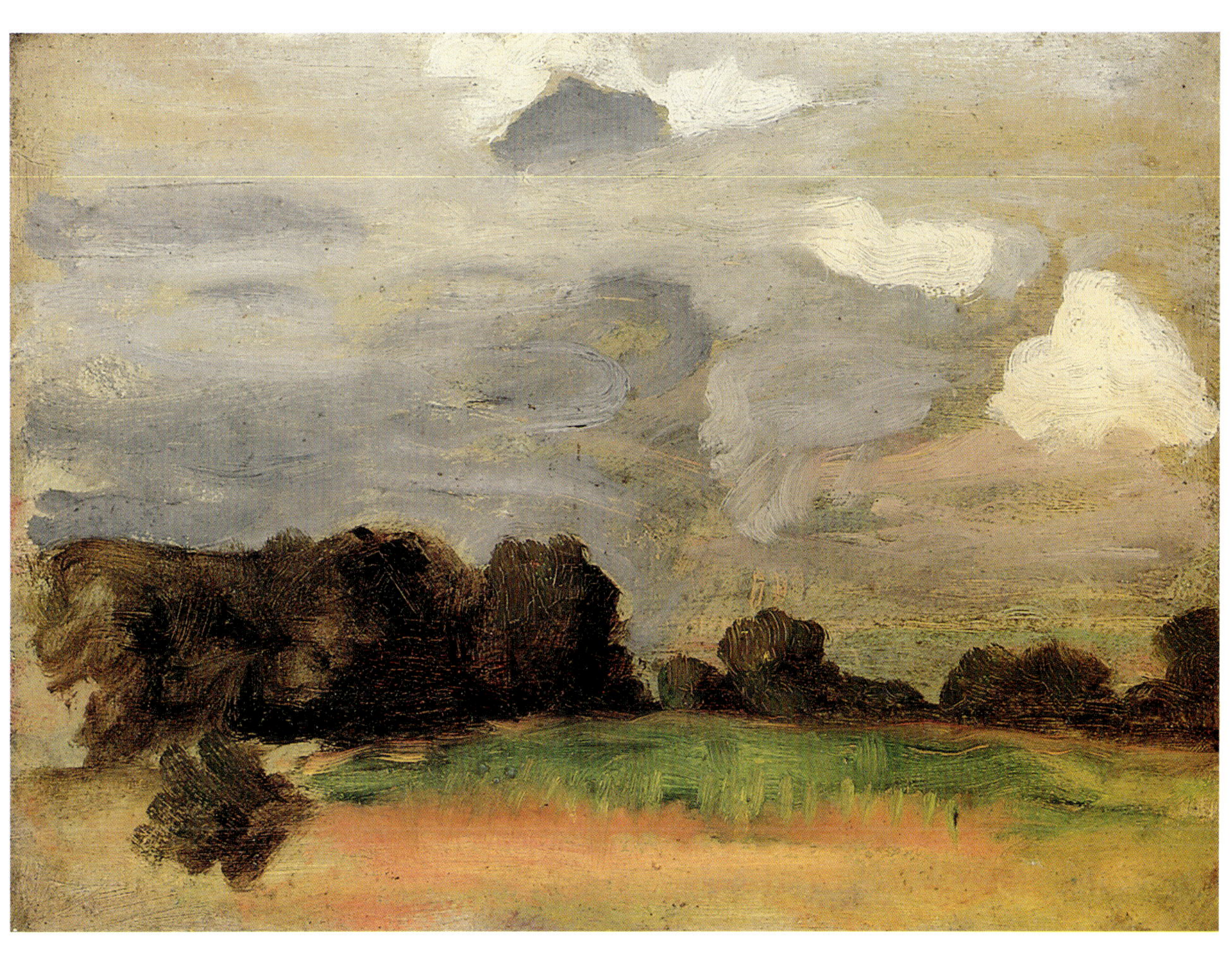

PLATE 17. *Landscape with Grey Sky*, ca. 1895
oil on board, 7½ × 10"
Collection of Mr. and Mrs. Samuel F. Mirabito

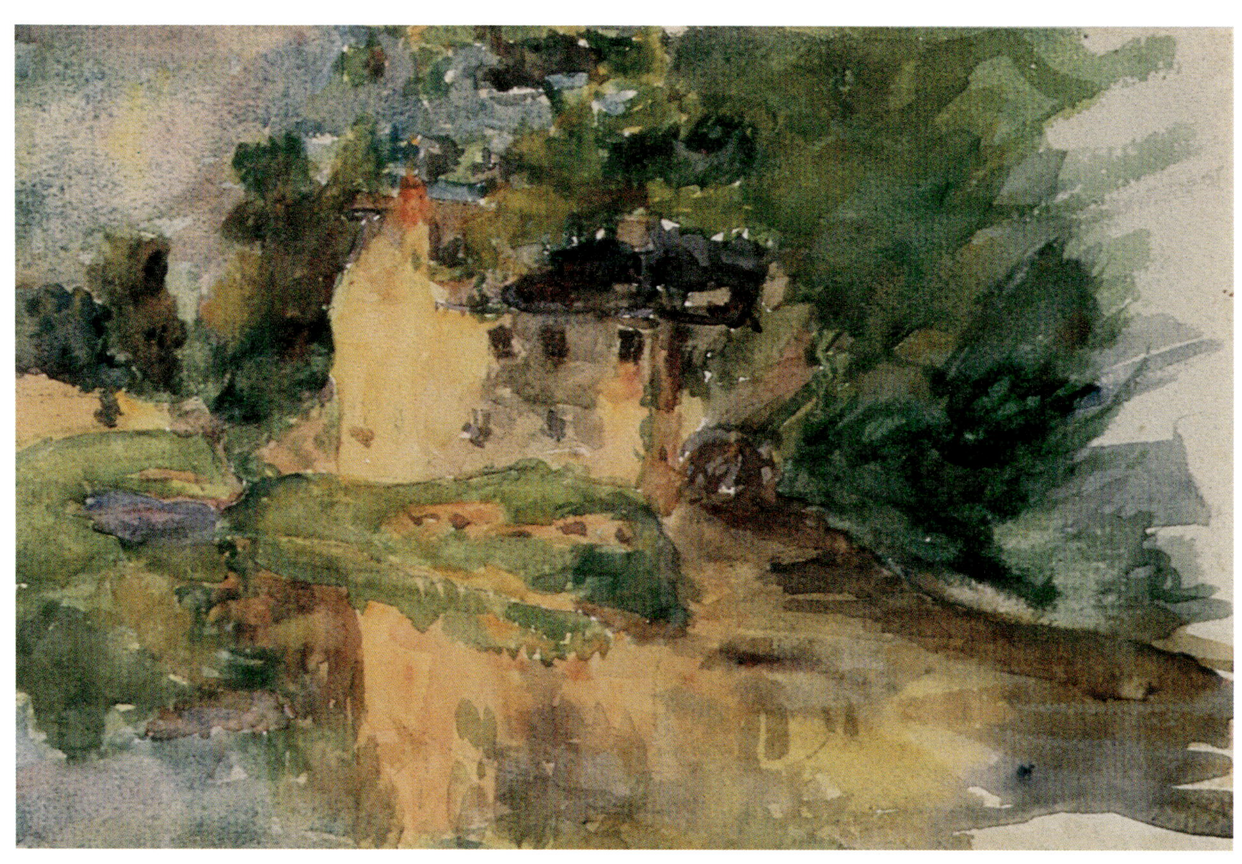

PLATE 18. *House by a Pond,* ca. 1900-05
watercolor, 7 × 10"
Location unknown

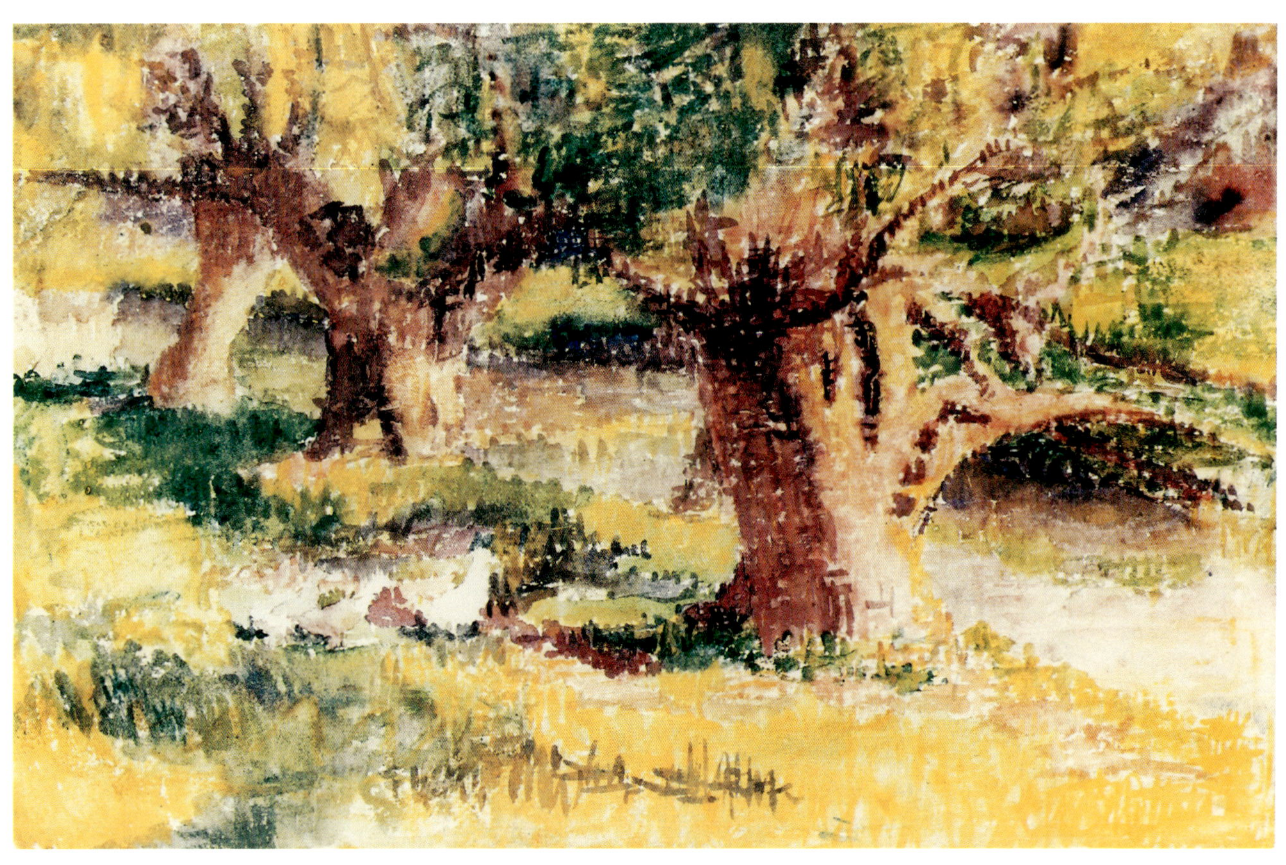

PLATE 19. *Three Trees by a Stream,* ca.1900-05
watercolor on paper, 13½ × 20¼"
The Hon. Joseph P. Carroll and Mrs. Carroll, New York

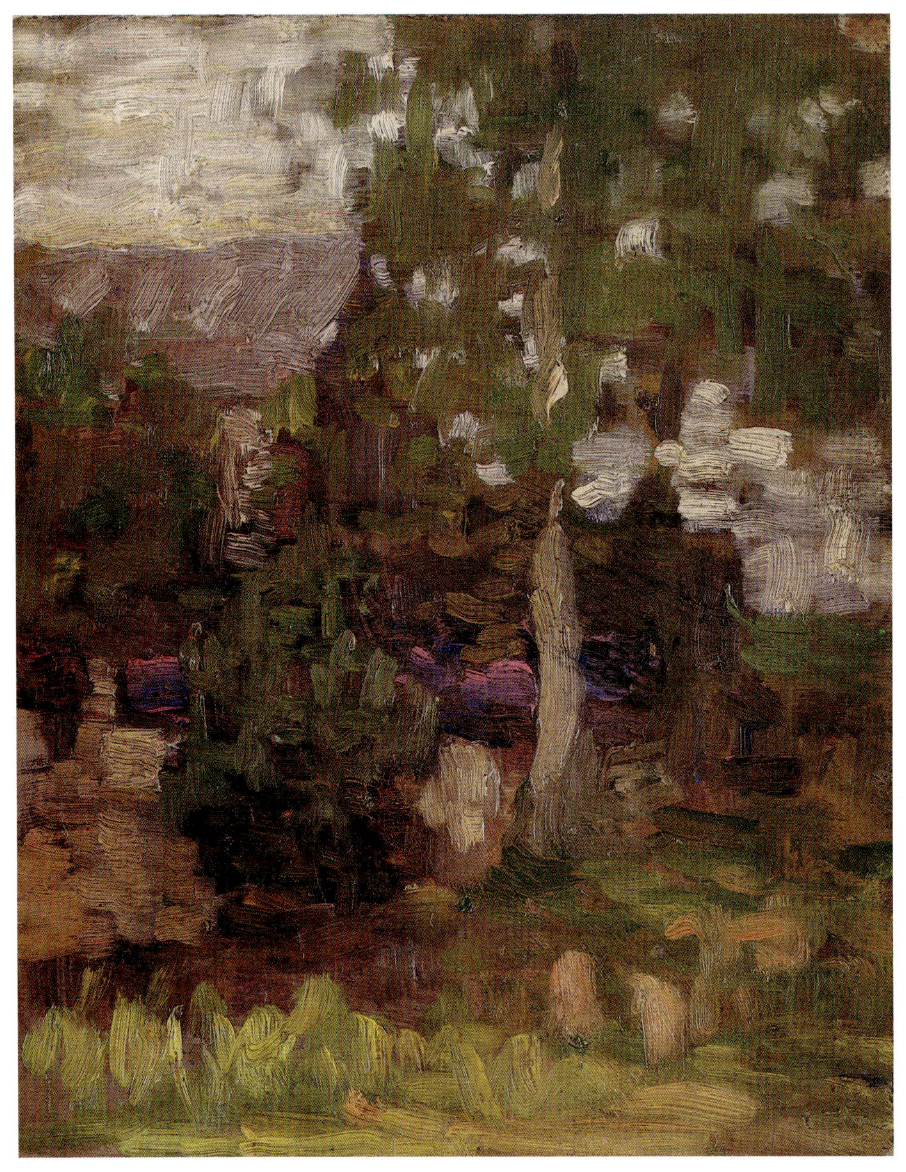

PLATE 20. *Garden,* ca. 1911
oil on board, 9½ × 7½"
The Hon. Joseph P. Carroll and Mrs. Carroll, New York

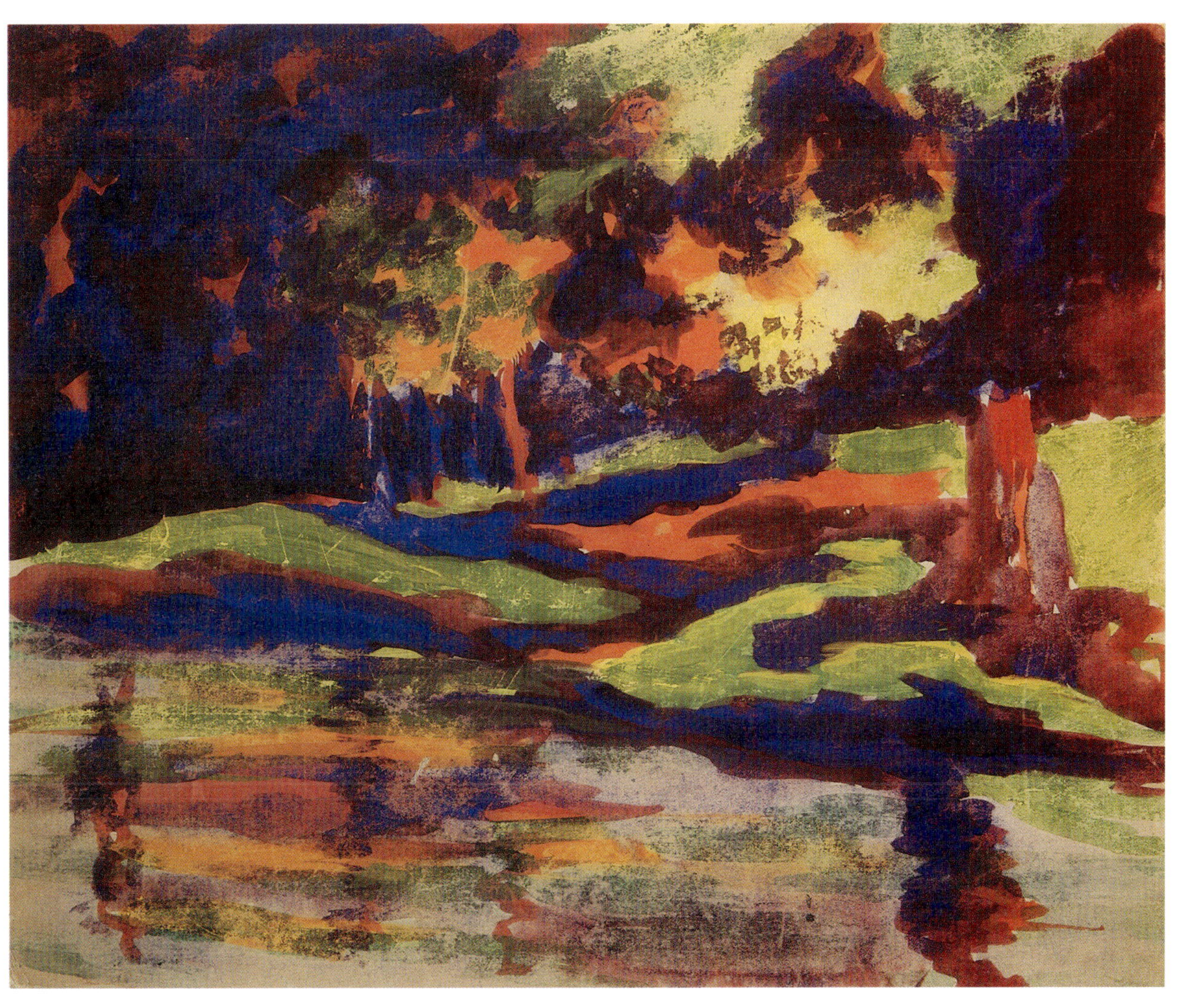

PLATE 21. *Landscape,* ca. 1911-12
watercolor on pulpboard, 10⅞ × 12"
The Pennsylvania Academy of the Fine Arts, Philadelphia.
Gift of Mrs. Edward R. Anshutz

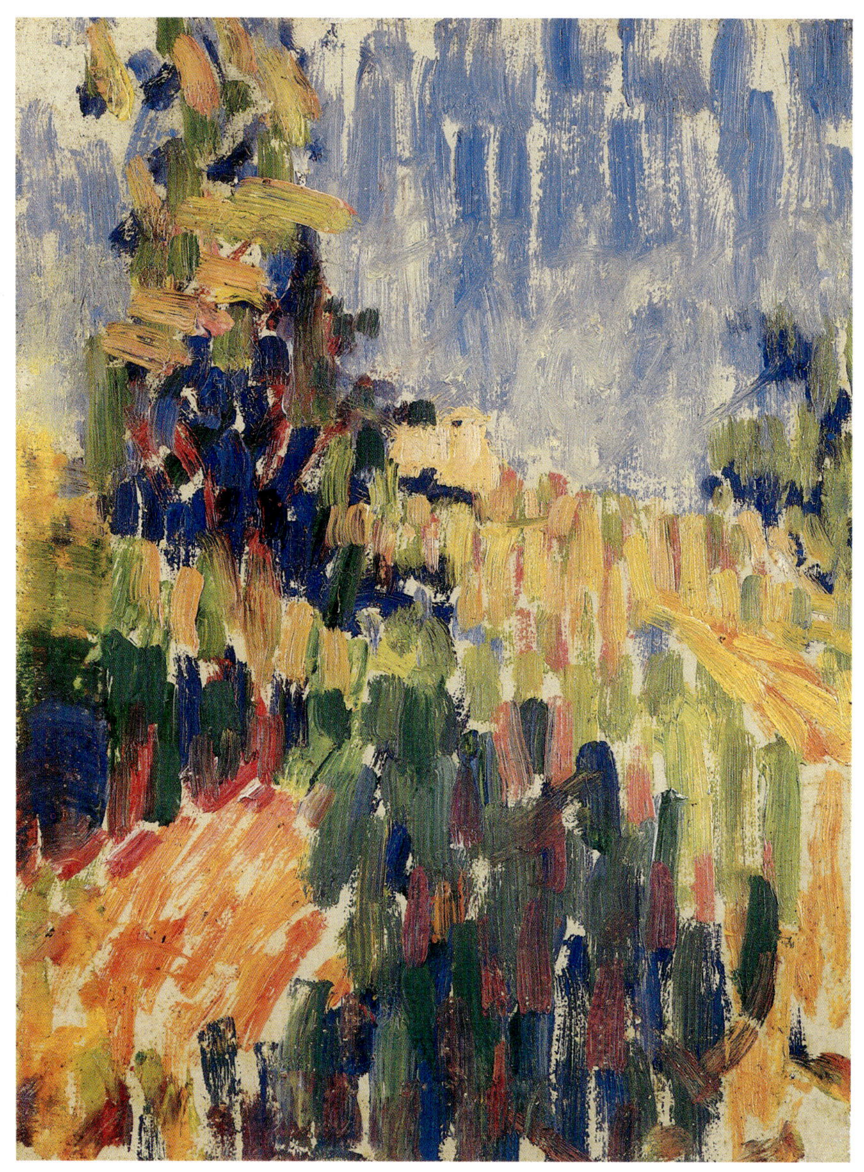

PLATE 22. *Landscape,* ca. 1911-12
oil on board, 8 × 5"
The Hon. Joseph P. Carroll and Mrs. Carroll, New York

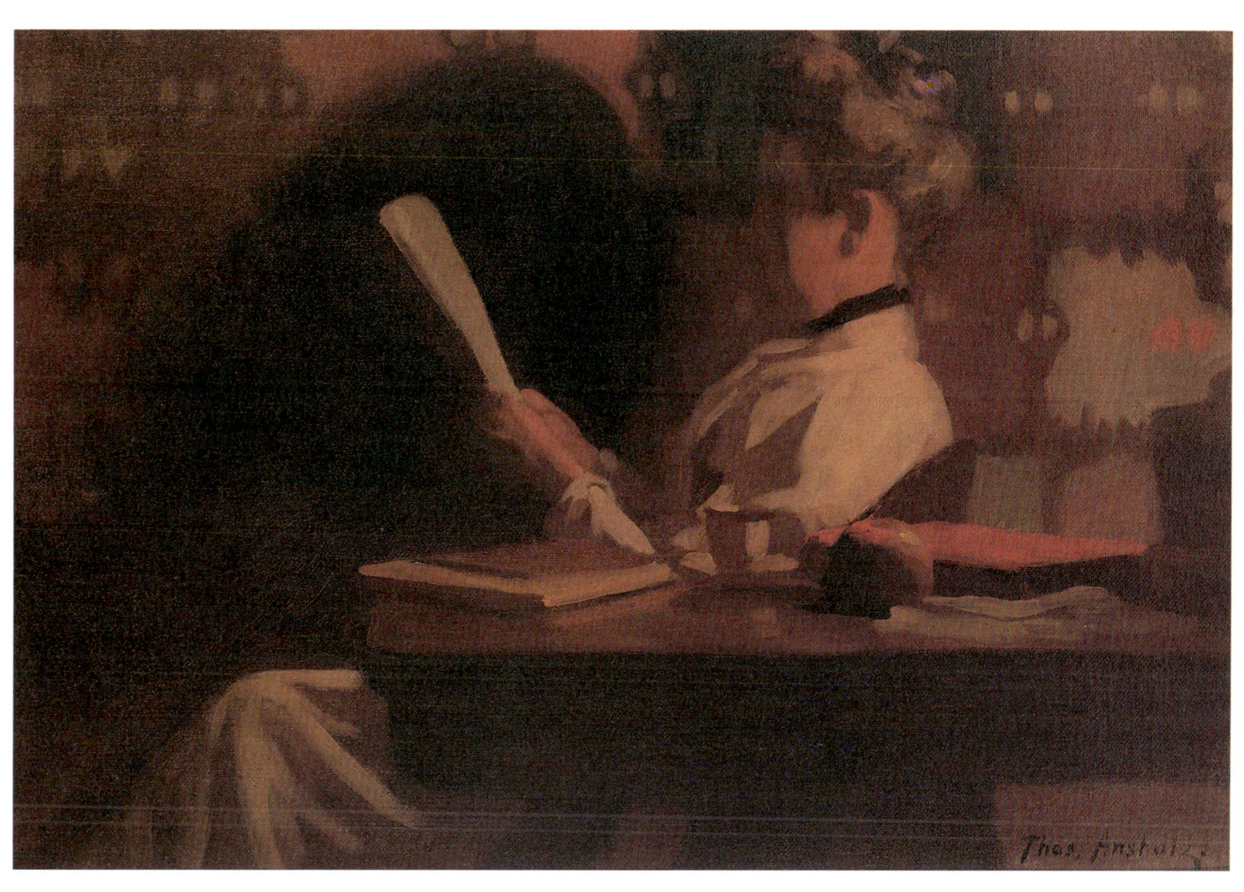

PLATE 23. *Woman in Interior Reading*, ca. 1910
oil on canvas, 16 × 23¼"
Location unknown

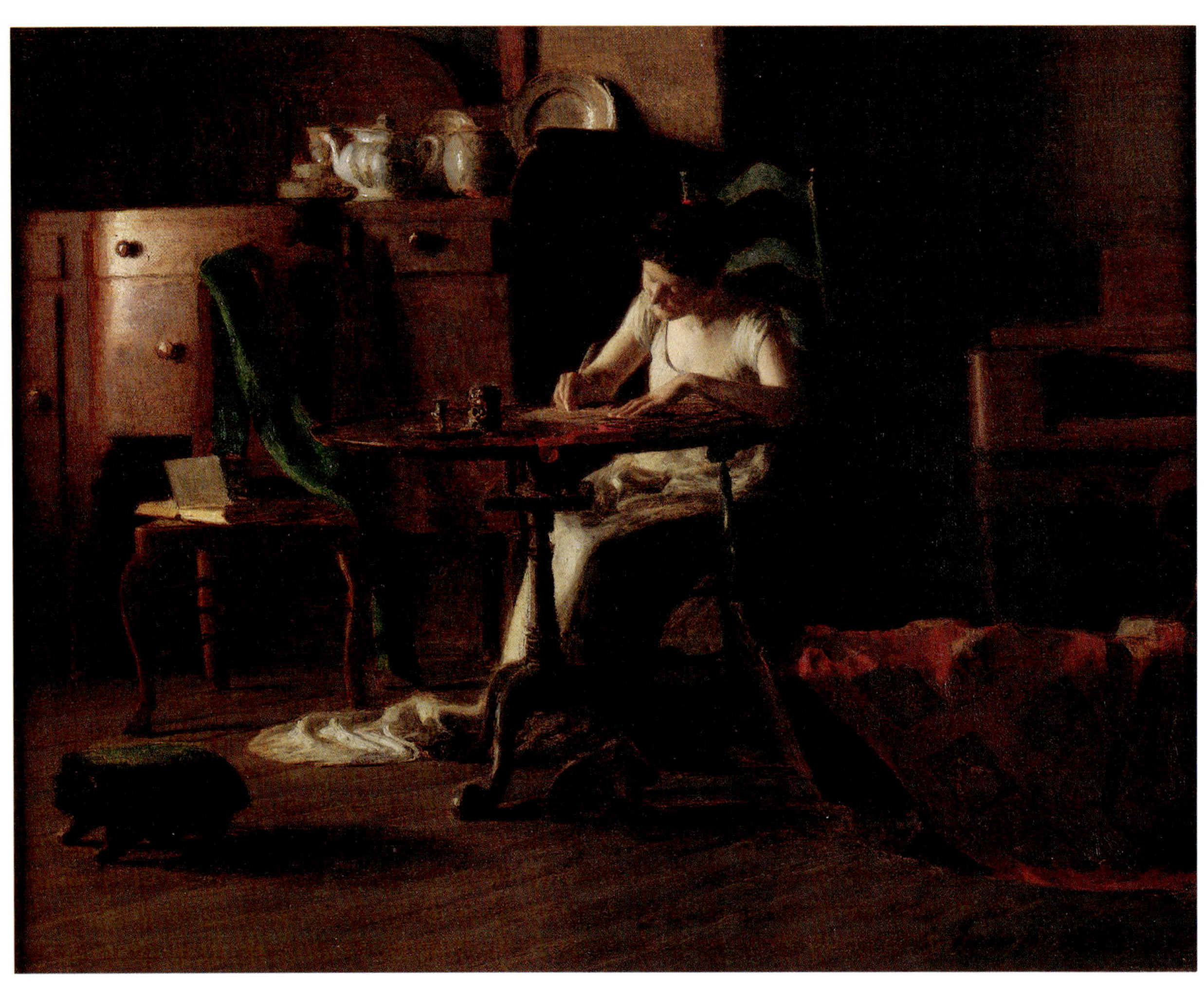

PLATE 24. *Woman Writing at a Table,* ca. 1905
oil on canvas, 16 × 20¼"
Byron Collection

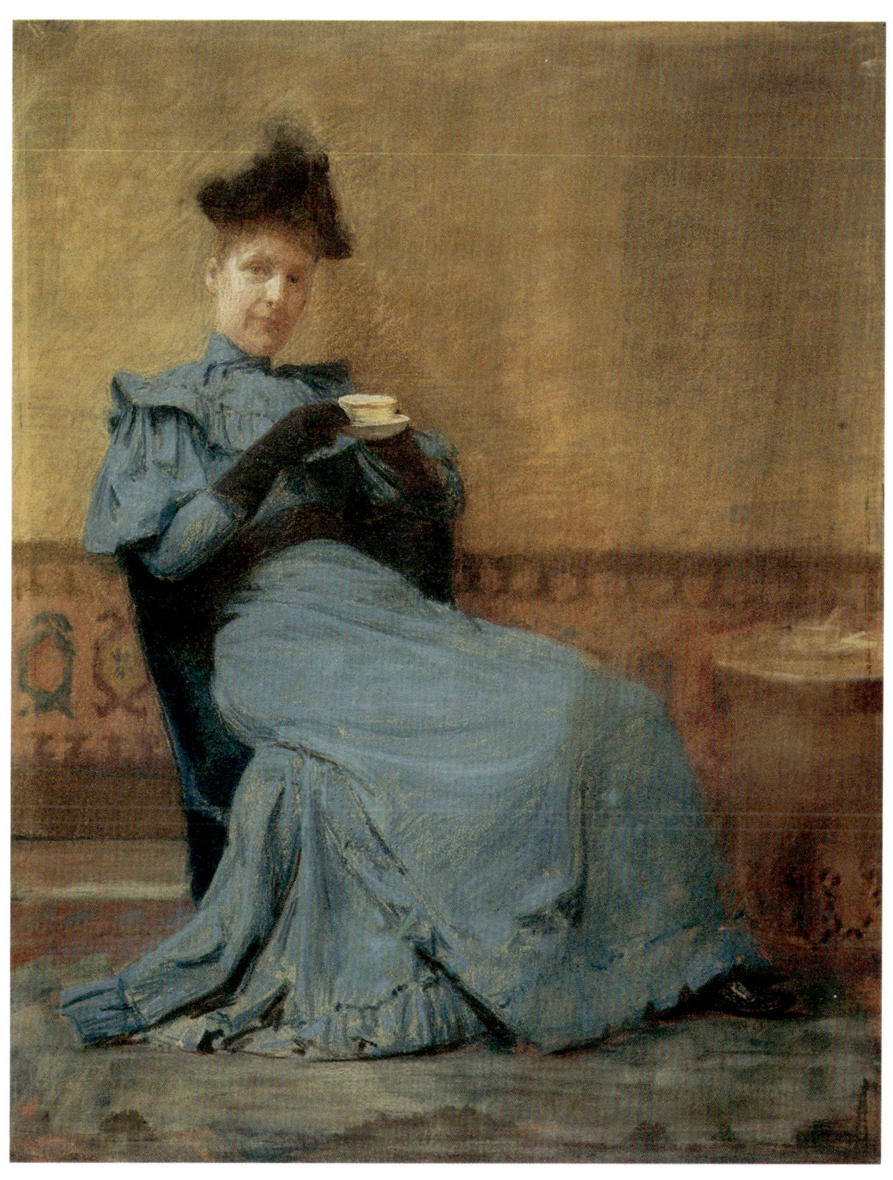

PLATE 25. *Portrait of Mrs. Anshutz,* 1893
pastel on paper, 26 × 20"
The Pennsylvania Academy of the Fine Arts, Philadelphia.
Gift of Mr. and Mrs. James H. Beal

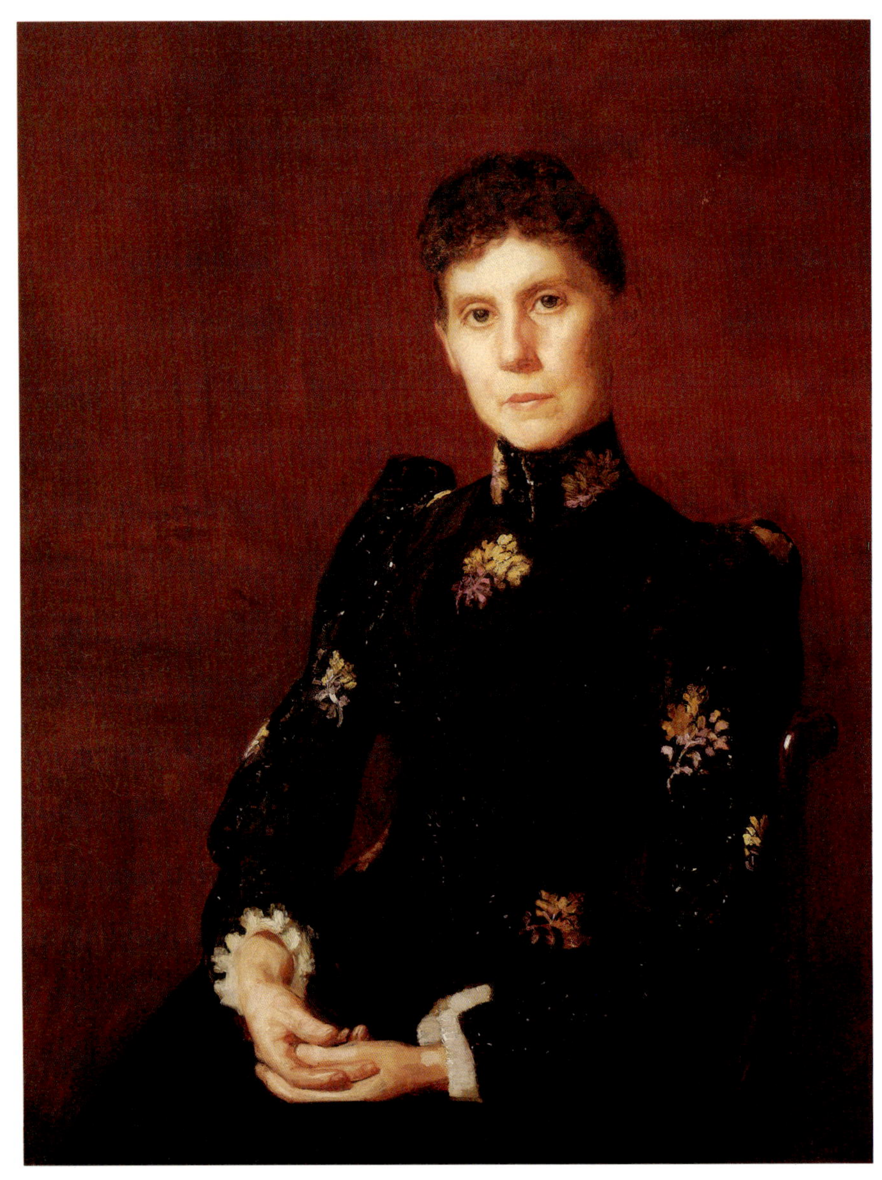

PLATE 26. *Portrait of Emily Fairchild Pollock,* ca. 1905
oil on canvas, 38 × 29"
The Hon. Joseph P. Carroll and Mrs. Carroll, New York

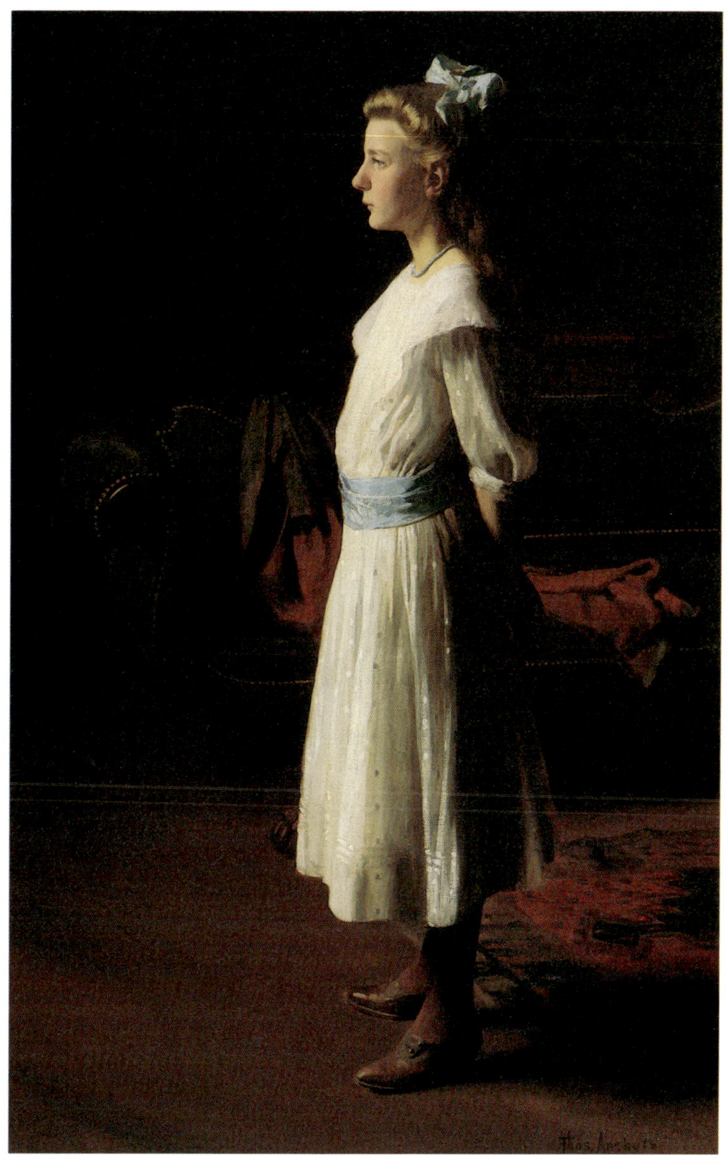

PLATE 27. *Portrait of Margaret Perot,* ca. 1908
oil on canvas, 64⅛ × 40"
Hirshhorn Museum and Sculpture Garden, Smithsonian Institution.
Gift of Joseph H. Hirshhorn, 1966.

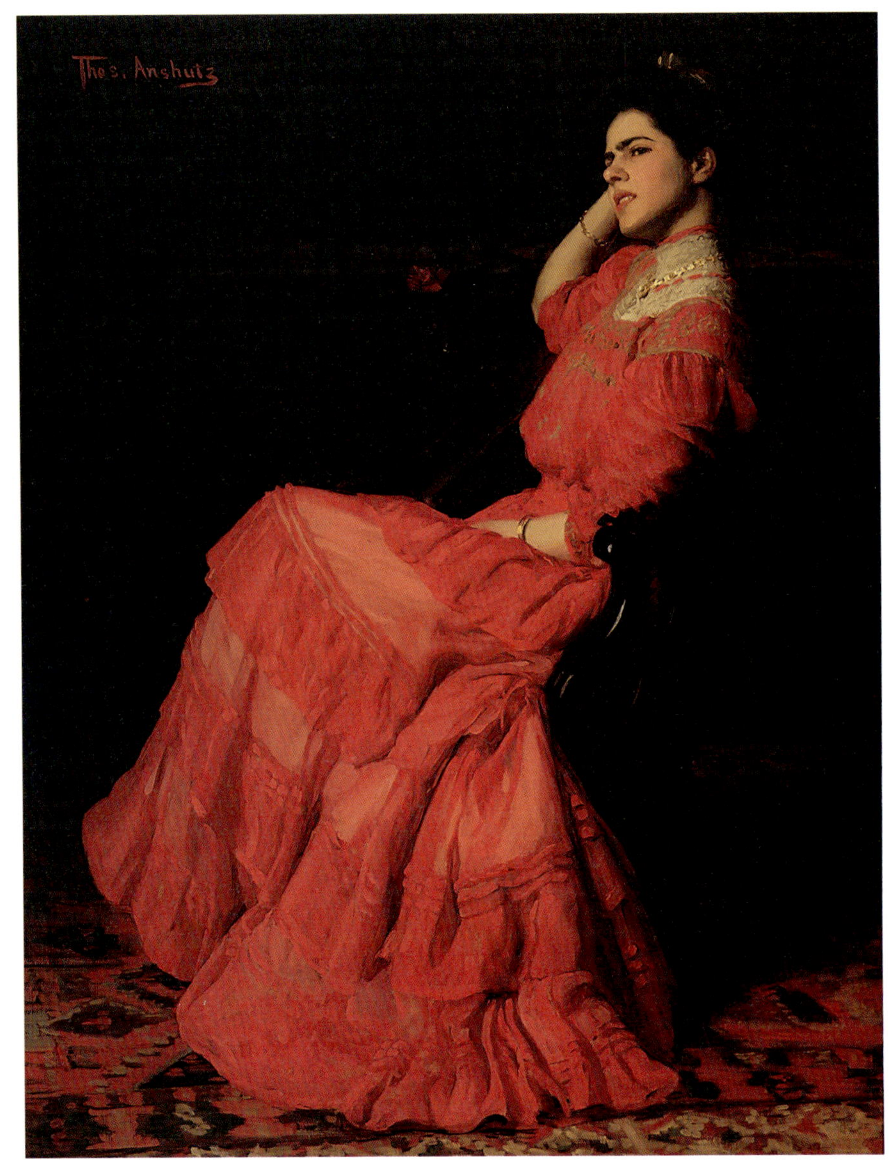

PLATE 28. *A Rose,* 1908
oil on canvas, $58 \times 43\frac{7}{8}$"
The Metropolitan Museum of Art,
Marguerite and Frank A. Cosgrove, Jr. Fund, 1993 (1993.324)

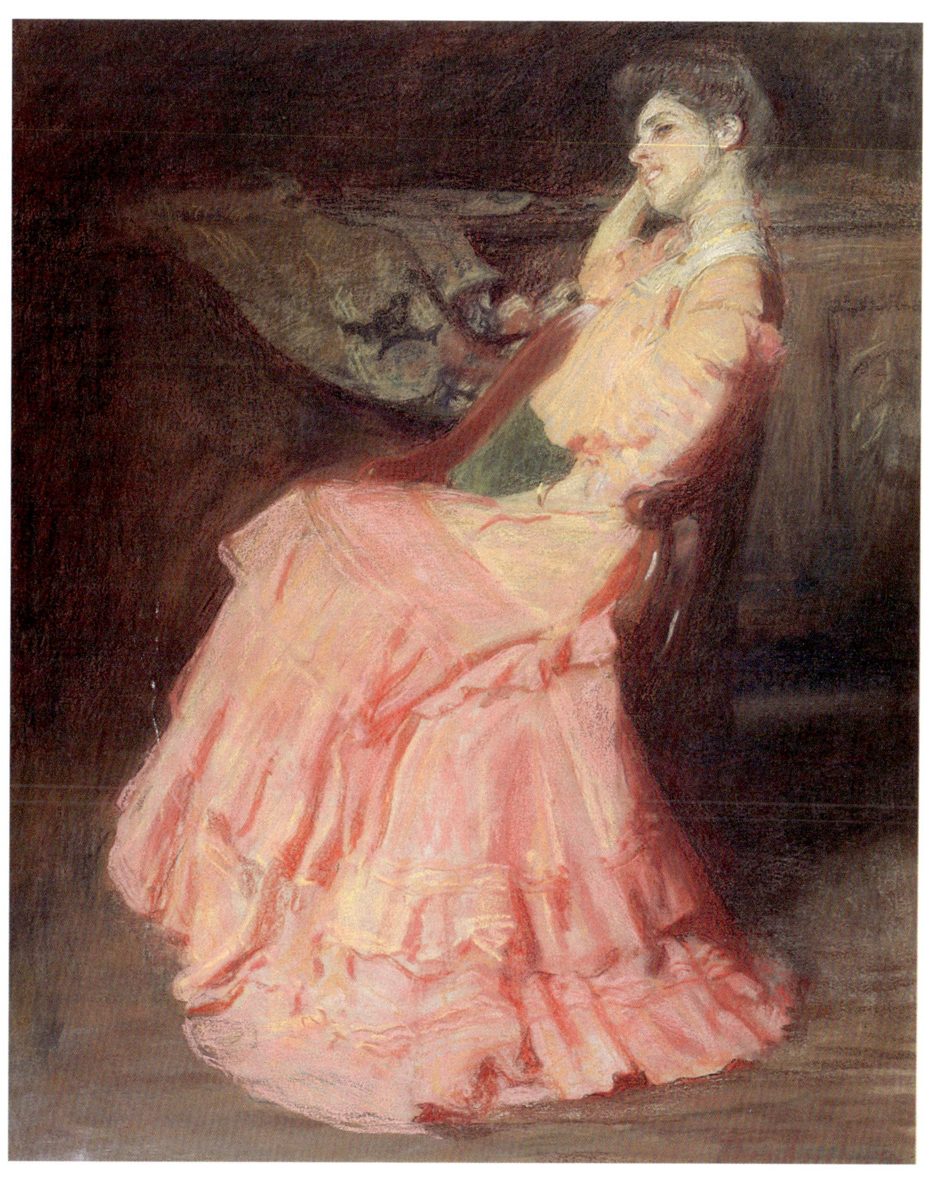

PLATE 29. *A Challenge,* ca. 1908
pastel on canvas, 30 × 24"
The Hon. Joseph P. Carroll and Mrs. Carroll, New York,
courtesy Berry-Hill Galleries, Inc., New York

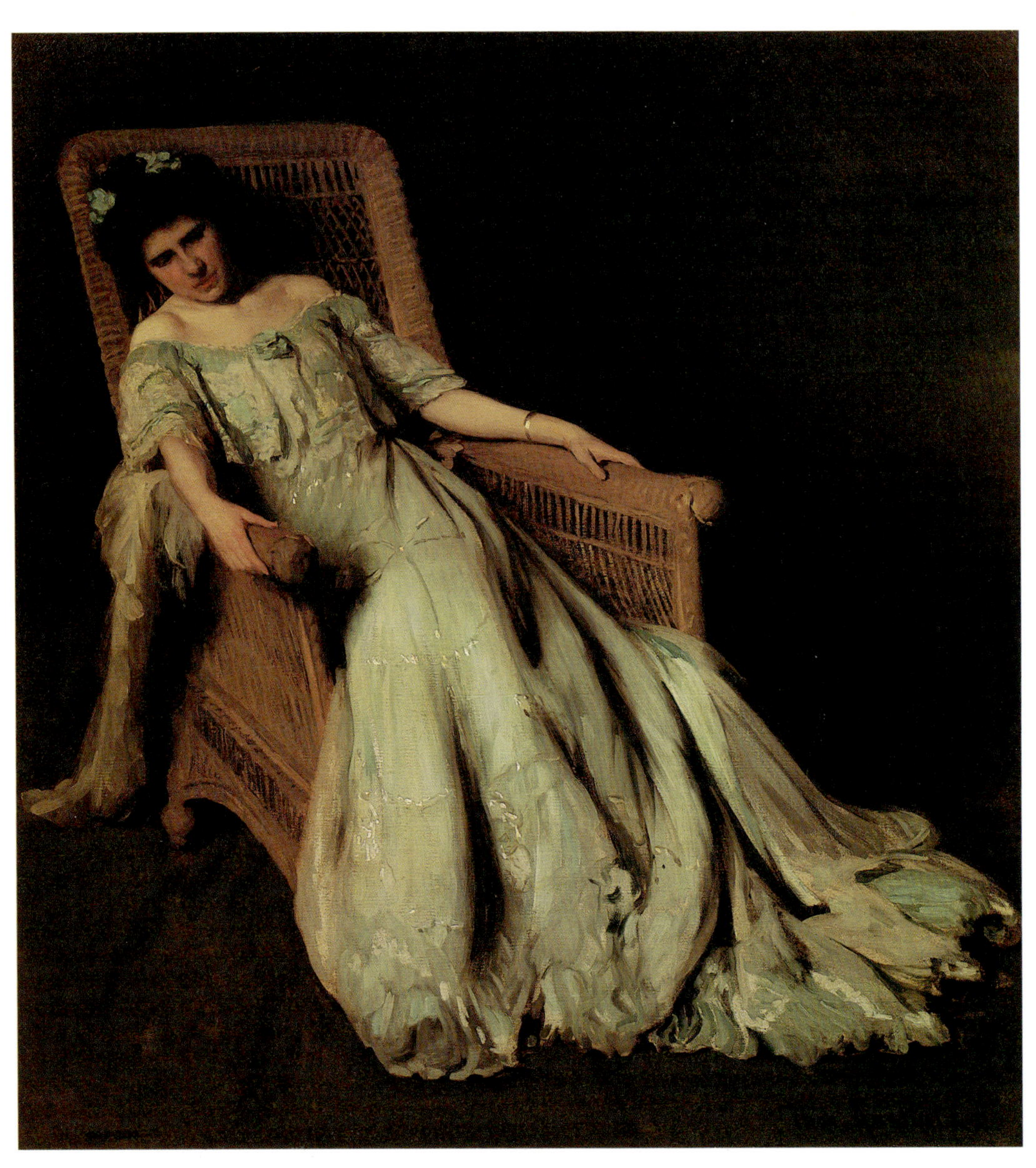

PLATE 30. *Figure Piece,* ca. 1909
oil on canvas, 40 × 36⅛"
National Academy of Design, New York

dents and critics thought him "always receptive to new methods and new ideas."[66]

These new approaches became evident in his teaching around 1900. In life-drawing classes he began asking his students to incorporate strong compositional croppings into their work. Student followers of Anshutz referred to themselves as "artists" and to others, Chase's students, as "mechanics."[67] Anshutz's students were also known as "the Smudgers" because of their technique of working charcoal dust with their moist fingers.[68] A former Anshutz student wrote:

> I was not an Anshutz fan. I was very Academic and did not appreciate his advanced breadth, etc.... There was a Thursday night sketch class in which some were interpreting the large plaster cast of "The Fates." One student saw the effect of dazzling light on the mass etc. To another this was the pulsating of life, the thrust of one figure against another.... "Tommy's" students seemed to have an emotional approach that might have the head half-way off the paper. It was time for a reaction to Academism and Tommy was a bold leader.[69]

In a 1905 summer portrait class at Fort Washington, Pennsylvania, his students produced relatively bold and idiosyncratic imagery. An anonymous—and typically for the time—sexist newspaper reviewer noted:

> There was one group of canvases in particular—those of a Chestnut Hill young lady—which showed most unusual student qualities, and which gave in their bold and striking color and line work no evidence of an effeminate origin. This and a series of three sketchy decorative panels of extraordinary virility and weird originality in conception and execution gave interest and distinction to the walls.[70]

As an instructor, Anshutz was not unique in his progressive teaching style, being one of several instructors at the Pennsylvania Academy who stressed the importance of artistic individuality and experimentation. For example, William Merritt Chase, a favorite of many Academy students, emphasized rapid sketching techniques, rejected lengthy study of the antique, and warned against succumbing to artistic convention.[71] During the period of Chase's tenure at the Pennsylvania Academy of the Fine Arts (1896-1909), the Academy also employed the progressively-minded Henry McCarter, Arthur B. Carles, and Hugh Breckenridge. Like Chase and Anshutz, these men sought to promote artistic self-expression, informing their students about new Parisian styles of painting.[72]

In conclusion, by acting to preserve many of Eakins' ideas, Anshutz shaped the development of American art. Yet Anshutz should equally be remembered as a teacher who was respected for many reasons. Among those most frequently mentioned were his admiration for students and his passion for allowing their individual artistic development. As one critic recorded,

> His greatest factor as a teacher was the complete suppression of his own mannerisms in painting, for he delighted to develop what he found inherent in the student rather than to insist upon his own ideas of art.[73]

Equally, Anshutz saw his students as a potential source for his own artistic renewal.

During the three decades Anshutz spent at the Academy, his instruction was always predicated on the belief that, above all else, an art school must provide its students with a set of basic skills. This was in spite of his increasingly progressive views on art, especially after 1900. He never wavered in his conviction that art schools should teach such traditional subjects as cast drawing and anatomical studies. As early as 1884, Anshutz attempted to combine this pragmatic approach with one that also attempted to encourage creativity and artistic autonomy. After 1900, influenced by the art of Hugh Breckenridge and the Nabis, Anshutz's teaching became more experimental. His beliefs that artistic truth was relative to the individual painter's feelings and impressions and that there was no one correct style led him to inspire in his students similarly unconventional notions of art.

NOTES

INTRODUCTION

1. For the most detailed previous studies on the painter, see my "Thomas Anshutz: A Study of His Art and Teaching," Ph.D. diss., University of Delaware, 1994; Sandra Lee Denney, "Thomas Anshutz: His Life, Art, and Teaching," unpublished master's thesis, University of Delaware, 1969; and Ruth Bowman, "Thomas Pollock Anshutz," unpublished master's thesis, Institute of Fine Arts, New York University, 1971. Ms. Bowman also published two excellent articles on Anshutz. See her "The Artist as Model: A Portrait of David Wilson Jordan by Thomas Anshutz," *The Register of the Spencer Museum of Art* 4 (Fall 1973): 4-34 and "Nature, the Photograph and Thomas Anshutz," *Art Journal 33* (Fall 1973): 32-40.

2. Virginia Woolf, *Orlando: A Biography* (New York: Harcourt, Brace and Company, 1933), 65.

CHAPTER 1

1. The information from this paragraph comes from a short unpublished history of the Anshutz family in the Archives of the Pennsylvania Academy of the Fine Arts (hereafter PAFA). P. J. Anshutz, "A Reminiscent History of the Anshutz Family," dated April 26, 1895. This history traces the Anshutz family patrilineally. For additional information on Anshutz's youth, see Martha Gyllenhaal, et al., *New Light: Ten Artists Inspired by Emanuel Swedenborg* (Bryn Athyn, PA: Glencairn Museum, Academy of the New Church, 1988), 16-17; John Cournos, "A Maker of Painters—Thomas P. Anshutz and His Service to American Art," *Boston Evening Transcript,* 10 February 1912; "American Portrait Painters of Today—Thomas P. Anshutz," *Vogue* 34 (17 June 1909): 1086; "Mrs. Jacob Anshutz," *New Church Life* 19 (1901): 104-5; Edward R. Anshutz (Thomas Anshutz's son) to William Innes Homer, 17 May 1963, Collection of William Innes Homer, Wilmington, DE; and an untitled note by Edward R. Anshutz, 13 May 1954, Archives of the PAFA, Philadelphia.

2. "American Portrait Painters of Today."

3. "Thos. P. Anshutz, the Painter, Dies," *Philadelphia Evening Bulletin*, 17 June 1912. The artist's son, Edward R. Anshutz, later stated that, by 1871, Thomas "was already up to his ears in art." Edward R. Anshutz to William Innes Homer, 26 March 1963, Collection of William Innes Homer, Wilmington, DE. See also "American Portrait Painters of Today."

4. Cited in Denney, "Thomas Anshutz: His Life, Art, and Teaching." In travelling to New York City, Anshutz spent the summer boating down the Ohio and Mississippi rivers to New Orleans, and after a brief stop in Cuba, took a ship up the Atlantic coast to New York, arriving on August 21. Edward R. Anshutz to William Innes Homer, 26 March 1963, Collection of William Innes Homer, Wilmington, DE.

5. For information on Anshutz at the National Academy of Design (hereafter NAD), see Anshutz to John E.D. Trask (Secretary and Manager of the PAFA), undated, Archives of the PAFA, Philadelphia and Bowman, "Thomas Pollock Anshutz." For a dis-

cussion of Lemuel E. Wilmarth, see H. Barbara Weinberg, *The American Pupils of Jean-Léon Gérôme* (Fort Worth, TX: Amon Carter Museum, 1984), 66.

6. See Archives of the NAD.

7. Anshutz's "Discourse on Art," ca. fall 1873, microfilm roll 140, Archives of American Art (hereafter AAA), Washington, DC.

8. Ibid.

9. For a discussion of Schussele, Eakins, and the PAFA, see Lloyd Goodrich, *Thomas Eakins,* 2 vols. (Cambridge, MA: Harvard University Press, 1982), 1: 169-73.

10. William C. Brownell, "The Art Schools of Philadelphia," *Scribner's Monthly* 18 (September 1897): 746.

11. Anshutz's cast of a horse followed Eakins' notions of art education. The older man believed in the importance of students producing sculpture in order to better understand three-dimensional form. This procedure was also advocated by Jean-Léon Gérôme, Léon Bonnat, and Jean-Louis-Ernest Meissonier. For a discussion of this matter, see William Innes Homer, *Thomas Eakins: His Life and Art* (New York: Abbeville Press Publishers, 1992), 35-36, 60.

12. Brownell, "Art Schools of Philadelphia," 737-50.

13. Eakins sometimes asked his students to produce wax casts of the human body. See Eakins to Edward Hornor Coates, 12 September 1886, Archives of the PAFA, Philadelphia; cited in Kathleen A. Foster and Cheryl Leibold, *Writing about Eakins: The Manuscripts in Charles Bregler's Thomas Eakins Collection* (Philadelphia: University of Pennsylvania Press, 1989), 239. As an instructor at the PAFA, Anshutz required similar class assignments.

14. For Courbet's statement about art, see Linda Nochlin, *Realism* (New York: Penguin Books, 1971), 23. See also Cournos, "A Maker of Painters."

15. Cited in David Sellin, "Eakins and the Macdowells and the Academy," in *Thomas Eakins, Susan Macdowell Eakins, Elizabeth Macdowell Kenton,* intro. by Betty Tisinger (Roanoke, VA: North Cross School Living Gallery, 1977), 25.

16. Cournos, "A Maker of Painters."

17. Brownell, "The Art Schools," 741.

18. Ibid.

19. Homer, *Thomas Eakins,* 165.

20. See John Sloan, *Gist of Art: Principles and Practice Expounded in the Classroom and Studio by John Sloan,* ed. Helen Farr Sloan (New York: Dover Publications, Inc., 1977), 12-13; Homer, *Thomas Eakins,* 165; and Sellin, "Eakins and the Macdowells," 24.

Among Anshutz's own works portraying simple sculptural objects is his still life of oranges, painted on the back of *Factory Study for The Ironworkers' Noontime,* plate 6 in this catalogue.

21. "American Portrait Painters of Today."

22. Anshutz to J. Laurie Wallace, 7 April 1884, Philadelphia Museum of Art Archives.

23. Anshutz painted river scenes of the Shenandoah, Ohio, Wissahickon, and Potomac rivers.

24. *On the Ohio* is very similar to *Mountain Landscape: West Virginia* (ca. 1879), formerly owned by James Graham & Sons Gallery and now in a private collection.

25. See Maria Chamberlin-Hellman, "Thomas Eakins as a Teacher," Ph.D. diss., Columbia University, 1981, 120.

26. Anshutz vacationed during his youth on a farm belonging to his uncle, John Peter Anshutz, near Moundsville, Ohio. See Edward R. Anshutz to William Innes Homer, 17 May 1963, Collection of William Innes Homer, Wilmington, DE.

27. See Christopher Kent Wilson, "Winslow Homer's *The Veteran in a New Field:* A Study of the Harvest Metaphor and Popular Culture, "*American Art Journal* 17 (Autumn 1985): 2-27.

28. *The Way They Live* was exhibited at the NAD in 1880. Anshutz also painted a larger version of this scene, which is no longer extant. See Julius Bloch Papers,

microfilm 3755, AAA, Washington, DC.

29. The four images include the oil paintings *The Chore* and *Aunt Hannah* (ca. 1888, Detroit Institute of Arts) and the watercolors *Ris* and *Negress with Broom* (ca. 1880, locations unknown).

30. *A Farmer Plowing* was painted on only a slightly larger canvas than *The Farmer and His Son at Harvesting, The Way They Live,* and *The Ironworkers' Noontime*: 18 x 25 inches instead of 17 x 24 inches. There is no record of the painting ever having been exhibited during Anshutz's lifetime.

31. For a fine historical reading of *The Ironworkers' Noontime,* see Thomas H. Pauley, "American Art and Labor: The Case of Anshutz's *The Ironworkers' Noontime,*" *American Quarterly* 40 (September 1988): 333-58. See also my essay, "Thomas Anshutz's *The Ironworkers' Noontime*: Remythologizing the Industrial Worker," *Smithsonian Studies in American Art* 4 (Fall/Spring 1990): 128-43.

32. For example, see Ashur B. Durand's *Progress* (1853, The Warner Collection of Gulf States Paper Corporation) and Jasper Cropsey's *Starrucca Viaduct, Pennsylvania* (1865, Toledo Museum of Art).

33. One American critic who encouraged fine artists to depict industrial scenes is T.H. Bartlett. See T.H. Bartlett, "Walter Shirlaw," *American Art Review* 2 (1881): 148. He wrote "none of our mighty manufacturing activities...have yet had their art expression." Nineteenth-century American artists who painted factory scenes included Bass Otis, John Ferguson Weir, Thomas Moran, and John Twachtman. For a discussion of European art and industrialism, see Francis D. Klingender, *Art and the Industrial Revolution,* edited and revised by Arthur Elton (London: Evelyn, Adams & Mackay, 1968).

34. See Anshutz, "A Reminiscent History." Anshutz's father's family was from the Alsatian village of Sinsville, France, on the Rhine near Strasbourg. That side of his family had a long history of work in iron manufacturing; many family members had managed iron factories.

35. Francis J. Ziegler, "An Unassuming Painter—Thomas P. Anshutz," *Brush and Pencil* 4 (September 1899): 279.

36. Such panoramic factory views were common in popular prints of the 1870s. In 1868 Anshutz had drawn a masthead for the *Wheeling Register,* a paper edited by his uncle Sidney . The masthead shows a panoramic river view of industrial Wheeling surmounted by brawny factory workers.

37. Ziegler, "An Unassuming Painter," 279. One critic described Anshutz's factory workers as "picturesque." See review of the Clarke collection, *New York News,* 30 December 1883. My thanks to Sarah Cash for informing me about this review.

38. For a discussion of the usage of the word "picturesque" in reference to the industrial landscape, see John F. Sears, *Sacred Places: American Tourist Attractions in the Nineteenth Century* (New York and Oxford: Oxford University Press, 1988), 198-206.

39. See Anshutz to J. Laurie Wallace, ca. fall 1883, Philadelphia Museum of Art Archives. For a similar usage of the word, see G.W. Sheldon, *American Painters* (London: D. Appleton and Company, 1878), 52.

40. For the most complete examination of late nineteenth-century American industrial illustration, see Emily Bardack Kies, "The City and the Machine: Urban and Industrial Illustration in America 1880-1900," Ph.D. diss., Columbia University, 1971.

41. For an excellent discussion of the elimination of trades, see Daniel T. Rodgers, *The Work Ethic in Industrial America: 1850-1920* (Chicago: The University of Chicago Press, 1978), 25.

42. Quoted in M.B. Schnapper, *American Labor: A Pictorial Social History* (Washington, DC: Public Affairs Press, 1972), 78.

43. See Rodgers, *The Work Ethic,* 19.

44. John Rule, "The Property of Skill," in *The Historical Meanings of Work,* ed. Patrick Joyce (Cambridge: Cambridge University Press, 1987), 107. See also David Leverenz, *Manhood and the American Renaissance* (Ithaca, NY: Cornell University Press, 1989), 74.

45. A large number of blacksmith images were produced beginning in the

1870s by artists such as John George Brown, Thomas Hovenden, and Frank Duveneck. Painters such as Brown also rendered nostalgic images of shoemakers and carpenters.

46. For romantic descriptions of factory work, see Henry Nash Smith, *Popular Culture and Industrialism: 1865-1890* (New York: Doubleday & Company, Anchor Books, 1967), 78-80. Also refer to Stephen Daniels, "Loutherbourg's Chemical Theater: Coalbrookdale by Night" in *Painting and the Politics of Culture: New Essays on British Art 1700-1850,* John Barrell, ed. (Oxford University Press, 1992), 213-16, 228.

47. J.O. Davidson, "Interior of a Southern Cotton Press by Night," *Harper's Weekly* 27 (24 March 1883): 181, cited in Smith, *Popular Culture and Industrialism: 1865-1890,* 78-80.

48. "The City of Pittsburgh," 56-59.

49. Ibid., 56.

50. The ironworkers themselves named their union "The Sons of Vulcan." See James M. Swank, *History of the Manufacture of Iron in all Ages, and Particularly in the United States from Colonial Times to 1891* (New York: Doubleday & Company, Anchor Books, 1967), 78-80.

51. Judging from articles in such magazines as *Harper's Weekly* and *Scribner's Monthly,* most Americans knew little about factory workers except that they often held highly paid, dangerous jobs. For example, see "The City of Pittsburgh," 56-58.

52. One reviewer wrote that "the painter presents them [the men] without affectation, with a vigorous and accurate hand." See review of the Clarke collection, *New York News,* 30 December 1883.

53. David Montgomery, *The Fall of the House of Labor: The Workplace, the State, and American Labor Activism, 1865-1925,* (Cambridge: Cambridge University Press, 1987), 14.

54. This provided a type of crude apprenticeship system. Fathers often handed on their furnace jobs to their sons. See ibid., 15.

55. Ibid., 15-16.

56. James Parton, "Pittsburgh," *Atlantic Monthly,* 21 (January 1868): 33, cited in ibid., 18.

57. Ibid., 18. By 1870 it was usual for a shift to consist of five separate "heatings" of 550 pounds each.

58. *The Dissecting Room* was the only multi-figure composition Anshutz had previously painted. It was illustrated in a magazine article concerning the PAFA. See Brownell, "The Art Schools of Philadelphia," 747.

59. Anshutz, after first using the title *The Ironworkers,* changed it to *Dinner Time*. Thomas B. Clarke, who purchased the painting in 1883, apparently changed the title to *The Ironworkers' Noontime*.

60. See Pauley, "American Art and Labor," 346 and Patricia Hills, *The Painters' America: Rural and Urban Life 1810-1910* (New York: Praeger Publishers, 1974), 115-18.

61. For a more detailed discussion of John George Brown's *The Longshoremen's Noon,* see Edward J. Nygren and Peter C. Marzio, *Of Time and Place: American Figurative Art from the Corcoran Gallery* (Washington, DC: Smithsonian Institution Traveling Exhibition Service and the Corcoran Gallery of Art, 1981), 64.

62. See review of the Clarke collection, *New York News,* 30 December 1883.

63. By late 1908, Anshutz had declared himself a socialist. See Bruce St. John, ed., *John Sloan's New York Scene* (New York: Harper & Row, 1965), 273. Few of Anshutz's paintings reflect any overt socialist influence. An exception may be the painter's *A Daughter of the Ghetto* (1902, location unknown), which was exhibited at the PAFA in 1902.

64. Ziegler, "An Unassuming Painter," 279.

65. See "Unique Exhibition," *Boston Herald,* 28 December 1883 and review of the Clarke collection, *New York Review,* 30 December 1883.

66. For discussions of industrial strikes in America, see Schnapper, *American Labor,* 115-117 and Sean Dennis Cashman, *America in the Gilded Age: From the Death of Lincoln to the Rise of Theodore Roosevelt* (New York: New York University Press, 1984), 244-53.

67. In May 1883, shortly before purchasing *The Ironworker's Noontime,* Clarke

bought Charles F. Ulrich's *The Glass Blowers of Murano*. See Pauley, "American Art and Labor," 350-52.

68. See an unidentified clipping, 15 November 1881, Archives of the PAFA, Philadelphia.

69. The drawings of equine anatomy interspersed with the preparatory drawings for *The Ironworkers' Noontime* are a sign of the closeness of Anshutz's interests to those of Eakins.

70. For a discussion of American late nineteenth-century interest in athletics, see Elizabeth Johns, *Thomas Eakins: The Heroism of Modern Life* (Princeton, NJ: Princeton University Press, 1983), 19-45; and Harvey Green, *Fit for America: Health, Fitness, Sport, and American Society* (New York: Pantheon Books, 1986), 181-215.

71. Sheldon, *American Painters,* 12, 16, 97, 228. For a discussion of masculinity and late nineteenth-century American culture, see Joe L. Dubbert, *A Man's Place: Masculinity in Transition* (Englewood Cliffs, NJ: Prentice Hall, 1979). My catalogue's discussion of artistic masculinity is an expanded version of my "Thomas Anshutz's *The Ironworkers' Noontime*," 139-42.

72. Sheldon, *American Painters,* 16.

73. Ibid., 228.

74. Cited in ibid., 92. Also refer to Sheldon, *American Painters,* 12, 16, 97, 228.

75. William Morris Hunt, *Talks on Art,* Compiled by H. M. Knowlton (Boston: Houghton Mifflin, 1875), 57.

76. "Art at the Paris Exhibition," *Scribner's Monthly* 17 (December 1878): 280. Also see Sidney Lomas, "History of the Sketch Club," 120, microfilm roll 3664, AAA, Washington, DC.

77. Anshutz to Cresson Schell, 22 June 1902, microfilm roll 140, AAA, Washington, DC.

78. Eakins to Edward Coates, 11 September 1886, Archives of the PAFA, Philadelphia.

79. Dubbert, *A Man's Place,* 87.

80. For a discussion of the blurring of gender roles and the feminization of American culture, see T. J. Jackson Lears, *No Place of Grace: Antimodernism and the Transformation of American Culture 1880-1920* (New York: Pantheon Books, 1981), 104. See also David Park Curry, *Winslow Homer: The Croquet Game* (New Haven, CT: Yale University Art Gallery, 1984) and George Peck, *Formation of a Manly Character: A Series of Lectures to Young Men* (New York: Carlton & Phillips, 1853).

81. Theodor Siegl, *The Thomas Eakins Collection* (Philadelphia: Philadelphia Museum of Art, 1978), 25-26. See also John Wilmerding, "Walt Whitman and American Painting," *Antiques* (November 1985): 998-1001.

For a discussion of the question of underlying homosexual desire present in homosocial visual and literary imagery, see Abigail Solomon-Godeau, "Male Trouble: A Crisis in Representation," *Art History* 16 (June 1993): 286-312; Alex Potts, "Beautiful Bodies and Dying Heroes: Images of Ideal Manhood in the French Revolution," *History Workshop Journal* 29 (Autumn 1990): 1-21; Eve Kosofsky Sedgwick, *Between Men: English Literature and Male Homosocial Desire* (New York: Columbia University Press, 1985); and David S. Reynolds, *Beneath the American Renaissance: The Subversive Imagination in the Age of Emerson and Melville* (New York: Alfred A. Knopf, 1989), 327-30.

82. In 1881 Anshutz failed to exhibit anything at either the NAD or the PAFA. Perhaps he only considered the oil a study for a larger painting. One critic called it a finished sketch. See unidentified clipping, 15 November 1881, Archives of the PAFA, Philadelphia.

83. Ziegler, "An Unassuming Painter," 279. Years later, Anshutz would recall that several times, because of the image's failure to sell, he came close to painting over *The Ironworkers' Noontime*.

84. This montage was the basis of one of the first American billboards, measuring approximately 100 x 160 inches, which was placed in Fountain Square, Philadelphia. See James C. Claypool, "An Unassuming Painter," *The Enquirer Magazine* (4 August 1985): 10. The self-contained character of the men in the soap

ad is markedly different from *The Ironworkers' Noontime*. None of the workers confronts the viewer. For an earlier discussion of this ad, see Bowman "Nature, The Photograph and Thomas Anshutz," 32.

85. Ziegler, "An Unassuming Painter," 277-84.

86. Anshutz had even posed nude for one of Eakins' photographs. My thanks to Cheryl Leibold for alerting me to this. The photograph is part of the Charles Bregler collection in the PAFA, Philadelphia.

87. Homer, *Thomas Eakins,* 147-53. See also William Innes Homer, "Eakins, Muybridge and the Motion Picture Process," *Art Quarterly* 26 (Summer 1963): 194-216, and Goodrich, *Thomas Eakins,* I: 260-78.

88. Goodrich, *Thomas Eakins,* I, 270-72.

89. Anshutz to J. Laurie Wallace, 18 June 1884, Philadelphia Museum of Art Archives.

90. Anshutz to J. Laurie Wallace, 7 April 1884, Philadelphia Museum of Art Archives.

91. Anshutz to J. Laurie Wallace, April 1884, Philadelphia Museum of Art Archives.

92. For instance, see Sheldon, *American Painters.*

93. Anshutz to Edward Hornor Coates, 3 June 1892, Archives of the PAFA, Philadelphia.

94. Anshutz to J. Laurie Wallace, 4 November 1885, Philadelphia Museum of Art Archives.

95. Anshutz to J. Laurie Wallace, 7 April 1884, Philadelphia Museum of Art Archives.

96. Ziegler, "An Unassuming Painter," 277. See also Anshutz to Cresson Schell, 25 August 1902, microfilm roll 140, AAA, Washington, DC. Anshutz stated "[I have the] same old feeling I had 25 years ago—I am just about to learn how to paint."

97. Although Anshutz exhibited seven paintings at the PAFA in 1879, he only exhibited a single work in 1880 and 1882.

98. Chamberlin-Hellman, "Thomas Eakins as a Teacher," 293, 294. See also Theodor Siegl, *The Thomas Eakins Collection,* 96.

99. For example, in 1886, Eakins asked his student Miss Van Buren to do outdoor sketching in order "to make color studies of outdoor effects." See Eakins to Edward Hornor Coates, 12 September 1886, Archives of the PAFA, Philadelphia; cited in Foster and Leibold, *Writing about Eakins,* 239.

100. Anshutz to J. Laurie Wallace, 7 April 1884, Philadelphia Museum of Art Archives.

101. In reference to this exhibition Helen Henderson later wrote that Anshutz and a friend (Jim Kelly) "were electrified by what they saw and felt that their eyes had opened upon a new world." See Helen W. Henderson, *Memorial Exhibition of the Work of Thomas Anshutz* (Philadelphia: Philadelphia Art Alliance, 1942).

102. Anshutz's *A Studio Study* is also reminiscent of a group of watercolor spinning scenes produced by Eakins in the late 1870s and early 1880s.

103. Anshutz to Mrs. Russell (his future mother-in-law), 11 November 1891, copy of letter in the collection of William Innes Homer, Wilmington, DE.

104. Barbara A. Wolanin, "Arthur B. Carles, 1882-1952: Philadelphia Modernist," Ph.D. diss., University of Wisconsin-Madison, 1981, 16.

105. Anshutz to the Board of Directors, spring 1892, Archives of the PAFA, Philadelphia.

Chapter 2

1. For information concerning the Académie Julian, see Lois Marie Fink, *American Art at the Nineteenth-Century Paris Salons* (Washington, DC: National Museum of American Art, Smithsonian Institution; Cambridge University Press, 1990), 134-35.

2. Anshutz to his brother Edward, spring 1893, microfilm roll 140, AAA, Washington, DC.

3. Ibid.

4. Anshutz to Edward Hornor Coates, 15 May 1893, microfilm roll 140, AAA, Washington, DC.

5. Alfred H. Barr Jr., *Matisse: His Art and His Public* (New York: Museum of Modern Art, 1951), 14.

6. Anshutz to his brother Edward, 3 February 1893, microfilm roll 140, AAA, Washington, DC.

7. Anshutz to his brother Edward, spring 1893, microfilm roll 140, AAA, Washington, DC.

8. Ibid.

9. See Anshutz to his brother Edward, spring 1893, microfilm roll 140, AAA, Washington, DC; Anshutz to Edward, 7 May 1893, microfilm roll 140, AAA, Washington, DC; Bowman, "Thomas Pollock Anshutz," 22; and Theodore Reff, ed., *Salons of the "Independants" 1892-1895* (New York: Garland Publishing, Inc., 1981), 17-81.

10. Robert Henri diary, 1 April 1891, microfilm roll 140, AAA, Washington, DC. See also Anshutz to his brother Edward, January 1893, microfilm roll 140, AAA, Washington, DC.

11. Anshutz to his brother Edward, 7 May 1893, microfilm roll 140, AAA, Washington, DC.

12. Anshutz to his brother Edward, 7 May 1893, microfilm roll 140, AAA, Washington, DC. There is no evidence that Anshutz ever sold or exhibited any of his Paris watercolors.

13. My reconstruction of Anshutz's travel itinerary is based on the painter's correspondence.

14. Anshutz to Effie Anshutz, 11 November 1893, microfilm roll 140, AAA, Washington, DC.

15. Most of Anshutz's charcoal drawings are in the collection of the PAFA. Charles Bregler, a former student of Anshutz's, stated "Let me note here, that this was exactly what that assistant professor [Thomas Anshutz] did a few years later, drawing from the antique night after night for several years—learning to draw—as if there were only one way to accomplish this." Cited in Chamberlin-Hellman, "Thomas Eakins as a Teacher," 197.

16. Ziegler, "An Unassuming Painter," 278.

17. Ibid., 279.

18. Anshutz had visited Holly Beach, New Jersey, with his family at least as early as the summer of 1874.

19. Anshutz to Effie Anshutz, 17 November 1893, microfilm roll 140, AAA, Washington, DC.

20. Seven of the Holly Beach watercolors were exhibited at the PAFA Annual in 1895. During the following two years, Anshutz showed no works at the PAFA.

21. Anshutz to Cresson Schell, ca. summer 1894, microfilm roll 140, AAA, Washington, DC.

22. Perhaps the recent or impending birth of his first and only child, Edward Russell Anshutz, known to the family as Ned, may have encouraged his choice of subject matter. His son, who was named after Anshutz's older brother Edward, was born sometime during 1894. See Gyllenhaal, *New Light,* 17.

23. Two of his Holly Beach watercolors were illustrated in Francis Ziegler's 1899 *Brush and Pencil* article on the artist. See Ziegler, "An Unassuming Painter," 280, 283.

24. The version of *Two Boys and a Boat* owned by the Carnegie Museum of Art is more detailed and finished than the version in the collection of Mr. and Mrs. Raymond J. Horowitz. The most finished and highly detailed of all these watercolors is *Sand Boys* (ca. 1894, Private Collection). A similarly finished watercolor entitled *Boys on the Beach* (ca. 1894-95, Barridoff Galleries, Portland, ME) shows three boys greeting someone coming ashore.

25. It was the first time since the early 1880s that he had exhibited large numbers of his paintings. See Peter Hastings Falk, ed., *The Annual Exhibition Record of The Art Institute of Chicago, 1888-1950* (New York: Sound View Press, 1990), 67. See

also Janice H. Chadbourne, Karl Gabosh, and Charles O. Vogel, eds., *The Boston Art Club: Exhibition Record, 1873-1909* (New York: Sound View Press, 1991), 58.

26. During the 1890s Anshutz took dozens of photographs of boats, fishermen, women in boats and on beaches, stretches of dunes, and rural houses. For the most detailed examination of Anshutz's use of photographs, see Bowman, "Nature, The Photograph and Thomas Anshutz." In 1971, Ruth Bowman rediscovered Anshutz's large collection of photographs. These photographs are now in the collection of the AAA, Washington, DC. Although Anshutz appears to have employed photographic sources infrequently for his watercolors, the photographs he did use, like all of his photographs, were printed from 4" x 5" glass negatives. The watercolor *Looking Seaward: Holly Beach* (ca. 1894, Private Collection) is based on the photograph *Two Women at Holly Beach* (ca. 1894, AAA, Washington, DC). See also Anshutz's watercolor *Mrs. Anshutz and Dog at Holly Beach* (ca. 1894, Collection of the Hon. Joseph P. Carroll and Mrs. Carroll), which is based on the photograph *Woman Seated on the Beach* (ca. 1894, AAA, Washington, DC).

27. Anshutz's Holly Beach scenes also resemble those of Robert V. V. Sewel, e.g., Sewel's *The Bathers* (1888, location unknown), illustrated in Carolyn Kinder Carr and George Gurney, *Revisiting the White City: American Art at the 1893 World's Fair* (Washington, DC: National Museum of American Art and National Portrait Gallery, 1993), 316.

28. Spanierman Gallery, *The Spencer Collection of American Art* (New York: Spanierman Gallery, 1990), 4.

29. The painter took more than ten photographs of ships along the Delaware River.See the Anshutz photographs in the collection of the AAA, Washington, DC.

30. Anshutz had also taken a boating trip in the summer of 1871 on the Ohio and Mississippi. One of his uncles, a P. J. Anshutz, was a steamboat captain and formerly a Union pilot during the Civil Ear. See Anshutz, "A Reminiscent History."

31. On the trip, Anshutz wrote that after rising at four in the morning, he "had a good big canvas—too big for a sketch requiring about three mornings." Anshutz to Effie Anshutz, 16 June 1897, microfilm roll 140, AAA, Washington, DC. See the Archives of the PAFA for the original letters.

32. Many of Anshutz's undated photographs of river life along the Delaware are reminiscent of Eakins' photographs of Gloucester shad fishermen.

33. Anshutz to Effie Anshutz, 29 June 1897, Archives of the PAFA, Philadelphia.

34. Anshutz to Effie Anshutz, 3 August 1897, microfilm roll 140, AAA, Washington, DC. None of his haying scenes are known to have survived.

35. Anshutz to Effie Anshutz, 22 August 1897, microfilm roll 140, AAA, Washington, DC.

36. Anshutz also took photographs of harbor areas. See the Anshutz photographs in the collection of the AAA, Washington, DC.

37. The steamboat pictured in Anshutz's photograph is the Hudson, which was constructed in 1886 and based in Pittsburgh. My thanks to the staff of the Smithsonian Institution's Museum of American History, Washington, DC, for providing me with this information. For a fine discussion of Anshutz's use of photographs for *Steamboat on the Ohio,* see Bowman, "Nature, The Photograph and Thomas Anshutz."

38. Anshutz produced one other pastel study for *Steamboat on the Ohio*. Located in a private collection, it is similar to the Westmoreland Museum of Art pastel, only lacking any foreground figures.

39. Anshutz did not date the painting. During his lifetime it was never exhibited, and none of his surviving letters mentions the image.

40. Anshutz also painted a related oil, *Two Indians on the Ohio* (ca. 1905, location unknown), which shows a pair of Native Americans watching a distant steamboat. For other pictured examples of this contrast between the arcadian and the industrial, see George Inness' *The Lackawanna Valley* (ca. 1855, National Gallery of Art), and Jasper Cropsey's *Starrucca Viaduct, Pennsylvania* (1865, Toledo Museum of Art).

41. The dramatic steamboat suggests passages in Mark Twain's *Life on the*

Mississippi (1883). See Mark Twain, *Life on the Mississippi* (New York: Bantam Books, 1988), 22, 25, 85.

42. Anshutz to his brother Edward, ca. spring 1893, microfilm roll 140, AAA, Washington, DC.

43. The summer art school first held classes at Darby, Pennsylvania, but Anshutz and Breckenridge soon moved the school to Fort Washington, Pennsylvania. For a description of the Fort Washington school, see "Thomas P. Anshutz—Brief Account of His Summer Art School at Historic Valley Forge," *Wheeling Register*, 10 September 1905. By 1910, Anshutz and Breckenridge had grown apart. Because Breckenridge was away in Europe during the summer of 1909, his last season with Anshutz was that of 1908. Anshutz kept the school going himself through the summer of 1910.

44. Henderson, *Memorial Exhibition of the Work of Thomas Anshutz*.

45. See the records of the Committee on Instruction, 26 May 1898, Archives of the PAFA, Philadelphia.

46. Bowman, "Thomas Pollock Anshutz," 47. According to Bowman, several of Ross' charts—from Ross' book *Theory of Pure Design: Harmony, Balance, Rhythm* (Boston and New York: Houghton Mifflin Co., 1907)—were found on the Anshutz property.

47. See Elizabeth Armstrong Handy, "H. G. Maratta's Color Theory and its Influence on the Painters—Robert Henri, John Sloan, and George Bellows," unpublished master's thesis, University of Delaware, 1969, 16.

48. Anshutz to Cresson Schell, 20 January 1902, microfilm roll 140, AAA, Washington, DC.

49. Anshutz to Cresson Schell, 11 December 1901, microfilm roll 140, AAA, Washington, DC.

50. Anshutz to Cresson Schell, 3 August 1900, microfilm roll 140, AAA, Washington, DC.

51. Ibid.

52. Ibid.

53. Albert Boime, *The Academy and French Painting in the Nineteenth Century* (New Haven, CT and London: Yale University Press, 1971), 73.

54. Anshutz to Cresson Schell, 20 January 1902, microfilm roll 140, AAA, Washington, DC.

55. Anshutz to J. Laurie Wallace, 7 April 1884, Philadelphia Museum of Art Archives.

56. The largest collection of these oil sketches is in the collection of the PAFA, Philadelphia.

57. Anshutz produced a watercolor of an antique cast in this same style around 1905 (location unknown).

58. Anshutz to Robert Henri, December 1906, copy of the letter in the collection of William Innes Homer, Wilmington, DE.

59. Anshutz's brother, Edward, was a prominent member of the New Church, and the artist's son, Edward, attended New Church services as a child.

60. Anshutz's second trip to Paris also led him to buy copies of the French avant-garde journal *Les Tendances Nouvelles.* This is according to William Innes Homer, who was informed of this by Anshutz's son, Edward R. Anshutz.

In the summer of 1910, while on a boat trip to Bermuda with his son Ned, Anshutz had produced several brightly colored landscapes, somewhat reminiscent of those of Hugh Breckenridge.

61. See "Art World Mourns Thomas P. Anshutz."

62. "Thos. P. Anshutz, Noted Artist, Dies," *Philadelphia Inquirer,* 18 June 1912.

63. The oil's Vlaminck-like quality bolsters the argument that the image could not have predated his trip to Paris in the summer of 1911. That the painter had become debilitatingly ill by the time of his return from Europe late that summer may account for his having produced only a small number of brightly-colored Nabis- or Fauves-inspired images. Anshutz was hospitalized in November 1911.

64. See "Thos. P. Anshutz, Noted Artist, Dies."

65. Ibid.

66. Cournos, "A Maker of Painters."

67. Henderson, *Memorial Exhibition of the Work of Thomas Anshutz.*

68. Anshutz owned a spinning wheel, which he kept in his studio.

69. Anshutz also painted *Woman Reading* (ca. 1896, Delaware Art Museum) and the Rembrandt-like *Woman Reading at Desk* (ca. 1908, location unknown). Anshutz owned a reproduction, now in the Archives of the PAFA, Philadelphia, of one of Vermeer's paintings of a woman reading a letter. He may have been prompted to explore a historical genre scene in this fashion by teaching costume classes at the PAFA (1900-02) and at the Darby School. Evidence of his interest in historical dress is found as well in his portrait of David Wilson Jordan, entitled *The Dutchman* (ca. 1905-06, Spencer Museum of Art). For an in-depth discussion of the Jordan portrait, see Bowman, "The Artist as Model," 4-34.

70. After 1900, Anshutz's portraits sold for $200-$500, depending on medium and size. See the Anshutz file, Archives of the PAFA, Philadelphia, for Anshutz's business records and correspondence with John E. D. Trask. Most of Anshutz's sitters were students, relatives, or people associated with the PAFA. For a good survey of Anshutz's portraiture, see Bowman "The Artist as Model."

71. These hang in the Philadelphia Sketch Club.

72. See Anshutz to Effie Anshutz, 5 November 1893, microfilm roll 140, AAA, Washinton, DC.

73. Dr. David Wilson to Theodor Siegl, undated, Philadelphia Museum of Art Archives.

74. For example, Anshutz produced oil studies for *The Dutchman* and *Incense Burner,* and a pastel drawing for *A Rose.* The prepatory pastel for *A Rose,* entitled *A Challange,* is illustrated in plate 29.

75. Throughout his career, Anshutz executed approximately a dozen portraits of family members in Wheeling and Fort Washington. What is presumably an oil study for this portrait is owned by the Sheldon Memorial Art Gallery, University of Nebraska, Lincoln.

76. "American Portrait Painters of Today."

77. John Cournos, "A Great Art Instructor: His Methods and Ideas," *Philadelphia Record,* May 29, 1910.

78. Cournos, "A Maker of Painters."

79. Anshutz to John E. D. Trask, undated, Archives of the PAFA, Philadelphia.

80. The NAD picture is one of two self-portraits he painted. The other, a slightly more cropped version, is in a private collection.

81. The portrait was commissioned by Annie Lovering Perot, an artist who had a summer studio next door to Anshutz's Fort Washington home and who was the aunt of Margaret Morris Perot, whose father was the Vice President of Francis Perot & Sons Malting Co.. The subject wrote that it was painted at Anshutz's Fort Washington studio when she was twelve years old. This would mean it was painted ca. 1908, since Ms. Perot was born in 1896. See Peggy Perot Fiero to Sandra Denney, undated, Collection of Sandra Denney, Wilmington, DE. See also the Anshutz file, Archives of the Hirshhorn Museum and Sculpture Garden, Washington, DC.

82. See Anshutz to Robert Henri, December 1906, copy of letter in the collection of William Innes Homer, Wilmington, DE. Henri painted two portraits of Anshutz in 1906. See Bowman, "The Artist as Model," 25; and Sloan, *John Sloan's New York,* 8.

83. For the most complete study of late nineteenth- and early twentieth-century American pastels, see Doreen Bolger, et al., *American Pastels in the Metropolitan Museum of Art* (New York: Harry N. Abrams, Inc., 1989).

84. In a similar style, Anshutz later produced two pastels of his student Becky Sharp (*The Incense Burner,* 1906, PAFA; and 1906, location unknown).

85. Anshutz's *A Passing Glance* (ca. 1907, Private Collection), which depicts a woman looking at her reflection in a mirror, is reminiscent of John White Alexander's *The Mirror* (ca.1896, location unknown), which had been shown at the PAFA's Annual in 1897, and Julian Alden Weir's *The Green Bodice* (ca. 1898, The Metropolitan Museum of Art).

86. Rebecca Whelan also posed for *The Tanagra* (1908, PAFA), *A Bird* (ca. 1908), *The Iris* (ca. 1908, location unknown), *Portrait of Rebecca Whelan* (ca. 1910, location unknown), and *The Spangled Gown* (ca. 1905, location unknown). See Helen W. Henderson, "Art World Feels Loss of Anshutz," *Philadelphia Inquirer*, 18 June 1912.

87. See "Latest News of Art and Artists," *The Philadelphia Inquirer*, 2 February 1908 and *The International Studio*, 34 (April 1908): 16, cited in *American Paintings from the Collection of James H. Ricau* (New York: Richard York Gallery, 1993). Anshutz's portraiture was also discussed in *Vogue*, "American Portrait Painters of Today."

88. *New York Evening Post*, 4 November 1909.

89. Why Anshutz gave *Figure Piece*, formerly titled *The Wave*, to the NAD is not known. *A Breaker*, by Anshutz, was exhibited at the NAD and the PAFA in 1908 and may have been this same painting. Concerning *Figure Piece*, Anshutz wrote in 1911 to Miss M. A. Nicholas, Assistant Librarian of the NAD, "The picture of mine that you want a title for was called in your exhibition *The Wave*. But, as that seems rather far fetched, call it a figure piece." Anshutz to Miss M.A. Nicholas, 29 March 1911, Archives of the NAD, New York.

90. During the last decade of his life, Anshutz began to explore other types of painting. As examples, he produced a watercolor illustrating a Greek myth—which myth is not known—titled *Illustration: Classical Drama* (ca. 1905, Private Collection); a watercolor titled *Illustration: Rip Van Winkle* (ca. 1905, Collection of the Hon. Joseph P. Carroll and Mrs. Carroll, New York); a Symbolist-like picture titled *Study* (ca. 1910, location unknown), which shows a woman standing in a landscape, backed by a huge conch shell; and a preparatory pencil sketch (1909, PAFA) for a never-completed mural project for the School of Industrial Arts, Trenton, NJ. For more information on this mural project, see Bowman, "Thomas Pollock Anshutz," 76-77.

91. By the end of his life he belonged to the Société Internationale des Beaux-Arts et Belles-Lettres, the Philadelphia Watercolor Club, the Philadelphia Sketch Club, the NAD, and the New York Watercolor Club. He was also first vice-president of the PAFA Fellowship. See "Art World Mourns Thomas P. Anshutz," *Evening Telegraph*, Philadelphia, 17 June 1912.

92. See "Thos. P. Anshutz, Noted Artist, Dies." The last picture Anshutz completed prior to his death was titled *Portrait* and was exhibited at the Philadelphia Watercolor Club in 1912. See Henderson, "Art World Feels Loss."

93. Anshutz died at 11:00 A.M., 16 June and was buried at Hillside Cemetery on 18 June. According to Helen Henderson, "hundreds of his students" came to the funeral. See Henderson, "Art World Feels Loss" and "Art World Mourns Thomas P. Anshutz."

Chapter 3

1. Cournos, "A Maker of Painters." For a more detailed discussion of Anshutz's teaching career, see Griffin, "Thomas Anshutz," chapter 4.

2. Anonymous editorial, *Philadelphia Inquirer*, 18 June 1912.

3. Elizabeth C. Bower to Sandra Denney, 13 October 1968, Collection of Sandra Denney, Wilmington, DE. See also Cournos, "A Great Art Instructor." Anshutz felt that dissection would make the student lose sight of dominant forms of the body.

4. Goodrich, *Thomas Eakins*, 1: 188-89. See also Homer, *Thomas Eakins*, 190. Anshutz had learned this technique from Eakins.

5. Brownell, "The Art Schools," 741; cited in Chamberlin-Hellman, "Thomas Eakins as a Teacher," 149.

6. Robert Henri Diary, 27 November 1886, microfilm roll 885, AAA, Washington, DC.

7. Homer, *Thomas Eakins*, 159. See also Sellin, *Thomas Eakins*, 25. For Anshutz's earliest reference to wax modeling, see the painter's sketchbooks in the collection of the PAFA. One page includes a recipe for making wax.

8. Homer, *Thomas Eakins*, 161, 165; and Sellin, "Eakins and the Macdowells," 24.

9. See Charles Bregler, "Thomas Eakins as a Teacher," *Arts* 17 (March 1931): 383-84; cited in Homer, *Thomas Eakins,* 165. For Anshutz, see Elizabeth C. Bower to Sandra Denney, 13 October 1968, Collection of Sandra Denney, Wilmington, DE and Anshutz to J. Laurie Wallace, 7 April 1884, Archives of the PAFA, Philadelphia.

10. Homer, *Thomas Eakins,* 161.

11. Anshutz to J. Laurie Wallace, 7 April 1884, Philadelphia Museum of Art Archives.

12. Ibid.

13. Robert Henri Diary, 17 February 1887, microfilm roll 885, AAA, Washington, DC.

14. Hunt, *Talks on Art,* 61-62. For a discussion of memory drawing in France, see Petra ten-Doesschate Chu, "Lecoq de Boisbaudran and Memory Drawing: A Teaching Course between Idealism and Naturalism," in *The European Realist Tradition,* ed. Gabriel P. Weisberg (Bloomington, IN: Indiana University Press, 1982), 242-89.

15. Robert Henri Diary, 20 March 1887, microfilm roll 885, AAA, Washington, DC.

16. Eakins, quoted in Lloyd Goodrich, *Thomas Eakins, His Life and Work* (New York: Whitney Museum of Art, 1933), 25. See also Homer, *Thomas Eakins,* 161-62.

17. Anshutz to John E. D. Trask, undated, Archives of the PAFA, Philadelphia.

18. Anshutz to J. Laurie Wallace, ca. 1883, Philadelphia Museum of Art Archives.

19. Eakins to his father, 29 October 1868, Archives of the PAFA, Philadelphia, cited in Foster and Leibold, *Writing about Eakins,* 208. Also see Anshutz to Edward Hornor Coates, 15 May 1893, microfilm roll 140, AAA, Washington, DC.

20. Anshutz to J. Laurie Wallace, 4 November 1885, Philadelphia Museum of Art Archives.

21. Anshutz to J. Laurie Wallace, 7 April 1884, Philadelphia Museum of Art Archives; cited in Homer, *Thomas Eakins,* 174.

22. Ibid., 163, 171, 173-75.

23. Ibid., 174-75. Members of the Sketch Club drew Whistlerian sketches and produced etchings.

24. See Foster and Leibold, *Writing about Eakins,* 75. Eakins also produced photographs of nude female students. See ibid., 77.

25. See Homer, *Thomas Eakins,* 175-79.

26. See Archives of the PAFA, Philadelphia. According to David Sellin, the letter was written by Frank Stephens. See Sellin, "Eakins and the Macdowells," 36.

27. See Chamberlin-Hellman, "Thomas Eakins as a Teacher," 351, 353.

28. For a discussion of American attitudes concerning the nude, see Robert Oliver Mellown, "Nineteenth-Century American Attitudes Towards the Nude Figure in Art," Ph.D. diss., The University of North Carolina at Chapel Hill, 1975, 163-67.

29. See "The Fiery Art Students," *North American,* 18 February 1886.

30. "Professor Eakins Resigns," *Philadelphia Evening Bulletin,* 15 February 1886, 6, cited in Chamberlin-Hellman, "Thomas Eakins as a Teacher," 360.

31. Chamberlin-Hellman, "Thomas Eakins as a Teacher," 312, 314-16.

32. Ibid., 358, 368. Anshutz and a fellow teacher, James P. Kelly were awarded salaries of $50.00 a month.

33. Throughout his career Anshutz probably played relatively little role in shaping the PAFA's educational policies. It was the Board of Directors that made it more difficult for students to advance from cast to life drawing class, a policy Anshutz wanted to change, but which was only liberalized during Chase's tenure; the Board, too, eliminated dissection classes while Anshutz was in Paris in 1892-93; and it was the Board that eliminated perspective classes as a requirement in 1899.

34. Anshutz to Edward Hornor Coates, 15 May 1893, microfilm roll 140, AAA, Washington, DC.

35. Ibid.

36. Ibid.

37. Cournos, "A Maker of Painters." See also, "American Portrait Painters of Today."

38. John Sloan's notes, 262, Delaware Art Museum, Wilmington, DE; cited in Elizabeth H. Hawkes, *American Painting and Sculpture: Delaware Art Museum* (Wilmington, DE: Delaware Art Museum, 1975), 78.

39. Sloan, *John Sloan's New York,* 621.

40. See Cournos, "A Maker of Painters."

41. Henri felt greater respect for Eakins' paintings than Anshutz's; he rarely mentioned Anshutz's work in descriptions of PAFA exhibitions. One of Henri's few mentions in writing of Anshutz's art is from 1886, when Henri was one of Anshutz's students: "I had never before seen or heard of a picture by Anshutz. Was anxious to see one and would have been favorably impressed with a good work. I like Anshutz as a teacher and expected something good of him. I did not like his picture." See Robert Henri Diary, 5 December 1886, microfilm roll 885, AAA, Washington, DC.

42. The only exception to this is *The Ironworkers' Noontime.*

43. Sloan, Luks, Glackens, Shinn, and Henri looked mainly for inspiration to the painting of Hals, Manet, and Velázquez; the cartoons of Daumier, Leech, and Keene; and the prints of Goya and Hogarth. The training many of them received in newspaper illustration also had an impact on their imagery. Henri had been a key influence, in the 1890s, on the work of Sloan and Shinn.

44. Robert Henri Diary, 20 March 1887, microfilm roll 885, AAA, Washington, DC.

45. Cournos, "A Maker of Painters." See also Ziegler, "An Unassuming Painter." Ziegler wrote, "Mr. Anshutz's art is strictly American."

46. Cited in Goodrich, *Thomas Eakins: His Life and Work,* 40-42.

47. For a discussion of Eakins' ideas concerning American art students abroad, see Homer, *Thomas Eakins,* 249.

48. Cournos, "A Great Art Instructor."

49. Sloan frequently mentions Anshutz in his correspondence during this period. See John Sloan's notes, 262, Delaware Art Museum; cited in Hawkes, *American Painting and Sculpture,* 78. At Fort Washington, sometimes "until dawn," Anshutz discussed art with Henri, Sloan, and Luks. See Henderson, *Memorial Exhibition of the Work of Thomas Anshutz.*

50. Sloan, *John Sloan's New York*, 333.

51. For Sloan's discussion of his etching *Anshutz on Anatomy,* see ibid., 606: "I've got a right good portrait of (memory) Tommy Anshutz." The only dates I have found for Anshutz's New York anatomy lessons are 12 January 1906 for the first lecture and 17 February 1906 for the fifth one. See Robert Henri Diary, 17 February 1906, microfilm roll 886, AAA, Washington, DC.

52. John Sloan's notes, 262, Delaware Art Museum; cited in Hawkes, *American Painting and Sculpture,* 78.

53. Henri to Mrs. Marjorie Henri, 6 July 1912, Robert Henri Materials, Beinecke Rare Book and Manuscript Library, Yale University, New Haven, CT.

54. Henri wrote that Anshutz had a "rationalistic influence" on him. See William Innes Homer, *Robert Henri and His Circle* (New York: Cornell University Press, 1969), 30, 120.

55. Nathaniel Pousette-Dart to William Innes Homer, 19 July 1964, Collection of William Innes Homer, Wilmington, DE.

56. Robert Henri Diary, 27 May 1890, microfilm roll 885, AAA, Washington, DC.

57. Ibid., 31 December 1886 and 8 January 1887.

58. Robert Henri Diary, 25 September 1910, microfilm roll 886, AAA, Washington, DC. Henri later stated, "In considering lines as a means of drawing, it is well to remember that the *line* practically does not exist in nature." See Henri, *The Art Spirit,* 113.

59. Henri, *The Art Spirit,* 27-28. Sloan also recommended memory exercises in his classes. See John Sloan, *The Gist of Art: Principles and Practice Expounded in the Classroom and Studio by John Sloan,* ed. Helen Farr Sloan (New York: Dover Publications, Inc., 1977), xxi, 2, 16, 17.

60. Henri, *The Art Spirit,* 139. For other Henri comments about the importance

of individuality, see pp. 93, 115, 129, 132, 135, 139. John Sloan felt the same way. See Sloan, *Gist of Art,* 5. As far as teaching, perhaps the most pronounced difference between Henri and Anshutz was his complete rejection of cast drawing classes. No class in cast drawing was ever offered at Henri's New York City school.

61. Anshutz was the only teacher John Marin later praised. See Sheldon Reich, *John Marin: A Stylistic Analysis and Catalogue Raisonné* (Tucson, AZ: The University of Arizona Press, 1970), 8. Also see E. M. Benson, *John Marin: The Man and His Work* (Washington, DC, 1935), 24. Charles Demuth liked Anshutz's teaching as well, and was, according to Barbara Haskell, influenced by his instructor's emphasis on observation. See Barbara Haskell, *Charles Demuth* (New York: Whitney Museum of Art, 1987), 17.

62. Jeannette Hope Saÿen wrote that Saÿen "admired Matisse immensely. I really think he had the greatest influence on his art." See Lyman Saÿen Papers, "Blossoms of Liberty," 35, AAA, Washington, DC.

63. Cournos, "A Maker of Painters."

64. Ibid.

65. Ibid.

66. Cournos, "A Great Art Instructor." See also Henderson, "Art World Feels Loss."

67. John Cournos to William Innes Homer, 17 June 1963, Collection of William Innes Homer, Wilmington, DE.

68. Denney, "Thomas Anshutz," 69. This technique of smudging charcoal was considered unorthodox.

69. Aimée E. Ortlip to Sandra Denney, undated, Collection of Sandra Denney, Wilmington, DE.

70. "Thomas P. Anshutz—Brief Account of His Summer Art School." The critic's remarks offer insight into the frequent intersection of artistic style with the construction of gender. Unorthodox, bold, and idiosyncratic painting was thought inherently "masculine" and virile, something not normally associated with a woman artist. In January 1906, John Sloan commented that Edwin Swift Clymer, one of Anshutz's students, was "after the full 'shock' of color and sunlight" in his landscapes. See Sloan, *John Sloan's New York,* 9.

71. Wilford W. Scott, "The Artistic Vanguard in Philadelphia, 1905-1920," Ph.D. diss., University of Delaware, 1983, 62; Wolanin, "Arthur B. Carles, 18; Ronald G. Pisano, "The Teaching Career of William Merritt Chase," *American Artist* 40 (March 1976): 64; and Katherine Metcalf Roof, *The Life and Art of William Merritt Chase* (New York, 1917), 179.

72. See Scott, "The Artistic Vanguard," 64.

73. "Thos. P. Anshutz, Noted Artist, Dies."

Bibliography

Archival Materials

New Haven, CT. Yale University. Beinecke Rare Book and Manuscript Library: Robert Henri Materials.

New York. Collection of Ruth Bowman: Thomas Anshutz archival materials.

New York. James Graham & Sons Gallery: Thomas Anshutz file.

New York. National Academy of Design Archives: Thomas Anshutz file.

Philadelphia. Pennsylvania Academy of the Fine Arts Archives: Alexander Stirling Calder Manuscript, Thomas Anshutz file, Hugh Breckenridge file, Minutes of the Board of Managers, Minutes of the Committee on Instruction, Board of Directors Annual Reports, Student Records, and Exhibition Records.

Philadelphia. Philadelphia Museum of Art Archives: Thomas Anshutz's letters to J. Laurie Wallace.

Philadelphia. Philadelphia Sketch Club: Annual Reports, Sidney Lomas, "History of the Sketch Club."

Washington, DC. Archives of American Art: Thomas Anshutz Papers, Lyman Saÿen Papers, Julius T. Bloch Papers, Robert Henri Papers, Hugh Breckenridge Papers, Sidney Lomas, "History of the Sketch Club."

Washington, DC. Hirshhorn Museum and Sculpture Garden Archives: Thomas Anshutz file.

Washington, DC. National Gallery of Art Photographic Archive: Victor Spark materials.

Washington, DC. National Museum of American Art: Index of American Painting.

Wilmington, DE. Collection of William Innes Homer: Thomas Anshutz archival materials.

Wilmington, DE. Delaware Art Museum: John Sloan Notes.

Books, Theses, and Dissertations

Abrams, Ann Uhry. "Catalyst for Change: American Art and Revolution, 1906-15." Ph.D. diss., Emory University, 1975.

Adams, Henry, et al. *American Drawings and Watercolors in the Museum of Art, Carnegie Institute*. Pittsburgh: University of Pittsburgh Press, 1985.

Allen, Frederick Lewis. *The Big Change: America Transforms Itself, 1900-1950*. New York: Harper & Row, 1964.

American Paintings V. New York: Berry-Hill Galleries, Inc., 1988.

American Paintings from the Collection of James H. Ricau. New York: Richard York Gallery, 1993.

American Paradise: The World of the Hudson River School. New York: The Metropolitan Museum of Art, 1987.

Banham, Reyner. *Theory and Design in the First Machine Age*. 2nd ed. Cambridge, MA: MIT Press, 1980.

Barnes, Lisa Tremper. *A Passion for Art: Selections from the Berman Collection*. Collegeville, PA: Philip and Muriel Berman Museum of Art, 1989.

Beaux, Cecilia. *Background with Figures*. Boston: Houghton Mifflin Company, 1930.

Benson, E. M. *John Marin: The Man and His Work*. Washington, DC: 1935.

Bermingham, Peter. *American Art in the Barbizon Mood*. Washington, DC: National Collection of Fine Arts, Smithsonian Institution Press, 1975.

Bizardel, Yvon. *American Painters in Paris*. Translated by Richard Howard. New York: The MacMillan Co., 1960.

Boime, Albert. *The Academy and French Painting in the Nineteenth Century*. New Haven, CT and London: Yale University Press, 1971.

Bolger, Doreen, et al. *American Pastels in the Metropolitan Museum of Art*. New York: Harry N. Abrams, Inc., 1989.

Boone, Joseph A., and Michael Cadden. *Engendering Men: The Question of Male Feminist Criticism*. New York: Routledge, 1990.

Bowman, Ruth. "Thomas Pollock Anshutz." M.A. thesis, Institute of Fine Arts, New York University, 1971.

Boyle, Richard J. *American Impressionism*. Boston: New York Graphic Society, 1974.

Breeskin, Adelyn D. H. *Lyman Saÿen*. Washington, DC: National Collection of Fine Arts, 1970.

———. *Pennsylvania Academy Moderns, 1910-1940*. Washington, DC: National Collection of Fine Arts, 1975.

Brooks, Van Wyck. *John Sloan: A Painter's Life*. New York: 1955.

Brown, Milton W. *The Modern Spirit: American Painting, 1908-1935*. London: Arts Council of Great Britain, 1977.

———. *The Story of the Armory Show*. Greenwich, CT: New York Graphic Society for the Joseph H. Hirshhorn Foundation, 1963.

Burke, Doreen Bolger et al. *American Paintings: A Catalogue of the Collection.* Vol. 3: *A Catalogue of Painters Born between 1846 and 1864.* New York: The Metropolitan Museum of Art, 1980.

Carr, Carolyn Kinder, and George Gurney. *Revisiting the White City: American Art at the 1893 World's Fair.* Washington, DC: National Museum of American Art and National Portrait Gallery, Smithsonian Institution, 1993.

Cashman, Sean Dennis. *America in the Gilded Age: From the Death of Lincoln to the Rise of Theodore Roosevelt.* New York: New York University Press, 1984.

Chadbourne, Janice H.; Karl Gabosh; and Charles O. Vogel, eds. *The Boston Art Club: Exhibition Record, 1873-1909.* New York: Sound View Press, 1991.

Chamberlin-Hellman, Maria. "Thomas Eakins as a Teacher." Ph.D. diss., Columbia University, 1981.

Chu, Petra ten-Doesschate. "Lecoq de Boisbaudran and Memory Drawing: A Teaching Course between Idealism and Naturalism." In *The European Realist Tradition.* Edited by Gabriel P. Weisberg. Bloomington, IN: Indiana University Press, 1982.

Clark, Eliot. *History of the National Academy of Design 1825-1953.* New York: Columbia University Press, 1954.

Clark, T. J. *Image of the People: Gustave Courbet and the 1848 Revolution.* Princeton, NJ: Princeton University Press, 1973.

Clarke Collection Sale Catalogue. New York, 1899.

Coke, Van Deren. *The Painter and the Photograph.* Albuquerque, NM: University of New Mexico Press, 1964.

Corcoran Gallery. *Of Time and Place: American Figurative Art from the Corcoran Gallery.* Washington, DC: Smithsonian Institution, 1981.

Corn, Wanda M. *The Color of Mood: American Tonalism, 1880-1910.* San Francisco, CA: M.H. de Young Memorial Museum, and California Palace of the Legion of Honor, 1972.

________ and John Wilmerding. "The United States." In *Post-Impressionism: Cross-Currents in European and American Painting, 1880-1906,* 219-40. Washington, DC: National Gallery of Art, 1980.

Curry, David Park. Winslow Homer: *The Croquet Game.* New Haven, CT: Yale University Art Gallery, 1984.

Davidson, Abraham. *Early American Modernist Painting, 1910-1935.* New York: Harper & Row, 1981.

Davidson, Marshall. *Life in America.* Boston: Houghton Mifflin Company, 1951.

Denney, Sandra Lee. "Thomas Anshutz: His Life, Art, and Teaching." M.A. thesis, University of Delaware, 1969.

________. *Thomas P. Anshutz, 1851-1912.* Philadelphia: Pennsylvania Academy of the Fine Arts, 1973.

d'Harnoncourt, Anne. *Philadelphia: Three Centuries of American Art.* Philadelphia: Philadelphia Museum of Art, 1976.

Dickerson, Scott Henry. *Iron & Steel in Wheeling.* Toledo, OH: Carlson Co., 1929.

Dickson, Harold E. *Pennsylvania Painters—Centennial Exhibition Commemorating the 100th Anniversary of the Pennsylvania State University.* Mineral Industries Gallery, University Park, PA, October 7-November 6, 1955.

Doezema, Marianne. *American Realism and the Industrial Age.* Cleveland, OH: Cleveland Museum of Art, 1980.

Dubbert, Joe L. *A Man's Place: Masculinity in Transition.* Englewood Cliffs, NJ: Prentice-Hall, 1979.

Falk, Peter Hastings, ed. *The Annual Exhibition Record of The Art Institute of Chicago, 1888-1950.* New York: Sound View Press, 1990.

________, ed. *The Annual Exhibition Record of the National Academy of Design, 1901-1950.* New York: Sound View Press, 1990.

________, ed. *The Annual Exhibition Record of the Pennsylvania Academy of the Fine Arts, 1876-1913.* New York: Sound View Press, 1989.

Farnham, Emily. *Charles Demuth: Behind a Laughing Mask.* Norman, OK: University of Oklahoma Press, 1971.

Fink, Lois Marie. *American Art at the Nineteenth-Century Paris Salons.* Washington, DC: National Museum of American Art, Smithsonian Institution; Cambridge University Press, 1990.

Foster, Kathleen A., and Leibold Cheryl. *Writing about Eakins: The Manuscripts in Charles Bregler's Thomas Eakins Collection.* Philadelphia: University of Pennsylvania Press, 1989.

Four Americans in Paris: The Collection of Gertrude Stein and Her Family. New York: Museum of Modern Art, 1970.

Frank E. Schoonover at Drexel: Illustration and the Academic Tradition, 1892-1903. Philadelphia: Drexel University Museum. 1986.

Fried, Michael. *Realism, Writing, Disfiguration on Thomas Eakins and Stephen Crane.* Chicago: The University of Chicago Press, 1987.

Goodrich, Lloyd. *Thomas Eakins, His Life and Work.* New York: Whitney Museum of American Art, 1933.

________. *Thomas Eakins.* 2 vols. Cambridge, MA: Harvard University Press, 1982.

________. *Winslow Homer.* New York: The MacMillan Co. for Whitney Museum of American Art, 1944.

Gordon, Donald. *Modern Art Exhibitions: 1900-1916.* 2 vols. Munich: Prestel, 1974.

Green, Harvey. *Fit for American: Health, Fitness, Sport, and American Society.* New York: Pantheon Books, 1986.

Gyllenhaal, Martha, et al. *New Light: Ten Artists Inspired by Emanuel Swedenborg.* Bryn Athyn, PA: Glencairn Museum, Academy of the New Church, 1988.

Halperin, David M. *One Hundred Years of Homosexuality and Other Essays on Greek Love.* New York: Routledge, 1990.

Handy, Elizabeth Armstrong. "H. G. Maratta's Color Theory and Its Influence on the Painters—Robert Henri, John Sloan, and George Bellows." M.A. thesis, University of Delaware, 1969.

Haskell, Barbara. *Charles Demuth.* New York: Whitney Museum of American Art, 1988.

Hawkes, Elizabeth H. *American Painting and Sculpture: Delaware Art Museum.* Wilmington, DE: Delaware Art Museum, 1975.

Henderson, Helen W. *Memorial Exhibition of the Work of Thomas Anshutz.* Philadelphia: Philadelphia Art Alliance, October 6-November 1, 1942.

———. *The Pennsylvania Academy of the Fine Arts.* Boston: L. C. Page and Co., 1911.

Hendricks, Gordon. *The Life and Work of Thomas Eakins.* New York: Grossman Publishers, 1974.

———. *The Photographs of Thomas Eakins.* New York: Grossman Publications, 1972.

Henri, Robert. *The Art Spirit.* Philadelphia and New York: J. B. Lippincott Co., 1939.

Hess, Thomas B., and Ashberry, John, eds. *Art News Journal: The Academy.* New York: The Macmillan Co., 1967.

Hills, Patricia. *The Painters' America: Rural and Urban Life, 1810-1910.* New York: Praeger Publications, 1974.

Hind, C. Lewis. *The Post-Impressionists.* London: Yale University Press, 1984.

Homer, William Innes. *Alfred Stieglitz and the American Avant-Garde.* Boston: New York Graphic Society, 1977.

———. *Avant-Garde Painting and Sculpture in America, 1910-1924.* Wilmington, DE: Delaware Art Museum, 1975.

———. "New Light on Thomas Eakins and Walt Whitman in Camden." In *Walt Whitman and the Visual Arts,* eds. Geoffrey M. Sill and Roberta K. Tarbell. New Brunswick, NJ: Rutgers University Press, 1992.

———. *Robert Henri and His Circle.* Ithaca, NY: Cornell University Press, 1969.

———. *Seurat and the Science of Painting.* Cambridge, MA: M.I.T. Press, 1964.

———. *Thomas Eakins: His Life and Art.* New York: Abbeville Press Publishers, 1992.

———, ed. *Eakins at Avondale and Thomas Eakins: A Personal Collection.* Foreword by James H. Duff. Chadds Ford, PA: Brandywine River Museum, 1980.

Hoopes, Donelson F. *Eakins Watercolors.* New York: Watson-Guptill Publications, 1971.

Hughes, Thomas. *The Manliness of Christ.* London: MacMillan and Co., 1880.

Hulten, Pontus K. G. *The Machine.* New York: Museum of Modern Art, 1968.

Hunt, William Morris. *Talks on Art.* Compiled by H. M. Knowlton. Boston: Houghton Mifflin Company, 1875.

Hunter, Louis C. *Steamboats on the Western Rivers: An Economic and Technological History.* Cambridge, MA: Harvard University Press, 1949.

In This Academy: The Pennsylvania Academy of the Fine Arts, 1805-1976. Philadelphia: Pennsylvania Academy of the Fine Arts, 1976.

Johns, Elizabeth. *Thomas Eakins: The Heroism of Modern Life.* Princeton, NJ: Princeton University Press, 1982.

Joyce, Patrick, ed. *The Historical Meanings of Work.* Cambridge: Cambridge University Press, 1987.

Kirven, Robert H. *Christian Living in the Swedenborgian Perspective.* Philadelphia: New Church Book Center, 1963.

Klingender, Francis D. *Art and the Industrial Revolution.* Edited and Revised by Arthur Elton. London: Evelyn, Adams & Mackay, 1968.

La Farge, John. *The Higher Life in Art.* New York: The McClure Company, 1908.

Larkin, Oliver W. *Art and Life in America.* New York: Doubleday & Co., 1949.

Lears, T. J. Jackson. *No Place of Grace: Antimodernism and the Transformation of American Culture 1880-1920.* New York: Pantheon Books, 1981.

Leff, Sandra. *Thomas Anshutz: Paintings, Watercolors and Pastels.* New York: James Graham & Sons Gallery, 1979.

Leverenz, David. *Manhood and the American Renaissance.* Ithaca, NY: Cornell University Press, 1989.

Levin, Gail. *Synchromism and American Color Abstraction 1910-1925.* New York: Whitney Museum of American Art and George Braziller, 1978.

Lindquist-Cock, Elizabeth. *The Influence of Photography on American Landscape Painting, 1839-1980.* New York: Garland Publishing, 1977.

Marx, Leo. *The Machine in the Garden: Technology and the Pastoral Ideal in America.* New York: Oxford University Press, 1941.

Mathey, François. *The Impressionists.* Translated by Jean Steinberg. New York: Frederick A. Praeger, Inc., 1967.

Matthiessen, F. O. *American Renaissance: Art and Expression in the Age of Emerson and Whitman.* Oxford: Oxford University Press, 1941.

McCoubrey, John W. *American Art, 1700-1960: Sources and Documents in the History of Art.* Englewood Cliffs, NJ: Prentice-Hall, 1965.

McElroy, Guy C. *Facing History: The Black Image in American Art, 1740-1940.* Washington, DC: Corcoran Gallery of Art, 1990.

McHenry, Margaret. *Thomas Eakins Who Painted.* By the Author, 1946.

Milroy, Elizabeth Lamotte Cates. "Thomas Eakins' Artistic Training, 1860-1870." Ph.D. diss., University of Pennsylvania, 1986.

Moffatt, Frederick C. *Arthur Wesley Dow (1857-1922).* Washington, DC: Smithsonian Institution Press, 1977.

Montgomery, David. *The Fall of the House of Labor: The Workplace, the State, and American Labor Activisim, 1865-1925.* Cambridge: Cambridge University Press, 1987.

Moore, George. *Impressions and Opinions.* New York: Charles Scribner's Sons, 1891.

Morgan, Wayne H., ed. *The Letters of Kenyon Cox, 1877-1882.* Kent, OH: Kent State University Press, 1989.

———. *New Muses: Art in American Culture, 1865-1920.* Norman, OK: University of Oklahoma Press, 1978.

Morrin, Peter, Judith Zilczer, et al. *The Advent of Modernism: Post-Impressionism and North American Art, 1900-1918.* Atlanta, GA: High Museum of Art, 1986.

Mourey, Gabriel. *Albert Besnard.* Paris, n.d.

Mumford, Lewis. *The Brown Decades: A Study of the Arts in America, 1865-1895.* New York: Harcourt, Brace, and Company, 1931.

Nochlin, Linda. *Realism.* New York: Penguin Books, 1971.

Novak, Barbara. *American Painting of the Nineteenth Century.* New York: Praeger Publishers, 1969.

Nygren, Edward J., and Peter C. Marzio. *Of Time and Place: American Figurative Art from the Corcoran Gallery.* Washington, DC: Smithsonian Institution Traveling Exhibition Service and the Corcoran Gallery of Art, 1981.

Onorato, Ronald J. "The Pennsylvania Academy of the Fine Arts and the Development of an Academic Curriculum in the Nineteenth Century." Ph.D. diss., Brown University, 1977.

Paint and Painting: An Exhibition and Working Studio Sponsored by Windsor and Newton to Celebrate their 150th Anniversary. London: Tate Gallery, 1982.

Peck, George. *Formation of a Manly Character: A Series of Lectures to Young Men.* New York: Carlton & Phillips, 1853.

Perlman, Bennard B. *Painters of the Ashcan School: The Immortal Eight.* New York: Dover Publications, Inc., 1962.

The Philadelphia Sketch Club in Its Ninetieth Year, 1950. Pamphlet in Sketch Club Library, Philadelphia.

Pisano, Ronald G. *William Merritt Chase.* New York: M. Knoedler & Co., 1976.

Porter, Fairfield. *Thomas Eakins.* New York: George Braziller, Inc., 1959.

Reich, Sheldon. *John Marin: A Stylistic Analysis and Catalogue Raisonné,* vol. 1. Tucson, AZ: The University of Arizona Press, 1970.

Richardson, E.P. *American Art: An Exhibition from the Collection of Mr. and Mrs. John D. Rockefeller 3rd.* San Francisco, CA: M.H. de Young Memorial Museum, 1976.

Rodgers, Daniel T. *The Work Ethic in Industrial America, 1850-1920.* Chicago: The University of Chicago Press, 1978.

Rosenblum, Robert. *Modern Painting and the Northern Romantic Tradition: Friedrich to Rothko.* New York: Harper & Row, 1975.

Rosenzweig, Phyllis D. *The Thomas Eakins Collection of the Hirshhorn Museum and Sculpture Garden.* Washington, DC: Smithsonian Institution Press, 1977.

Saldern, Axel von. *Triumph of Realism—An Exhibition of European and American Realist Paintings, 1850-1910.* Brooklyn, NY: Brooklyn Museum, 1967.

Savelle, Max. *A Short History of American Civilization.* New York: The Dryden Press, 1957.

Scharf, Aaron. *Art and Photography.* London: Allen Lane, 1968.

Schendler, Sylvan. *Eakins.* Boston: Little, Brown and Company, 1967.

Schnapper, M. B. *American Labor: A Pictorial Social History.* Washington, DC: Public Affairs Press, 1972.

Scott, Wilford W. "The Artistic Vanguard in Philadelphia, 1905-1920." Ph.D. diss., University of Delaware, 1983.

Sears, John F. *Sacred Places: American Tourist Attractions in the Nineteenth Century.* New York and Oxford: Oxford University Press, 1989.

Sellin, David. *The First Pose, 1876: Turning Point in American Art: Howard Roberts, Thomas Eakins, and a Century of Philadelphia Nudes.* New York: W. W. Norton & Company, Inc., 1976.

________. "Eakins and the Macdowells and the Academy." In *Thomas Eakins, Susan Macdowell Eakins, Elizabeth Macdowell Kenton.* Introduction by Betty Tisinger. Roanoke, VA: North Cross School Living Gallery, 1977.

Sheldon, G. W. *American Painters.* London: D. Appleton and Company, 1878.

Siegl, Theodor. *The Thomas Eakins Collection.* Introduction by Evan H. Turner. Philadelphia: Philadelphia Museum of Art, 1978.

Simmons, Edward. *From Seven to Seventy.* New York and London: Harper and Brothers, 1922.

Simpson, Marc, et al. *Eastman Johnston: The Cranberry Harvest, Island of Nantucket.* San Diego, CA: Timken Art Gallery, 1990.

Sloan, John. *The Gist of Art: Principles and Practice Expounded in the Classroom and Studio by John Sloan.* Edited by Helen Farr Sloan. New York: Dover Publications, Inc., 1977.

________. *John Sloan's New York Scene.* Edited by Bruce St. John, with an Introduction by Helen Farr Sloan. New York: Harper and Row, 1965.

Smith, Henry Nash, ed. *Popular Culture and Industrialism, 1865-1890.* New York: Doubleday Anchor Books, 1967.

The Spencer Collection of American Art. New York: Spanierman Gallery, 1990.

Stebbins, Theodore E., Jr. *American Master Drawings and Watercolors: A History of Works on Paper from Colonial Times to the Present.* New York: Harper & Row, 1976.

Swank, James M. *History of the Manufacture of Iron in All Ages, and Particularly in the United States from Colonial Times to 1891.* Philadelphia: The American Iron and Steel Association, 1892.

Tagg, John. *The Burden of Representation: Essays on Photographs and Histories.* Amherst, MA: The University of Massachusetts Press, 1988.

Tashjian, Dickran. *Skyscraper Primitives.* Middleton, CT: Wesleyan University Press, 1975.

Taylor, Joshua. *America as Art.* Washington, DC: Smithsonian Institution Press for the National Collection of Fine Arts, 1976.

Thomas Anshutz Retrospective. New York: James Graham & Sons Gallery, 1963.

Thomas Eakins: His Photographic Works. Philadelphia: Pennsylvania Academy of the Fine Arts, 1969.

Troyen, Carol. *A Private Eye: Fifty Nineteenth-Century American Paintings, Drawings, & Watercolors from the Stebbins Collection.* Huntington, NY: The Heckscher Museum, 1977.

Tsujimoto, Karen. *Images of America: Precisionist Painting*

and Modern Photography. Seattle, WA: University of Washington Press, 1982.
Twain, Mark. *Life on the Mississippi* (1883). New York: Bantam Books, 1988.
Vogel, Margaret. *The Paintings of Hugh H. Breckenridge (1870-1937).* Dallas, TX: Valley House Gallery, 1967.
Webster, Noah. *A Dictionary of the English Language.* Springfield, MA: G. & C. Merriam, 1881.
Weinberg, H. Barbara. *The American Pupils of Jean-Léon Gérôme.* Fort Worth, TX: Amon Carter Museum, 1984.
———. *The Lure of Paris: Nineteenth-Century American Painters and Their French Teachers.* New York: Abbeville Press Publishers, 1991.
Whitman, Walt. *Leaves of Grass.* Brooklyn, NY, 1855.
———. *The Portable Walt Whitman.* Selected and introduced by Mark Van Doren. New York: The Viking Press, 1945.
Wilson, Richard Guy. *The Machine Age in America, 1918-1941.* New York: Brooklyn Museum in Association with Abrams, 1986.
Wolanin, Barbara A. *Arthur B. Carles (1882-1952): Painting with Color.* Philadelphia: Pennsylvania Academy of the Fine Arts, 1983.
———. "Arthur B. Carles, 1882-1952: Philadelphia Modernist." Ph.D. diss., University of Wisconsin-Madison, 1981.
Wunsch, William F. *What Is A Swedenborgian?* Chicago: The Swedenborgian Press, n.d.
Young, Art. *On My Way.* New York: Horace Liveright, 1928.
Young, Dorothy Weir. *The Life and Letters of J. Alden Weir.* New Haven, CT: Yale University Press, 1960.
Zilczer, Judith K. "The Aesthetic Struggle in America, 1913-1918: Abstract Art and Theory in the Stieglitz Circle." Ph.D. diss., University of Delaware, 1975.

Periodicals and Newspapers

Adlow, Dorothy. "Anshutz Rejoins Company of Worthies." *Christian Science Monitor,* 23 February 1963.
"American Portrait Painters of Today—Thomas P. Anshutz." *Vogue* 34 (17 June 1909): 1086.
Anonymous article on the Thomas B. Clarke collection. *Boston Herald,* 28 December 1883.
Anonymous article on the Thomas B. Clarke collection. *New York News,* 30 December 1883.
"Anshutz, Famous Painter Is Dead." *Philadelphia Press,* 17 June 1912.
"Anshutz's 'Tanagra' Given At Academy." *Philadelphia Inquirer,* 21 August 1912.
"Art at the Paris Exhibition." *Scribner's Monthly*, December 1878, 280.
"Art Debits and Credits—Lambert Lincolniana." *Quaker City Crier,* Minneapolis, MN, 29 June 1912.
"Art World Feels Loss of Anshutz." *Philadelphia Inquirer,* 18 June 1912.
"Art World Mourns Thomas P. Anshutz." *Evening Telegraph,* Philadelphia, 17 June 1912
"Artist Anshutz Honored." *Philadelphia Ledger,* 3 May 1895.
Banks, Marissa; Lorraine Glennon; and Jeffery Schaire. "The 25 Most Undervalued American Artists." *Art & Antiques* 3 (October 1986): 63-79.
Bartlett, T. H. "Walter Shirlaw." *The American Art Review* 2 (1881): 148.
Benjamin, G. W. "Tendencies of Art in America." *The American Art Review* 1 (1880): 196-202.
Binyon, Laurence. "Post-Impressionists." *Saturday Review* 110 (1910): 609-10.
Bowman, Ruth. "The Artist as Model: A Portrait of David Wilson Jordan by Thomas Anshutz." *The Register of the Spencer Museum of Art* 4 (Fall 1973): 4-34.
———. "Nature, the Photograph and Thomas Anshutz." *Art Journal* 33 (Fall 1973): 32-40.
Bregler, Charles. "Thomas Eakins As a Teacher." *Arts* 17 (March 1931): 378-86.
———. "Thomas Eakins as a Teacher, Second Article." *Arts* 18 (October 1931): 28-42.
Brownell, William C. "The Art Schools of Philadelphia." *Scribner's Monthly* 18 (September 1879): 737-50.
Burgess, Gelett. "The Wild Men of Paris." *Architectural Record* 27 (May 1910): 400-14.
Carpenter, Horace T. "An Art School At Valley Forge." *New York Herald,* 3 September 1905.
Carr, Gerald L. "Hugh Henry Breckenridge (1870-1937)." *The American Art Review* 4 (May 1978): 92-99, 119-22.
Childs, George W. "Thomas Pollock Anshutz." *Public Ledger-Philadelphia Times,* 18 June 1912.
"The City of Pittsburgh." *Harper's New Monthly Magazine* 62 (December 1880): 56-58.
Claypool, James C. "An Unassuming Painter," *The Enquirer Magazine* (4 August 1985): 8-10.
Clutton-Brock. "Post-Impressionists." *Burlington Magazine* 18 (1911): 216.
Cournos, John. "A Great Art Instructor: His Methods and Ideas." *Philadelphia Record,* 29 May 1910.
———. "A Maker of Painters—Thomas P. Anshutz and His Service to American Art." *Boston Evening Transcript,* 10 February 1912.
Davidson, J. O. "Interior of a Southern Cotton Press by Night." *Harper's Weekly* 27 (24 March 1883): 181.
Dinnerstein, Lois. "The Iron Worker and King Solomon: Some Images of Labor in American Art." *Arts Magazine* 54 (September 1979): 112-17.
Goodyear, Frank H., Jr. "Ironworkers: Noontime." *The American Art Review* 1 (January-February 1974): 39-48.
Griffin, Randall C. "Thomas Anshutz's *The Ironworkers' Noontime:* Remythologizing the Industrial Worker." *Smithsonian Studies in American Art* 4 (Fall/Spring 1990): 128-43.
Homer, William Innes. "Eakins, Muybridge and the Motion Picture Process." *Art Quarterly* 26 (Summer 1963): 194-216
"How It Goes." *Wheeling Register,* 17 December 1911.
"In Commemoration." *Art Digest* 17 (15 October 1942): 19.
"In Turkey-Chawed Country." *Time* 81 (22 March 1963): 72.
Katz, Leslie. "The Breakthrough of Anshutz." *Arts Magazine* 37 (March 1963): 26-29.

"Latest News of Art and Artists." *Philadelphia Inquirer,* 9 February 1908.

Les Tendances Nouvelles. Paris: (1906-11).

Lester, William R. "Great Artists Show Works of Distinction." *North American,* Philadelphia, 12 July 1900.

"M'Dougall Joins the Summer Sketching Class at Darby Creek." *North American,* Philadelphia, 21 January 1906.

"Memorial To Thomas Anshutz." *New York Herald Tribune,* 4 October 1942.

"More Fame for the Famous." *Bulletin,* Philadelphia, 17 October 1942.

"New Honor for an American Artist." *Brooklyn Daily Times,* 6 March 1909.

"News of Art and Artists." *Philadelphia Inquirer,* 2 February 1908.

Onorato, Ronald J. "Photography and Teaching: Eakins at the Academy." *The American Art Review* 3 (July-August 1976): 127-40.

Parry, Ellwood C., III. "Thomas Eakins and the Everpresence of Photography." *Arts Magazine* 51 (June 1977): 111-15.

________. "Thomas Eakins's 'Naked Series' Reconsidered: Another Look at the Standing Nude Photographs Made for the Use of Eakins's Students." *American Art Journal* 20 (1988): 53-77.

"Pastel Painting." *Art Amateur* 13 (October 1885): 95.

Patterson, James. "Pittsburgh." *Atlantic Monthly* 21 (January 1868): 33.

Pauley, Thomas H. "American Art and Labor: The Case of Anshutz's *The Ironworkers' Noontime*," *American Quarterly* 40 (September 1988): 333-58.

Peck, Robert McCracken. "Thomas Eakins and Photography: The Means to an End." *Arts Magazine* 53 (May 1979): 113-17.

Pitz, Henry C. "The Turning Wheel." *American Artist,* 28 (March 1964): 23.

"Professor Eakins Resigns." *Philadelphia Press,* 15 February 1886.

"Reviews and Previews—Thomas P. Anshutz." *Art News* 61 (February 1963): 14.

Rogers, Fairman. "The Schools of the Pennsylvania Academy of the Fine Arts." *Penn Monthly* 12 (June 1881): 453-62.

Simpson, Marc. "Thomas Eakins and His Arcadian Works." *Smithsonian Studies in American Art* 1 (Fall 1987): 71-95.

"'Study in Scarlet' by Thomas P. Anshutz." *Daily Evening Telegraph,* Philadelphia, 15 February 1909.

"Thomas P. Anshutz." *Evening Post,* Philadelphia, 17 June 1912.

"Thomas P. Anshutz—Brief Account of His Summer Art School at Historic Valley Forge." *Wheeling Register,* 10 September 1905.

"Thomas P. Anshutz, Noted Artist, Dies." *Philadelphia Inquirer,* 18 June 1912.

Thouron, Henry Joseph. "Correction of an Official Bulletin." *Public Ledger,* 9 February 1913.

"Wealth of New Material Marks Academy's 103rd Annual Exhibition." *Philadelphia Inquirer,* 19 January 1908.

Webster, Sally. "Thomas Anshutz: The Philadelphia Connection." *Arts Magazine* 54 (November 1979): 138-40.

Wilmerding, John. "Walt Whitman and American Painting." *Antiques* 128 (November 1985): 998-1001.

Wilson, Christopher Kent. "Winslow Homer's *The Veteran in a New Field:* A Study of the Harvest Metaphor and Popular Culture." *American Art Journal* 17 (Autumn 1985): 2-27.

Ziegler, Francis J. "An Unassuming Painter—Thomas P. Anshutz." *Brush and Pencil* 4 (September 1899): 277-84.

Interviews

Bowman, Ruth, New York, NY, 25 October 1988.

Bowman, Ruth, New York, NY, 10 May 1989.

Denney, Sandra L., Wilmington, DE, 1 November 1989.

Sloan, Helen Farr, Wilmington, DE, 10 October 1989.

Sloan, Helen Farr, Wilmington, DE, 20 May 1990.

Spark, Victor, New York, NY, 16 February 1990.

*L*ist of Illustrations

Color Plates

Frontispiece
Self-Portrait, ca. 1909
oil on canvas, 30 × 25"
National Academy of Design, New York

1. *The Ironworkers' Noontime*, 1880
oil on canvas, $17\frac{1}{8} \times 24$"
The Fine Arts Museums of San Francisco, Gift of Mr. and Mrs. John D. Rockefeller 3rd, 1979.7.4

2. *The Farmer and His Son at Harvesting*, 1879
oil on canvas, $24\frac{1}{4} \times 17\frac{1}{4}$"
Courtesy Berry-Hill Galleries, Inc., New York

3. *The Way They Live*, 1879
oil on canvas, 24 × 17"
The Metropolitan Museum of Art, Morris K. Jesup Fund, 1940

4. *The Chore*, 1888
oil on canvas, $14\frac{1}{16} \times 9\frac{7}{8}$"
Allentown Art Museum: Gift of J. I. and Anna Rodale, 1961 (61.26)

5. *Steamboat on the Ohio*, ca. 1900-08
oil on canvas, $27\frac{1}{4} \times 48\frac{1}{4}$"
The Carnegie Museum of Art; Patrons Art Fund, 57.36

6. *Factory-Study for The Ironworkers' Noontime*, 1880
oil on paperboard, $8\frac{1}{2} \times 12\frac{7}{8}$"
Hirshhorn Museum and Sculpture Garden, Smithsonian Institution. Gift of Joseph H. Hirshhorn, 1966.

7. *St. Cloud near Paris*, ca. 1893
watercolor on paper, $10\frac{1}{2} \times 8\frac{1}{4}$"
The Hon. Joseph P. Carroll and Mrs. Carroll, New York

8. *North East Weather*, ca. 1893
watercolor on paper, $10\frac{3}{4} \times 14\frac{1}{2}$"
Baker/Pisano Collection

9. *Two Boys by a Boat*, ca. 1894
watercolor on paper, $10 \times 13\frac{3}{8}$"
The Carnegie Museum of Art; Gift of Mrs. Carl Selden, 82.100

10. *Boys Playing with Crabs*, ca. 1894
watercolor on paper, 14 × 20"
Private Collection

11. *Boys by a Fire*, ca. 1894
watercolor on paper, $9\frac{3}{4} \times 13\frac{1}{4}$"
Location unknown

12. *Down the Delaware Bay*, ca. 1897
oil on canvas, 26 × 36"
Location unknown

13. *The Lumber Boat*, ca. 1897
oil on canvas, $16\frac{1}{4}" \times 24\frac{1}{8}$"
Private Collection, Riverhead, New York

14. *On the Delaware at Tacony*, ca. 1897
oil on canvas, $16\frac{1}{8} \times 23\frac{1}{8}$"
The Hon. Joseph P. Carroll and Mrs. Carroll, New York

15. *Steamboat on the Ohio*, ca. 1900
oil on canvas, 10 × 15"
Mr. and Mrs. Richard Waitzer

16. *Landscape*, ca. 1898
oil on board, dimens. unknown
Location unknown

17. *Landscape with Grey Sky*, ca. 1895
oil on board, $7\frac{1}{2} \times 10$"
Collection of Mr. and Mrs. Samuel F. Mirabito

18. *House by a Pond*, ca. 1900-05
watercolor, 7 × 10"
Location unknown

19. *Three Trees by a Stream*, ca.1900-05
watercolor on paper, $13\frac{1}{2} \times 20\frac{1}{4}$"
The Hon. Joseph P. Carroll and Mrs. Carroll, New York

20. *Garden*, ca. 1911
oil on board, $9\frac{1}{2} \times 7\frac{1}{2}$"
The Hon. Joseph P. Carroll and Mrs. Carroll, New York

21. *Landscape*, ca. 1911-12
watercolor on pulpboard, $10\frac{7}{8} \times 12$"
The Pennsylvania Academy of the Fine Arts, Philadelphia. Gift of Mrs. Edward R. Anshutz

22. *Landscape*, ca. 1911-12
oil on board, 8 × 5"
The Hon. Joseph P. Carroll and Mrs. Carroll, New York

23. *Woman in Interior Reading*, ca. 1910
oil on canvas, 16 × 23¼"
Location unknown

24. *Woman Writing at a Table*, ca. 1905
oil on canvas, 16 × 20¼"
Byron Collection

25. *Portrait of Mrs. Anshutz*, 1893
pastel on paper, 26 × 20"
The Pennsylvania Academy of the Fine Arts, Philadelphia. Gift of Mr. and Mrs. James H. Beal

26. *Portrait of Emily Fairchild Pollock*, ca. 1905
oil on canvas, 38 × 29"
The Hon. Joseph P. Carroll and Mrs. Carroll, New York

27. *Portrait of Margaret Perot*, ca. 1908
oil on canvas, 64⅛ × 40"
Hirshhorn Museum and Sculpture Garden, Smithsonian Institution. Gift of Joseph H. Hirshhorn, 1966.

28. *A Rose*, 1908
oil on canvas, 58 × 43⅞"
The Metropolitan Museum of Art, Marguerite and Frank A. Cosgrove, Jr. Fund, 1993 (1993.324)

29. *A Challenge*, ca. 1908
pastel on canvas, 30 × 24"
The Hon. Joseph P. Carroll and Mrs. Carroll, New York, courtesy Berry-Hill Galleries, Inc., New York

30. *Figure Piece*, ca. 1909
oil on canvas, 40 × 36⅛"
National Academy of Design, New York

Black and White Figures

1. *The Dissecting Room*, 1879
oil on canvas on wood, 10 × 12½"
The Pennsylvania Academy of the Fine Arts, Philadelphia. Gift of the Artist

2. John Sloan (1871-1951)
Anshutz on Anatomy, 1912
etching, 8th state, 12¾ × 14½" (sheet)
The Pennsylvania Academy of the Fine Arts, Philadelphia. Gift of Helen Farr Sloan

3. *On the Ohio*, ca. 1880
oil on fabric on composition board, 9 × 13½"
In the Collection of The Corcoran Gallery of Art, Washington, DC, Museum Purchase through the Gift of Joseph Sanders

4. *Rooftop Scene, Philadelphia*, ca. 1883
watercolor, 7 × 11"
Location unknown

5. Winslow Homer (1836-1910)
Crossing the Pasture, ca. 1872
oil on canvas, 26⅛ × 38⅛"
Amon Carter Museum, Fort Worth

6. *A Farmer Plowing*, 1880
oil on canvas, 18¼ × 25¼"
Collection of the Brandywine River Museum

7. John Ferguson Weir (1841-1926)
Forging the Shaft, 1877
oil on canvas, 52 × 73¼"
The Metropolitan Museum of Art, Purchase, Lyman G. Bloomingdale Gift, 1901 (01.7.1)

8. Anonymous artist
Wheeling Iron and Nail Company, 1877
lithograph on paper
Illustration from Henry Dickerson Scott, *Iron and Steel in Wheeling*, 1929

9. *Factory Study*, 1880
Sketchbook #2, graphite on off-white wove leaves, 4¼ × 6½"
The Pennsylvania Academy of the Fine Arts, Philadelphia. Gift of Mr. and Mrs. Daniel W. Dietrich, II

10. Walter Shirlaw (1838-1909)
Emptying the Crucible, 1880
Harper's New Monthly Magazine, December 1880

11. J. Liberty Tadd (dates unknown)
Large Antique Class (#3), 1901
albumen print
The Pennsylvania Academy of the Fine Arts, Philadelphia. Archives

12. J. Liberty Tadd
Large Antique Class (#3) (detail)
albumen print
The Pennsylvania Academy of the Fine Arts, Philadelphia. Archives

13. *The Ironworkers' Noontime* (detail)
oil on canvas, 17⅛ × 24"
The Fine Arts Museums of San Francisco, Gift of Mr. and Mrs. John D. Rockefeller 3rd

14. *Figure Study for The Ironworkers' Noontime*, 1880
Sketchbook #1, graphite on buff wove leaves, 4⁹⁄₁₆ × 7¹³⁄₁₆"
The Pennsylvania Academy of the Fine Arts, Philadelphia. Gift of Mr. and Mrs. Daniel W. Dietrich, II

15. John George Brown (1831-1913)
Longshoremen's Noon, 1879
oil on canvas, 33¼ × 50¼"
In the Collection of The Corcoran Gallery of Art, Washington, DC, Museum Purchase, Gallery Fund

16. Thomas Eakins (1844-1916)
The Biglin Brothers Turning the Stake-Boat, 1873
oil on canvas, 40¼ × 60¼"
The Cleveland Museum of Art, Hinman B. Hurlbut Collection, 1984.27

17. Thomas Eakins
The Swimming Hole, ca. 1883-85
oil on canvas, $27\frac{5}{16} \times 36\frac{5}{16}$"
Purchased by the Friends of Art, Fort Worth Art Association, 1925; acquired by the Amon Carter Museum, 1990, from the Modern Art Museum of Fort Worth through grants and donations from the Amon G. Carter Foundation, the Sid W. Richardson Foundation, the Anne Burnett and Charles Tandy Foundation, Capital Cities/ABC Foundation, Fort Worth Star-Telegram, The R. D. and Joan Dale Hubbard Foundation and the people of Fort Worth.

18. Maxfield Parrish (1870-1966)
The Artist, Sex, Male, 1909
oil on stretched paper, $19\frac{3}{4} \times 16$"
Illustration for *Collier's*, May 1, 1909
Collection of the Brandywine River Museum. The Betsy James Wyeth Fund

19. *Poster by Proctor & Gamble to introduce Ivory Soap*, ca. 1883
lithograph on paper, 100×160"
Collection of The New-York Historical Society

20. *A Studio Study*, ca. 1891
oil on canvas, $22\frac{1}{16} \times 36\frac{1}{8}$"
The Pennsylvania Academy of the Fine Arts, Philadelphia. Bequest of Helen W. Henderson

21. *Nude Model*, ca. 1892-93
charcoal, $24\frac{3}{4} \times 18\frac{3}{4}$"
Location unknown

22. *Cast Drawing with Woman Student Drawing*, ca. 1895
charcoal on paper, $24 \times 18\frac{1}{2}$"
Collection of Mr. and Mrs. Raymond J. Horowitz

23. *Cast Study: Reclining Torso*, ca. 1895
charcoal on paper, $18\frac{3}{4} \times 24\frac{1}{2}$"
The Hon. Joseph P. Carroll and Mrs. Carroll, New York

24. *Cast Drawing of Milo of Croton*, ca. 1895
charcoal, $24\frac{1}{4} \times 18\frac{3}{4}$"
Private Collection

25. *Women by a Boat*, ca. 1893
photograph
Thomas Anshutz Papers, Archives of American Art, Smithsonian Institution

26. *Woman on Beach*, ca. 1894
watercolor on paper, $8\frac{5}{8} \times 12\frac{1}{2}$" (sight)
Yale University Art Gallery, Collection of Mary C. and James W. Fosburgh, B.A. 1933, M.A. 1935.

27. *Two Boys by a Boat*, ca. 1894
photograph
Thomas Anshutz Papers, Archives of American Art, Smithsonian Institution

28. *Thomas Eakins and J. Laurie Wallace*, ca. 1883
photograph
Thomas Anshutz Papers, Archives of American Art, Smithsonian Institution

29. *Two Men by a Boat*, ca. 1897
photograph
Thomas Anshutz papers, Archives of American Art, Smithsonian Institution

30. *Figures by the Ohio River, Wheeling, West Virginia,* ca. 1890
photograph
Thomas Anshutz Papers, Archives of American Art, Smithsonian Institution

31. *Figures by the Ohio River, Wheeling, West Virginia*, ca. 1890
photograph
Thomas Anshutz Papers, Archives of American Art, Smithsonian Institution

32. *Steamboat on the Ohio*, ca. 1897
pastel on paper, $7\frac{1}{4} \times 11\frac{1}{2}$"
Westmoreland Museum of Art, Greensburg, Pennsylvania, Gift of William A. Coulter Fund, 59.73

33. *Landscape with House*, ca. 1895
oil on board, $7\frac{1}{4} \times 9\frac{5}{8}$"
Location unknown

34. *Seated Figure in Landscape*, ca. 1904
watercolor, 7×10"
Location unknown

35. *In a Garret*, 1891
oil on canvas, $10\frac{1}{16} \times 16\frac{1}{16}$"
The Pennsylvania Academy of the Fine Arts, Philadelphia. Gift of pupils of the artist in the Pennsylvania Academy School

36. *Self-Portrait*, ca. 1909
oil on canvas, 30×25"
National Academy of Design, New York

37. Thomas Eakins
The Pathetic Song, 1881
oil on canvas, $45 \times 32\frac{1}{2}$"
In the Collection of The Corcoran Gallery of Art, Washington, DC, Museum Purchase, Gallery Fund

38. *Portrait of Edwin S. Clymer*, ca. 1900
pastel on paper, 48×39"
Courtesy of the Reading Public Museum, Reading, Pennsylvania

39. *The Tanagra*, ca. 1908
oil on canvas, 80×40"
The Pennsylvania Academy of the Fine Arts, Philadelphia. Gift of Friends and Admirers of the Artist

Endplate
Photographer Unknown
Thomas Anshutz, ca. 1885
photograph
Private Collection

Checklist of the Exhibition

The Art of Thomas Anshutz

The Farmer and His Son at Harvesting, 1879
oil on canvas, 24¼ × 17¼"
Courtesy Berry-Hill Galleries, Inc., New York
[Cover, color plate 2]

The Way They Live, 1879
oil on canvas, 24 × 17"
Lent by The Metropolitan Museum of Art, Morris K. Jesup Fund, 1940
[Color plate 3]

Factory Study, 1880
Sketchbook #2, graphite on off-white wove leaves, 4¼ × 6½"
The Pennsylvania Academy of the Fine Arts. Gift of Mr. and Mrs. Daniel W. Dietrich, II
[fig. 9]

Factory-Study for "The Ironworkers' Noontime," 1880
oil on paperboard, 8½ × 12⅞"
Hirshhorn Museum and Sculpture Garden, Smithsonian Institution. Gift of Joseph H. Hirshhorn, 1966.
[Color plate 6]

A Farmer Plowing, 1880
oil on canvas, 18¼ × 25¼"
Collection of the Brandywine River Museum
[fig. 6]

Figure Study for The Ironworkers' Noontime, 1880
Sketchbook #1, graphite on buff wove leaves, 4⁹⁄₁₆ × 7¹³⁄₁₆"
The Pennsylvania Academy of the Fine Arts. Gift of Mr. and Mrs. Daniel W. Dietrich, II
[fig. 14]

The Ironworkers' Noontime, 1880
oil on canvas, 17⅛ × 24"
The Fine Arts Museums of San Francisco, Gift of Mr. and Mrs. John D. Rockefeller 3rd, 1979.7.4
[Color plate 1; detail, fig. 14]

On the Ohio, ca. 1880
oil on fabric on composition board, 9 × 13½"
In the Collection of The Corcoran Gallery of Art, Washington, DC, Museum Purchase through the Gift of Joseph Sanders
[fig. 3]

Cast Study with Students, ca. 1885
charcoal on white laid paper, 24⅜ × 18⅝"
Lent by The Metropolitan Museum of Art, Rogers Fund, 1967

The Chore, 1888
oil on canvas, 14¹⁄₁₆ × 9⅞"
Allentown Art Museum: Gift of J.I. and Anna Rodale, 1961 (61.26)
[Color plate 4]

In a Garret, 1891
oil on canvas, 10¹⁄₁₆ × 16¹⁄₁₆"
The Pennsylvania Academy of the Fine Arts, Philadelphia. Gift of the pupils of the artist in the Pennsylvania Academy School
[fig. 35]

North East Weather, ca. 1893
watercolor on paper, 10¾ × 14½"
Baker/Pisano Collection
[Color plate 8]

St. Cloud near Paris, ca. 1893
watercolor on paper, 10½ × 8¼"
The Hon. Joseph P. Carroll and Mrs. Carroll, New York
[Color plate 7]

Boys Playing with Crabs, ca. 1894
watercolor on paper, 14 × 20"
Private Collection
[Color plate 10]

Woman on Beach, ca. 1894
watercolor on paper, 8⅝ × 12½" (sight)
Yale University Art Gallery, Collection of Mary C. and James W. Fosburgh, B.A. 1933, M.A. 1935.
[fig. 26]

Cast Drawing of Milo of Croton, ca. 1895
charcoal on paper, 24¼ × 18¾"
Private Collection
[fig. 24]

Cast Drawing with Woman Student Drawing, ca. 1895
charcoal on paper, 24 × 18½"
Collection of Mr. and Mrs. Raymond J. Horowitz
[fig. 22]

Cast Study: Reclining Torso, ca. 1895
charcoal on paper, 18¾ × 24½"
The Hon. Joseph P. Carroll and Mrs. Carroll, New York
[fig. 23]

Hunter Seated by Boat with Dog, ca. 1895
watercolor on paper, 9⅞ × 13½"
The Hon. Joseph P. Carroll and Mrs. Carroll, New York

Landscape with Grey Sky, ca. 1895
oil on board, 7½ × 10"
Collection of Mr. and Mrs. Samuel F. Mirabito
[Color plate 17]

The Lumber Boat, ca. 1897
oil on canvas, 16¼ × 24⅛"
Private Collection, Riverhead, New York
[Color plate 13]

On the Delaware at Tacony, ca. 1897
oil on canvas, 16⅛ × 23⅛"
The Hon. Joseph P. Carroll and Mrs. Carroll, New York
[Color plate 14]

Steamboat on the Ohio, ca. 1897
pastel on paper, 7¼ × 11½"
Westmoreland Museum of Art, Greensburg, Pennsylvania, Gift of William A. Coulter Fund, 59.73
[fig. 32]

Landscape, ca. 1900
oil on cardboard, $8\frac{13}{16} \times 5\frac{7}{16}$"
The Pennsylvania Academy of the Fine Arts, Philadelphia. Gift of Mrs. Edward R. Anshutz

Landscape with Buildings, ca. 1900
oil on academy board, $9\frac{15}{16} \times 7\frac{1}{2}$"
The Pennsylvania Academy of the Fine Arts, Philadelphia. Gift of Mrs. Edward R. Anshutz

Landscape with White Clouds, ca. 1900
oil on board, 7½ × 10"
James Graham & Sons Gallery, New York

Portrait of Edwin S. Clymer, ca. 1900
pastel on paper, 48 × 39"
Courtesy of the Reading Public Museum, Reading, Pennsylvania
[fig. 38]

Steamboat on the Ohio, ca. 1900
oil on canvas, 10 × 15"
Mr. and Mrs. Richard Waitzer
[Color plate 15]

Three Trees by a Stream, ca. 1900-05
watercolor on paper, 13½ × 20¼"
The Hon. Joseph P. Carroll and Mrs. Carroll, New York
[Color plate 19]

Portrait of Emily Fairchild Pollock, ca. 1905
oil on canvas, 38 × 29"
The Hon. Joseph P. Carroll and Mrs. Carroll, New York
[Color plate 26]

Tree Study, ca. 1905
watercolor on paper, 10¼ × 13½"
The Hon. Joseph P. Carroll and Mrs. Carroll, New York

Woman in Red, ca. 1905
oil on canvas, 34 × 30½"
Courtesy of the Reading Public Museum, Reading, Pennsylvania

Woman Writing at a Table, ca. 1905
oil on canvas, 16 × 20¼"
Byron Collection
[Color plate 24]

A Challenge, ca. 1908
pastel on canvas, 30 × 24"
The Hon. Joseph P. Carroll and Mrs. Carroll, New York, courtesy Berry-Hill Galleries, Inc., New York
[Color plate 29]

Portrait of Margaret Perot, ca. 1908
oil on canvas, 64⅛ × 40"
Hirshhorn Museum and Sculpture Garden, Smithsonian Institution. Gift of Joseph H. Hirshhorn, 1966.
[Color plate 27]

Figure Piece, ca. 1909
oil on canvas, 40 × 36⅛"
National Academy of Design, New York
[Color plate 30]

Self-Portrait, ca. 1909
oil on canvas, 30 × 25"
National Academy of Design, New York
[Frontispiece, fig. 36]

Garden, ca. 1911
oil on board, 9½ × 7½"
The Hon. Joseph P. Carroll and Mrs. Carroll, New York
[Color plate 20]

Landscape, ca. 1911-12
oil on board, 8 × 5"
The Hon. Joseph P. Carroll and Mrs. Carroll, New York
[Color plate 22]

Photographs by Thomas Anshutz

All photographs courtesy of the Thomas Anshutz Papers, Archives of American Art, Smithsonian Institution

Figures by the Ohio River, Wheeling, West Virginia, ca. 1890
photograph
[fig. 30]

Figures by the Ohio River, Wheeling, West Virginia, ca. 1890
photograph
[fig. 31]

Two Figures by the Ohio River, Wheeling, West Virginia, ca. 1890
photograph

Women by a Boat, ca. 1893
photograph
[fig. 25]

Two Boys by a Boat, ca. 1894
photograph
[fig. 27]

Two Men by a Boat, ca. 1897
photograph
[fig. 29]

*I*NDEX

(References to figures and plates are in italic typeface.)

Photo Credits

All photographs, except where otherwise noted, have been provided by the owners with permission granted to reproduce.

James Graham & Sons Gallery - plates 11, 13, 14, 23
Randall C. Griffin - figs. 8, 10, 34, plates 16, 18
Greg Heins - plate 10
Gerald T. Mancini - fig. 26
Lee Stalsworth - plates 6, 28
Richard Stoner - plate 5
Jim Strong - fig. 22
Charles B. Tyler - fig. 21
Ed Watkins - plate 8
Richard York Gallery - plate 29

Endplate:
Photographer Unknown, *Thomas Anshutz*, ca. 1885, photograph, Private Collection

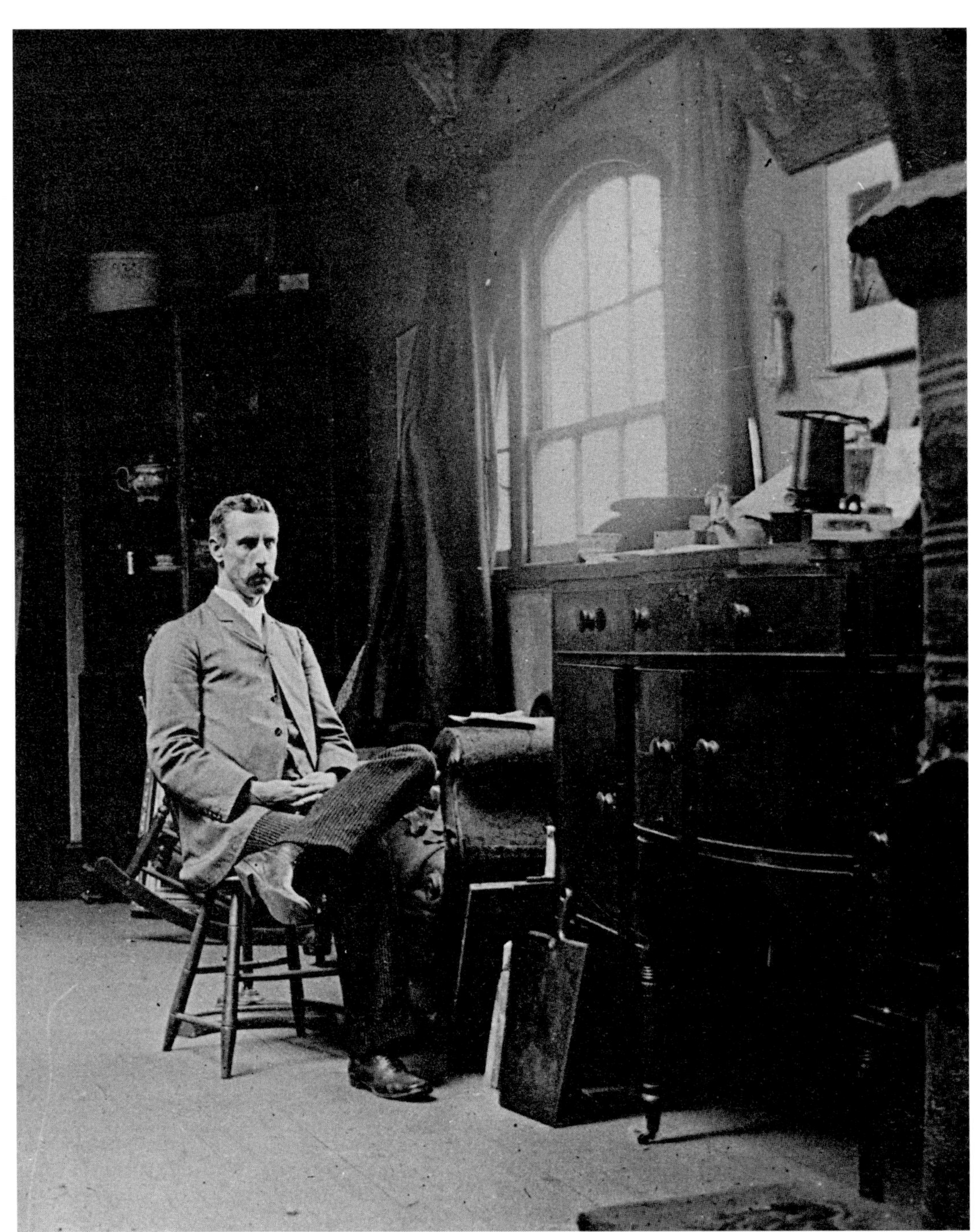